W9-BYM-911

MAXIMUM SECURITY

John Devine

MAXIMUM SECURITY
The Culture of Violence in Inner-City Schools

The University of Chicago Press

Chicago and London

371.58
1996

JOHN DEVINE is director of the School Partnership Program and teaches at the Metropolitan Center for Urban Education at New York University's School of Education.

The University of Chicago Press, Chicago 60637
The University of Chicago Press, Ltd., London

© 1996 by The University of Chicago
All rights reserved. Published 1996

Printed in the United States of America

05 04 03 02 01 00 99 98 97 96   1 2 3 4 5

ISBN: 0-226-14386-4 (cloth)
        0-226-14387-2 (paper)

Library of Congress Cataloging-in-Publication Data

Devine, John (John Francis)
    Maximum security: The culture of violence in inner-city schools/
John Devine.
        p.   cm.
    Includes bibliographical references and index.
    ISBN 0-226-14386-4 (alk. paper).—ISBN 0-226-14387-2 (pbk.:
alk. paper)
    1. School violence—United States.   2. Urban schools—United
States—Sociological aspects.   3. Educational anthropology—United
States.   I. Title.
    LB3013.3.D48   1996
    371.5'8—dc20   96-8910
                                                                 CIP

For Elizabeth
animae dimidium meae

CONTENTS

ACKNOWLEDGMENTS

Neither increased public awareness of the anguish and human tragedies associated with school violence nor the recent surge in what is euphemistically known as school restructuring has done much to ameliorate the complex of problems that have come to be called the school safety issue. Given the intensity of the national spotlight—which envelops everything from congressional hearings to Internet conversations on the subject—it would be arrogant in the extreme for me to suggest that the observations contained in the following chapters might bring about a significant curtailment of this epidemic. At the same time, there is an obvious urgency to assess the efficacy of current pragmatic approaches for making schools safer and to critique the dominant theoretical paradigms that would explain this social pathology. Catalogs of the metal-detector companies keep rolling off the presses as rapidly as the scholarly articles on symbolic violence and multiculturalism, but the sickening headlines chronicling the latest school-related atrocities have not abated.

The central proposition that will be drawn from this ethnography of corridor space, security guards, and school violence is that the mentality that relies on paramilitary measures and technological devices to achieve "safe" schools is only the latest fallout from a long-term hierarchization of the institution of the school and a more recent professionalization of the role of the teacher. I hope to show that both of these processes are buttressed and partially concealed by educational philosophies that distance adult society more and more from the everyday experiences and practical (that is, messy) issues that adolescents face—a novel division of pedagogical labor that would have no doubt surprised John Dewey but that follows logically and precisely from his premises.

In order to appreciate what is happening in the corridors of today's inner-city high schools, anthropology's participant-observation techniques are far more useful than research that, armed with surveys, questionnaires, and standardized instruments, is in hot pursuit of data collection. It is only prolonged exposure to the lives of the students—facilitated in my case by our program's daily presence in the schools—that fulfills cultural anthropology's prerequisite for authentic fieldwork. But, as I try to suggest throughout, it would be naive to think that such contact is unproblematic. Anthropology's self-critique in recent years is all about just such issues of representation and cultural hubris: "I was there and let me tell you what it was like." I hope the reader will also detect in these pages an awareness of this danger and a movement in another direction.

For many years, the Harry Frank Guggenheim Foundation has been concerned with the reduction of violence and aggression in our society, "our" understood in a global sense; I am most grateful for the foundation's generous support of this project. I would especially like to thank Karen Colvard and Joel Wallman for their attentive understanding and ever-friendly encouragement.

If one thing is clear from the text, it is that the always fresh and unusually revealing weekly journals of my graduate students have been essential for the production of this book. My own ethnography is interwoven with my commentary on the daily journals of Shirley Fennessey, Tricia Glynn, Pedro Mateu-Gelabert, Laurie Jacoby, Barbara Miller, David Mueller, Romilia Ramirez, Julia Rennenkampf, Candace Reyes-Dandrea, Dawn Ward, Roxanne Warner, Carla Zilber, Michael Zilber, and the many other tutors who have made significant contributions to our work with adolescents. The few who have asked that their writings not be used did so primarily out of a concern for the confidentiality of their relationship with their students, and of course I have respected this concern. I also appreciate the encouragement and support of Peter and Anneli Lax and of Janet Mindes, whose friendship has provided access to a constant stream of literature, clippings, and insights. I am deeply grateful for the comments of Philippe Bourgois and Allen Feldman, who read the manuscript when it was still in preparation. Many friends and colleagues have been a constant source of encouragement by showing their continued interest. I especially want to thank John Cleary, Clare Coombs, Kathryn Edmundson, Zhimin Gu, Eve Levy, Frank Schneiger, Gloria Singer, and Dick Starkey.

I am genuinely indebted to Peter Lucas, with whom my conversations on school issues have been continuous over the past several years, as well as to the principals, superintendents, teachers, counselors, guards, and of course the students of the several schools that form the subject of this work and who of necessity must remain anonymous. Peter Lucas also took a number of the photographs that are part of the book. My thanks also to Dr. LaMar P. Miller, Executive Director of the Metropolitan Center for Urban Education of New York University, for his support of my research efforts. To T. David Brent of the University of Chicago I express my warmest thanks for the generous devotion of his time and skill to the preparation of this book. I also wish to thank Kathryn Kraynik and Karen Peterson of the University of Chicago Press and David Severtson, copy editor, for the many helpful suggestions and the careful editing.

I am particularly fortunate in having a family whose members have all been unfailing in their interest, support, and love. The contributions of my wife, Frances Elizabeth Devine, go far beyond the editing and commenting she did and extend into a multitude of hidden pathways of which even she is unaware and for which I am particularly appreciative.

INTRODUCTION

New York City TV reporter: "How do you like this school?"
Inner-city high school student: "O.K. Security treat us right!"

The response of this New York City high school student summarizes the discourse I try to problematize in the pages that follow.[1] When most people—Americans or foreigners, even those who live in economically impoverished lands—think about schools, they ordinarily do not think of uniformed security guards, high-tech devices for weapons searches, or the use of police tactics for corridor surveillance. Students attending New York City's most troubled high schools do so automatically.

The central thesis of this book, based on my ten years of working in New York's inner-city high schools, can be described as an attempt to outline the process by which violence becomes normalized in everyday school life, to examine the inner logic of its accompanying ethos of fear, and to suggest that this phenomenon may be growing more widespread throughout American education, even in suburban and rural schools—wherever, in fact, a techno-security apparatus is relied on as the primary mechanism for achieving schoolwide discipline. My basic claim is that the collective imagination of the New York City high school system, fed over the past several decades on an amalgam of real and invented student crime, treacheries, and rampages, has reacted with intensive paramilitary practices that have engendered an antagonistic terrain where traditional public schooling and urban street culture mingle—the latter conceptualized as both transforming and transformed by the educational institution. I will contend that state, school, and street languages are merging into a koine of corporeal experiences (the attendant emotions of this koine are suspicion, loneliness, anger, terror, fear, and grief, although it also allows for the negation of those feelings). This emerging etiquette has so radically shattered the standard concept of the school and affected the historical teacher-student bond that a novel

1

duality has arisen, assigning to teachers an exclusively cognitive role while delegating to security forces the responsibility for supervising the body, controlling student behavior, and managing school discipline. When I ask teachers in these schools how they maintain classroom control, their response is, "I can always call security if the kids get too rough." The chapters that follow question these kinds of responses, now taken for granted, through an anthropology of the body that takes as its starting point Feldman's (1994, 407) observation that "relations of domination are spatially marked by the increase of perceptual (and thus social) distance from the body of the Other."

But the hallways of urban schools are not spaces in which educational researchers and theoreticians have been comfortable. Their preference for the classroom as the locus of investigation reflects their interest in the cognitive aspects of teacher training, their fascination with the "hidden curriculum," their rush to create "effective" schools before adequately diagnosing why schools have become ineffective, and their desire to recount success stories about "transferable" experiments "that work." This study will focus on that most contested of spaces, the high school corridor, understood here—in opposition to the increasingly privatized universe of the classroom—as emblematic of the whole public dimension of the institution. The corridor calls into question that vast body of literature that centers on the enclosed realm of the classroom and its curriculum, those twin preoccupations of most educational research journals. The social topography of the urban corridor implies infinitely deferred presence (Derrida's *différance*), multiplicity, a dispersion of temporality, constant distraction, and the random occurrence of events; the classroom still holds out the promise of dialogue, unity, a coherent configuration of time, concentration, and the possibility of narrative.

By refusing to consider the processes whereby the student's body becomes transformed into a proactive instrument of violence, by disdaining to theorize about the politically incorrect topic of discipline, research has bolstered those tendencies of the "system" that pretend there are some facile answers to the overwhelmingly complex problems associated with urban school reform. Such sweeping assertions will rightfully elicit a host of objections from informed readers. I will address some of these objections at the outset.

Since I start by attempting to establish that violence does exist in the schools that are the subject of this study and that its discovery is not simply the result of racist interpretation, nostalgic exaggeration about the "good old days," or general adult squeamishness about adolescent culture, perhaps the first question that might arise is precisely why it is necessary to begin in this way—merely confirming the existence of a conspicuous phenomenon. Is it not obvious, one might object, to anyone who watches the news or reads the papers that the schools, especially the public schools, are, like the streets surrounding them, saturated with stabbings, muggings, and worse?

The problem is that in attempting to interpret the phenomenon of violence, one immediately encounters a discourse of denial coexisting alongside this discourse of frank admission. The same high school principal who confides to a visitor that half of the students in his school routinely carry weapons is also able to maintain, almost in the same breath, that "things have been getting much better lately." It is therefore necessary to situate the problem of violence, as I attempt to do in chapter 1, to confirm its existence, isolate its components, and circumscribe it, even though it stays one step ahead and forces researchers to realize their own complicity in constructing the very object to be studied.

I shall maintain that this discourse of denial manifests itself on two levels—the practical as well as the theoretical. Since my project aims at addressing both levels, my audience perforce includes scholars interested in analyzing the American educational scene as well as parents, teachers, and the general public, for whom school violence has become an authentic concern. These reflections are primarily meant to start practical and useful conversations with anyone interested in shaping urban educational policies, in discussing how highly troubled schools can be converted into safer, more respectful places of learning. But I am also arguing that the culture of school violence—whose exact demarcations I shall at this point leave undefined—is undertheorized. In reacting to right-wing views, many academicians have, for some time now, portrayed the inner-city adolescent as pure victim. Without denying the validity of their insights, I will be claiming that the realities of inner-city schooling are far more convoluted.

Although my argument builds toward a concluding set of propositions in chapter 8, I do not attempt to formulate any simple antiviolence checklist or to write a how-to manual that educators can put to immediate use. I have not set out to write a school-management text; what I have attempted is an ethnographic reflection on my ten years' presence in inner-city schools.

One of my underlying assumptions is the now rather old-fashioned concept that, before we begin to solve social problems, it is a good idea to question our assumptions. One way to accomplish this is through the experience of long-term ethnography. That notion has been rightly called into question, since it smacks of a quasi-colonialist brand of anthropology that believed the anthropologist could shed her or his ethnocentric biases and "study" the "cultural Other" before recommending ways of "intervening." If my methodological self-consciousness is only too apparent, it stems from a desire to avoid the dual pitfalls of presuming to represent others and pretending to solve their problems. The inferences I draw are proffered more as invitations to a dialogue about one's fundamental presuppositions concerning school violence. The point I am striving to make throughout is that one of the main reasons school violence is not properly dealt with is that it is not being sufficiently analyzed; furthermore, that analysis will always be open to question, because it cannot be separated from the ongoing fabrication and dissolution of the narrative of modernity, on which narrative the educational system itself is based, or from our own complicity with that narrative.

My conclusions, however, are not predetermined hypotheses that I set out to prove; rather, they unfolded over ten years in the context of a tutorial program in which New York University's Metropolitan Center for Urban Education collaborated with inner-city high schools. During this time, my experiences and those of my graduate students clashed with our received (and my rather traditional) notions on schools and adolescent development. As we tried, in our weekly seminars, to make sense of what we were encountering in the everyday life in the schools, we consulted a broad range of the educational literature—from traditional "positivistic" studies to critical ethnography to feminist scholarship—only to end up feeling that most of it, though enlightening in many ways, did not relate to what we were encountering. As I began to write, this mix of ideas became further entangled with the opinions I anticipated my readers might espouse on these same topics. Somewhere along the way the distinction between writing for an academic audience and writing for the general public got lost. Perhaps that is just as well, since the issue of school violence is too important to sacrifice on one side of a prosaic distinction.[2]

The continued presence of violence in American schools represents more than just a challenge to the way each school is managed; it calls into question the administrative infrastructure of the entire educational system as well as the more basic philosophy that purports to undergird it. Everyday life in these schools does not correspond with any of the currently fashionable models, certainly not with those of right-wing theorists (who think of these schools as totally chaotic and place blame on students, their families, and uninspired principals), nor with those of radical theorists (who fixate exclusively on the "symbolic violence" perpetrated by the educational establishment), nor with those of mainstream liberal theorists (who ordinarily choose to avoid the most painful problems and to focus on disseminating prototypes of "effective schools," which are presumably free of violence).

One question that presents itself concerns the legitimacy of extrapolating my findings beyond the handful of New York inner-city public high schools and of extending my thesis to schools elsewhere in New York and other cities. This question, though reasonable, betrays a crypto-positivist outlook that accepts the assumptions of a statistically oriented social science. The present work lays no claims to being a scientific study. It aspires to reject the ideology of "observer-observed" (see Tyler 1986, 126) and strives to forgo the notion of a transcendental, all-knowing scientific gaze that would definitively establish for the "reader" what "objectively" goes on in "troubled schools" for predominantly "at risk" inner-city youth. My methodological stance is not just a convenient way for a white, middle-class male ethnographer to circumvent the thorny question of how to "represent" the behavior of black, Asian, and Hispanic youths in schools situated in the city's most violent neighborhoods. The ideal for which I have striven is to avoid authoritative "representations" of the youth with whom we work. Instead, I offer, as much as possible, daily journal reflections on our work of tutoring and mentoring—my interactions, as well as those of my graduate assistants, with students and school staff. Each log snippet also needs to be placed in its context and its writer briefly described.

Our primary purpose in the schools was not to "study" them, their students, or their teachers but to perform a support service. In this book, I reflect on that service and on the privileged vantage point it affords us to mature our perceptions about what is going on in the schools as a whole. This approach runs the risk of being labeled disingenuous, since ultimately we *do,* willy-nilly, represent the Other, the world of the student—but the shift in the angle of observation is nonetheless important, if only because its ambition is to be less doctrinaire.

In a work in which I am attempting to identify various factors as contributing causes of school violence, I am acutely aware that my own texts, the texts of the tutors' daily logs, and my own interpretations of these can easily stand accused of helping to construct the very social categories we are examining: "youth," "youth culture," "youth violence," "culture of school violence"—and this in the context of schools with no white students. If the "cultural studies" literature has done anything, it has sensitized us to these issues of representation. My very commentary on the presence or absence of the adult gaze may be an example of a gaze that creates a taxonomy of violent youth at the same time as it purports to observe it and comment on it.

It may also be, however, that the field of cultural studies, as important as it is, should not have the final word. In detailing how hegemonic power— through racist, sexist, and classist discursive formations—constructs America's understandings of crime, it often minimizes the magnitude of crime itself and belittles efforts to create a world in which crime is less likely. In writing about his interest in "the circulation of ideas about American youth," for example, Charles Acland (1995) reassures the reader, as an aside, that "violence is deplorable" and that there is indeed a "crisis of youth," although his main point seems to be that this crisis is a journalistically constructed "moral panic" that has now become common sense. In a similar vein, Henry Giroux (1996, 57) apparently believes that black youth violence is merely a representation of the media. Would such authors allow anyone to think, say, or write anything about youth violence? Still, I have to be concerned, given the bulk of the log material and the range of tutors' backgrounds, what social literacy is here being reproduced: the tutors are not just multiple "eyes" recording the events faithfully and impartially. I recognize that I am asking the reader to participate actively in the task of decipherment, of reading between the lines at times.

In the end, I have had to be satisfied with trying to stage the kind of compromised representational performance that Nancy Scheper-Hughes (1992) has called a "good enough" ethnography—that is to say, a middle ground between saying nothing at all and representing inner-city schools in an apodictic way.

Since, then, my subjectivity as a researcher is ancillary to my subjectivity as a service provider in the schools, the purpose of chapter 2 is to set up the baseline data, as it were, on my own values and attitudes and some of the presuppositions on which our program is structured. Similarly, the epilogue on Jesuit education is merely intended to present a non-nostalgic autobiographical picture of the pedagogical "baggage" I carried with me as I began to approach inner-city public schools. Like all baggage, it has been both useful and weighty.

Chapter 2, located within the intimate confines of one of our small tutoring rooms, sets the stage for the unorthodox data-collection methodology. It should not be read as a public relations item that would seek to convince the reader of the powerful impact of our program; on the contrary, the message is precisely that programs such as ours—however successful— are not *the* answer to school violence. Since our intervention program is an explicit attempt to communicate values, attitudes, and interpretations of reality as much as to improve basic academic skills and to nudge students toward graduation and beyond, our subjectivities—like those of anyone who works with adolescents—are on the line every day to the extent that we hold ourselves open to be molded by and to mold the next student encounter. Put simply, if we think that we are grasping student attitudes or "capturing student voice," we may find that it is our own voice that we are "capturing," since, after all, our central reason for being in the schools is precisely to affect student motivation, attitudes, and values—as well as to impart skills. When our research is going at its best, our "data" are "collected" serendipitously and are subject to being changed by the very gathering process. Questionnaires, formal and informal interviews—all the claptrap from which dissertations are constructed—have been strenuously avoided.[3]

To answer the anticipated question more directly: readers will have to judge what the parallels are, if any, between the New York situation and school systems elsewhere in the country. I hope I do not have such a narrow view of the world that I believe the trends in school antiviolence policies have to emanate from New York. All the schools referred to are located in highly troubled New York City neighborhoods, but one does not need acute cultural antennae to surmise that these kinds of problems are not confined to New York. School violence has been amply described as a crisis of the 1990s not just for urban schools but for rural and suburban schools as well (see Friedlander 1992; New York State Department of Education 1994; U.S.

Department of Health and Human Services 1993; American Psychological Association 1993; Leitman & Binns 1993; Carnegie Corporation of New York 1994). A National School Boards Association survey found that 82 percent of the responding school districts said violence had increased at their schools over the previous five years. Indeed, one of the National Education Goals, as enunciated in the *Goals 2000* (16) report, is "to make every school in America free of drugs and violence."

What I am certain of is how debatable these chapters will be even to teachers working in the inner-city neighborhoods from which they are culled. Violence seems to erupt so sporadically and randomly that, at the very site of enactment, wildly differing interpretations are exposed. I recall traveling back to Manhattan from a Brooklyn high school one afternoon after a long day in which a near riot had taken place in the cafeteria, replete with police intervention. My companion was a teacher from the same school who had been teaching her class on the other side of the building, oblivious to the whole thing. Hers was a "normal" school day, whereas mine was a "violent" one. My graduate students debate incessantly among themselves, and with me, whether one or the other of us is overreacting or underreacting to what is perceived as violence and often labeled such. How does one go about interpreting students' interpretations of violence, especially when both interpreter and interpreted are two parts of the same event? What to one observer (or participant) is merely playful shadow boxing is, to another, a clear case of aggression. Tom Landry, the former Dallas Cowboys' football coach, is reputed to have placed in the players' locker room a sign that read, "Only the trained eye can see fat." Perhaps violence is in a category similar to fat: it may take a special set of qualifications just to recognize it. Then, again, one must be careful, since anorexics think they see fat where it is not.

We are left, then, with what Stephen Tyler (1986, 130) has called an "evocation" of reality rather than with a scientific verification of "facts" or a tabulation of violent incidents. Traditional psychological accounts of the educational process once commonly explained "deviant" student behavior as an individual phenomenon. For several years now, educational researchers have chosen to define conflict in schools in terms of the interplay among powerful social, linguistic, political, and cultural forces or as the collision between an oppressive dominant culture and a counterculture of resistance. The most powerful of these paradigms are the various forms of "social reproduction theory" (Giroux 1983) or of "critical pedagogy" (Anderson 1989; Ellsworth 1989). For Foucault (1977), it was the whole enterprise of modern society itself that produced both deviancy and normality not only in schools but throughout all of Western culture.

The lobbies and hallways of inner-city schools, epitomized most concretely in the icon of the student's concealed weapon meeting the guard's hand-held metal detector, reveal that none of these educational theories is any longer particularly germane for the task of mapping the school culture. The question that arises, then, is whether any narrative can replace these formulations and adequately interpret these agitated and fragmented social texts of mimetic violence that masquerade as contemporary schools.

I will argue that none of the discourses of present currency is relevant for the job of reflecting this cutting edge of postmodern experience, the inner-city public school space. If this claim is even partially correct, what line of commentary is left for us to make? As an exercise in cultural decipherment, postmodernism by its very nature eschews any kind of theory building, social activism, or participation in the political process. Some postmodernists dismiss the very possibility of making policy recommendations (Rosenau 1992, 3). But the ruined edifice of the metropolitan school bears a postmodern message that differs radically from that of the collages of advertising or of boutique windows. At issue is the task of finding effective and democratic, if limited, responses to the ritualized violence—even if these responses run the risk of being labeled neo-humanistic.

In chapter 8, therefore, I advance some proposals, the two most important of which are the creation of smaller schools and a concomitant reconceptualization of the role of the teacher. In doing so, however, I will strongly criticize certain key aspects of the small school movement, at least in the way it is being currently implemented on the New York scene.

Unquestionably, if humanism is to be identified with a modernity that scorned diversity and difference, it cannot and should not be resurrected as such; neither is it sufficient merely to purge it of its Eurocentric and capitalistic biases. But to reject it completely, as William Spanos (1993) appears to want to do, is to accept what I define as a culture of school violence as normal and to give up on the educational project altogether, thereby hurting the educationally disadvantaged more than they have already been hurt.

In discussing the origins of school violence, I do not conceive of a specified time at which the violence began; rather, I see an evolutionary dynamic at work whose roots are deeply intertwined with several aspects of American schooling and economics throughout this century. I will also make the point that teachers' traditionally complex and multifaceted roles have now become splintered among security guards, guidance counselors, "special education" staff, the police, community-based organizations, and programs such as ours. I will be suggesting that the supervision of the minutiae of human behavior and the hierarchical surveillance, which Foucault associates with bourgeois society, humanism, and the modern era, have been breaking down drastically for some decades now. The fact that they have "always already" been breaking down throughout modernity, which is the very reason for their appearance, does not contradict the previous statement. But at the present historical juncture, these controls over student behavior have all but disappeared—paradoxically so, given the plethora of "school safety officers" and security devices that jam the lobbies and corridors.[4]

If my interpretation of the spread of school violence and the corresponding waning of the desire for disciplinary enforcement rings true, the question facing followers of Foucault is whether his basic paradigm, although perhaps valid as an approach for exploring and explaining modernity, has become inapplicable to our era. One is further entitled to ask whether the older humanist social order, which Foucault conceived to be constructed by the panoptic gaze, with all its oppressive contradictions, did not have something to recommend it, compared to the violent regime currently being produced by antipanopticism, the lack of disciplinary enforcement, and constant fear. Asking the question in this way, as I indicated earlier, is not identical with a call for a restoration of all the elements of the older humanism as such.

The message American society has been sending to teachers and schools is that they should focus on improving academic skills. The teaching profession, led on by its unions, has been only too happy to listen to this advice and to absorb its not-so-subliminal message: steer clear of the nonacademic, do not get involved in imparting ("imposing" is the more usual verb) your own standards of conduct or values on students or, certainly, in entering into direct confrontations about etiquette or behavior. Briefly, the message is: distance yourself from the body of the student. And what could be more commonsensical, especially since half the students are carrying weapons?

Dealing with students who are armed or who threaten teachers or other students is a serious predicament for contemporary secondary education. Teachers' unions, with their legitimate concerns for the safety of their members, have taken a hands-off policy: teachers are specifically directed not to get in the middle of the fray or attempt to break up fights. I am certainly not proposing anything that would contravene what is only common sense. I am suggesting only that we not flinch from looking at how current practice became commonsensical in the first place, that we analyze how the whole educational system is structured—and not just individual schools—and that we re-think, in a fresh way, what educators and policymakers must do to contain, reduce, and control the violence.

Chapter 8 is not meant to be an agenda for action in this regard but rather—in the light of what comes before it—to be a critique of what are currently considered enlightened strategies for reform. The principal "education" message issuing from the conservative camp—of which William Bennett (1992) is the most strident representative—is that the public schools are chaotic beyond repair and that they should be abandoned in favor of some form of a voucher scheme. Alternatively, Bennett dangles one lusciously elite scholastic model after another before starving urban populations—all of which are beyond their financial reach. The risk one runs in developing a discourse on the phenomenon of school violence is to appear to support these political forces that paint such a hopeless picture, give lectures on virtue, and propose simplistic solutions. Sensational inner-city school horror stories that appear daily in our newspapers give ammunition to those whose only solution is to close down the whole enterprise of public education. My ten years' experience in public schools—after my twenty-eight years' commitment to Jesuit education—has led me to conclusions that are the polar opposite of those of William Bennett. It is clear to me that the public system, despite all its shortcomings, is and will remain the only possible refuge for the truly poor and the marginalized and that public schools are *not* hopelessly beyond salvation. At the same time, their extreme vulnerability, which permits the consistent penetration of violence, reveals that the deterioration of the system is far more extensive than the existing literature would lead us to believe and that the task of reform is far more complex and challenging.

Chapter 3 roams the school corridors with the security guards and raises the question of whether the new technology throughout the school building is just a new form of panopticism or if, on the contrary, it should cause us to have some misgivings about Foucault's whole thesis. It argues that the "network of gazes," so feared by Foucault, is, in reality, disappearing and that the embodying of self-supervision in the individual adolescent is vanishing along with it. In chapter 4, I extend Philippe Bourgois's (1989) analysis of "street culture" into the space of the school; its central demeanor— a display of toughness by a population much older than the teenagers we see—begins to hold sway in the school as teachers progressively withdraw from their former disciplinary role and from confrontations with students.

But this infiltration of the culture of violence through the porous perimeters of the school is traceable to a level deeper than that of everyday managerial routines within the school itself. Pedagogical theory, I maintain in chapter 5, contributes to and legitimates the silence surrounding the issue of violence that one finds in everyday life. A dualism can be discerned in the writings of critical ethnographers, sociolinguists, and other theorists, who, perhaps for fear of lapsing back into cultural deficit theory, refuse to attribute a true agency of violence to their romanticized and glorified versions of the "body" of the inner-city student. One finds no real adolescent aggression in the commentaries and studies of most critical ethnographers. They encounter only "feisty" teenagers who suffer—and resist—the symbolic violence of the system, and they refuse to conceive of their prototypical ideal teacher as anything other than a disembodied, intellectualized persona. More precisely, the questions I am raising here are the exact opposite of those advanced by the social reproductionists yet do not on that account negate their thesis. Bourdieu (1977, 94) seeks to unearth a whole concealed political philosophy in the transmittal of what he has famously called cultural capital, passed down by schools and families from one generation to the next:

> The principles em-bodied in this way are placed beyond the grasp of consciousness, and hence cannot be touched by voluntary, deliberate transformation, cannot even be made explicit; nothing seems more ineffable, more incommunicable, more inimitable, and therefore, more precious, than the values given the body, *made* body by transubstantiation achieved by the hidden pedagogy, capable of instilling a whole cosmology, an ethic, a metaphysic, a political philosophy, through injunctions as insignificant as "stand up straight" or "don't hold your knife in your left hand."

Reduced to its simplest form, the question I am suggesting needs to be posed is, What happens to cultural transmission and to Bourdieu's notion of cultural capital when adults stop telling youth to stand up straight, when they withdraw from the game? What response can pedagogical theory make when pedagogical praxis—for many legitimate reasons—has become remote from the embodiment of the student? And it is a measure of the reproductionists' distance from the realities of inner-city schools that they apparently believe that teachers are still seeking to imprint their values onto students.

Mainstream reaction to school violence lies somewhere between the radical right- and left-wing responses. In almost every public information release announcing expansion of the metal detector system, the New York City Board of Education simultaneously declares an increase in "conflict-resolution classes," as if to reassure us that the old humanism is still alive and well with every embarrassing upgrade in technology. "Conflict-resolution classes," "peer mediation sessions," and "violence-prevention seminars" have become firmly acceptable buzzwords for the 1990s. Attacking these trends, now solidly funded by governmental educational agencies, is tantamount to maligning apple pie and motherhood, but in chapter 6 I venture not only to question their worth but also to assert their capacity to distract us from the real issues surrounding violence and schooling. Pinning one's hopes for school safety on the twin towers of techno-security devices and conflict-resolution sessions is simply a way of abdicating responsibility while pretending to "do something" about the problems. As James Q. Wilson says in *The Moral Sense* (1993, 249):

> children do not learn morality by learning maxims or by clarifying values. . . . A moral life is perfected by practice more than by precept; children are not taught so much as habituated. In this sense, the schools inevitably teach morality, whether they intend to or not, by such behavior as they reward or punish. A school reinforces the better moral nature of a pupil to the extent it insists on the habitual performance of duties, including the duty to deal fairly with others, to discharge one's own responsibilities, and to defer the satisfaction of immediate and base motives in favor of more distant and nobler ones.

My only gloss on Wilson's sound comments is that schools also teach morality by choosing to ignore certain behavior and that, today, deliberately choosing "not to see" a good deal of adolescent misbehavior has become a major tendency in the schools we work in. The conflict-resolution classes in question and the new curricula they are spawning (for example, those of Prothrow-Stith 1991) should be seen, I would maintain, as attempts to deal with asocial behaviors *before* the fact, or *after* the fact, while ignoring them *in actu ipso*. Carol Gilligan's (1982; Gilligan, Ward, and Taylor 1988) emphasis on "listening to the voices" of adolescent girls, in a similar way, downplays the values teachers have to offer and neglects the insidious ways in which an unchecked culture of violence can and does permeate teenage girls' (and boys') subjectivities. The students we encounter, like those Gilligan and her associates describe, want to be listened to, but they also seek—and need—structure, direction, and even the occasional admonition.

The constant exposure to youth that occurs in a one-on-one tutoring and mentoring program discloses the need for adults to reenter the initiation rites of adolescents in our society. But to some authors this philosophy masks a hidden hegemony. William Spanos (1993, 199) regards any validation of the maturity-immaturity dichotomy as just one more oppressive way by which the dominant society subjugates youth, especially minority youth. In chapter 7, the bankruptcy of Spanos's position becomes evident when contrasted with an extended log excerpt in which one of our former tutors reflects on her experiences as she accompanies one of her students to and from an abortion clinic.

The main obstacle, however, in attempting to gain a fresh and privileged theoretical vantage point for addressing the issue of school violence in a more satisfying way is that the language has already been preempted by vocabularies that have a priori reduced violence to a scientific object to be described, studied, analyzed, and corrected by the observing scholar-anthropologist. Various causal explanations (poverty and economic factors), linguistic models (radical discontinuities between school and home cultures), psychosocial interpretations (early child abuse, student alienation), origin myths (tracing the statistical increase of violent incidents over time), social reproductionist schemata (symbolic violence), structural patterns of control (by federal and state governments) are all necessary but insufficient grounds for explaining violent school scenarios. They all turn away from what is disclosed through concrete occurrences and from the actual production of violence and place the emphasis on what Feldman (1991, 3) calls the legitimation rationality of an archic center—a "cause" that is narrated as having occurred at an earlier epoch or at a distance far removed from the actual performance of the violence.

Violence within the schools is said, for example, to have arisen from the lax disciplinary attitudes of the 1960s or from dozens of other earlier conditions. These social-science constructs tend to assume the existence of an idyllic state prior to the arrival of violence or a future utopian eschatological condition that would occur if only a certain prescribed agenda is followed. A "culture of school violence" is thus introduced into the scene as a deus ex machina to explain how violence erupts within an otherwise stable academic community. This structuralist-functionalist accounting imagines the school as a past or future stable society that is interrupted by a culture of school violence, which itself becomes a reified entity narrated from the perspective of a spectator who has observed an already terminated process.

It is extremely important, instead, to attempt to delineate this contextualized mix of violence and serenity as a medium of communication inhabiting all dimensions of today's inner-city school as it clings to a precarious existence on the edge of two clashing traditions—the received pedagogy and the policing function of the state, which has by now entirely saturated the school site—as the two erupt, overlap, and expand within given spatial contexts and bodily comportments.

Two images, both extracted from the Arcades Project[5] of Walter Benjamin, will serve as antidotes to these purely short-term causal explications. The glass-ceilinged arcades erected in Paris and other major cities during the early nineteenth century—the original shopping malls that fascinated Benjamin—may seem at a distant architectural remove from the urban school space with which we are concerned here. But, for Benjamin, the displays of merchandise and the luxury shops along these interior passageways that attracted even the peasants and the working classes—the first customers—represented all that was duplicitous in the bourgeois modern world: commodity fetishism, the false hope of advancement, and dreams of an infinitely progressing utopian society based on capitalism's promises (Buck-Morss 1989). His task as a cultural critic, as he saw it, was to awaken his contemporaries from their bourgeois daydreams and from the delusions of indefinite progress that the perspective of the glass ceilings—open to the expanse of the heavens and to imaginary infinite opportunities—had induced in the crowds. Long before Benjamin's time (the 1930s) the arcades had fallen into ruin, thereby revealing, as he perceived it, their true (i.e., their hypocritical) nature. By his day, and even earlier, the cult of commodities had burst out of the narrow confines of the original arcades and into the department stores, streets, and boulevards of the entire Parisian scene (Buck-Morss 1995).

The original pattern of one of the urban schools under consideration in this book offers an interesting clue to a possible linkage to the Benjaminian prototypes. The original ceiling of the auditorium, covered over by plaster and green paint many years ago, was originally designed in 1912–13 by the renowned school architect of the day, C. B. J. Snyder; like the Paris arcades, it was fabricated of pure glass and iron, as was the ceiling of the school lobby.[6] One can only speculate on the extent to which the dreams and hopes of those earlier generations of mostly working-class youth of European extraction—whom one can imagine sitting in that auditorium in the early part of this century, gazing up at the sky—were fulfilled by the jobs they later occupied, mostly in New York City's factories (now also in ruins) and offices. These World War I-era schools did not need security guards or police squads to patrol the corridors, but the glass-ceilinged auditorium and the dubious vision it offered provides us with a hint that the school and societal structures were not as stable as is usually presumed during this so-called golden age of American schooling.

The second image is that of the *flâneur,* that jaunty denizen of the arcades who so captivated Benjamin. For him, the flâneur was more than just a dandy wandering alone among the crowds; he was a creature of that very space of the arcades, a stroller-artist detached from yet mesmerized by the phantasmagoria of consumption and the deceptive prospects of window shopping and people watching. But the flâneur's trancelike and ecstatic state of worship before the commodity cult objects had a flip side: his loneliness, boredom, alienation, and shock—the "truth" that lay hidden inside these commodities once their deceptive natures had been revealed. The resemblance of the ruined arcades to the public spaces of today's inner-city schools and that of the flâneur to the student hallwalker, that bane of every high school principal's existence, is more than merely metaphorical. The hallwalker, the "internal dropout," as we shall see, is the student who comes into the building only to cut classes and wander the halls most of the day, playing and roaming as if totally at home in the space but also disrupting classrooms and generally causing havoc. These baggy-panted, Reebok-shod adolescents are the so-called at-risk students, defined as such by federal and state dropout prevention programs—the students our program attempts to serve, acting as a cultural bridge (see Heath 1989, 369) between the peer group and the school. Their very presence in the halls poses the question of whether, like Benjamin's flâneurs, they serve as oppositional figures, culture critics themselves of an unjust and failing system.

Now the ceiling of the lobby and the auditorium are covered with plaster, and there is no way to stare out at the heavens. In fact, since the lobby is too small to contain the burgeoning weapons-searching activity, the large staff required for its operation, and the long lines of students waiting to be scanned, the whole enterprise has been moved into the auditorium, right up onto the stage. Now, during their first, second, and third periods, students sit watching the first scholastic performance of the day: their classmates being searched for weapons by squads of security guards with hand-held metal detectors. The scene proceeds on a daily basis, at one moment routinely, at another tumultuously; the routine tumult becomes standardized. Of those who manage to pass through this gauntlet, some will proceed to classrooms, others will wander the halls all day, every day, rarely going to class. Are we merely witnessing a traditional puberty rite in this liminal space, preliminary to later stages, when youths will become socialized into the stable roles of a structured society? Or are we in the presence of a Benjaminian dialectical image in which the adult educators have absented themselves from the puberty rites and in which the rites themselves are no longer preliminary to full incorporation into society—a world in which liminality is permanent, stability of school and society are no longer even utopian hopes, and the youth are being prepared not, as the social reproductionist narrative insists, for the lowest jobs on the factory floor but for a space of violence entirely outside and beyond what used to be called mainstream culture?

CHAPTER ONE

SCHOOLS OR "SCHOOLS"?: COMPETING DISCOURSES ON VIOLENCE

Two teenagers were shot to death at point-blank range in the hallway of a
Brooklyn high school yesterday morning, little more than an hour before
Mayor David N. Dinkins was to visit the troubled school to tell students they
had the power to break free of the world of violence and drugs.
                                                    —*New York Times,* Feb. 27, 1992

Tuesday we were arriving at the school. The beginning of the day couldn't
have been worse. We saw one of our students handcuffed and escorted by two
police officers. . . . Her face was all scratched. I talked to K, another one of
our students and the other girl who was in the fight. She was on her way to the
police car so I couldn't find out what happened. It's the fourth time I have
seen a student leaving the school handcuffed. The image is truly painful. What
can be so wrong in the school, or outside the school, that makes these things
happen?
                                —Excerpt from daily journal of Hispanic male tutor

Two Conflicting Discourses

Both of the violent events recounted above took place in large New York
City high schools.[1] Accidental or intended, perpetrated with handguns,
knives, or boxcutters, such episodes are no longer even front-page news in
American newspapers. To begin to understand why such tragic incidents
keep happening, one has to be willing to defer judgment on a range of
presuppositions by which we explain American culture and schooling to
ourselves. One extreme conservative view portrays the public schools as
sites of total anarchy. In response, one liberal view chides us for manifesting
any concern about school violence and unearths examples of how bad the
schools were at the beginning of this century. Thus, a set of preliminary
questions arises. Before we can inquire into ways of curing school violence,
we must question why we are engaged in that inquiry. Are today's schools
really violent? Are they that much worse than they were fifty years ago? Is

not the phenomenon of violence confined to a few tough inner-city schools? Or is that view racist? Does not our focus on the negative just detract from all the good things that are happening in schools?

In the forefront of those who avow the existence of an ethos of violence in schools, one finds the right-wing politicians and journalists. To the questions above, the most conventional American response is represented by people such as Pat Robertson and William Bennett; this response discerns a moral and behavioral deterioration over the course of the twentieth century in all of American life—most especially in the public schools. Horace long ago taught us to beware of this *laudator temporis acti* mentality,[2] the attitude of the man who extols the past as he imagines it was when he was a boy. To these traditionalists, anyone holding out hopes for reforming the corrupt and chaotic urban school systems of today is a naive liberal. Vouchers, choice, and the creation of "proprietary" (i.e., business-run) or parochial schools are seen as our only hope for the future.

In reaction to the reactionaries, some authors deny that any problem exists, at least any that should be of serious interest. This opposing argument has the appeal of the counterintuitive. To the annoyance of many older Americans with fond memories of their school days, these authors assert that schools are not much more violent now than they were fifty or seventy-five years ago and that there never was a golden age in American public education (Graham 1992). To prove their point, high turn-of-the-century dropout rates are resurrected, and lists of current school crimes (assaults, rapes, robberies) are downplayed as mere jeremiads concocted by fundamentalists and moralists (see, e.g., O'Neill 1994). We are told that we should be concentrating on school reform and on positive—and often-cited—models such as Theodore Sizer's Coalition of Essential Schools or James Comer's New Haven Plan rather than on merely dissecting failures. Even the mention of the word "violence" in connection with inner-city schools—especially when the topic is raised by a white male writer—is apt to bring cries of racism. In brief, many liberal academicians and intellectuals, for a variety of reasons, shy away from this painful topic of school violence. They are able to enforce this silence by accusing all those who want to raise the issue of being ideologically committed conservatives or worried hand-wringers who are unwilling to appreciate the many successes of our public educational system. Another variation of this thesis would

hoods who are serious about getting an education. "Ed op," therefore, means "magnet." In fact, one can conceptualize the top and middle strata together as a gigantic magnet drawing the best students to the top, as far away as possible from the worst students at the bottom. It is crucial to understand this most fundamental feature of the system. It is not only the private schools of Manhattan and the Catholic schools of the archdiocese that siphon the best and the brightest—and the wealthiest—away from the public system, as is often stated; rather, the system itself does the most thorough job of drawing "the best" to the top.

DEFINING "LOWER TIER"

Occupying the bottom stratum of the pyramid are the lower-tier schools. Since no one has a precise definition of "lower tier," it is impossible to pin down the number of schools that can be so classified. But people well acquainted with the system have their own private listings of which schools fit into this most undesirable category: "lower tier" means more than just low test scores and poor attendance. By 1992, the board had installed weapons-scanning metal detector systems in the forty-one high schools with the highest number of violent incidents, partly to forestall potential lawsuits by teachers, students, and parents who might, after a weapons incident, claim that the board had not done all it could to protect them. In the 1991–92 school year, the teachers' union counted 129 gun incidents, most of them in these schools.[6] By 1994, the number of "metal detector" high schools had grown to forty-seven; many were predicting that it was only a question of time until all high schools would have the "security package," which includes the full array of very expensive technological hardware. Most of these forty-seven are the very large, overcrowded neighborhood schools located in the most highly segregated, most deteriorated, and most violent neighborhoods. They either have no ed op programs or very mediocre ones and therefore have trouble drawing students from other parts of the city. In these neighborhoods, one finds most of the schools that are staffed with the greatest numbers of security guards.[7]

These schools are seen by teachers, students, and parents as the least attractive from every perspective. Inevitably, they are referred to as the worst in the city—even by their own teaching staffs. All the "objective" measurements support these "subjective" impressions: they have the highest dropout rates, the lowest graduation rates, the worst scores on standardized tests, the poorest attendance patterns, and the worst statistics on assaults and possession of weapons. Each of these schools is saddled with the burden of its reputation in the community. A fifteen-year-old Puerto Rican student who had dropped out of one of the specialized high schools and whose father—in full view of his wife and family—was killed on his way home from work by a local drug dealer told me that, in contemplating returning to school, he had ruled out going to the local (lower tier) high school because "it has a bad reputation" and because he knew too many kids there with whom it would be too easy to hang out and to cut classes. He was looking for a good ed op school, the euphemism for "safe" in the board's vocabulary of violence. This reluctance to call fear of violence by its proper name also infects the ethnographer. From my fieldnotes: "Once past 6–8 guards at the front desk, I began thinking how placid, how 'traditional' the school appeared today. Then one woman tutor told me about the very bright boy who was coming down to see them who wants desperately to leave because a gang in the school is threatening him, but that he cannot get a transfer until January."

Within the school reform movement, "magnet school" is an unproblematic concept. In enthusiastic press releases and in news stories, the concept of magnetism has retained its physical, almost magical, meaning: the power to attract. Magnet schools—strongly promoted by the U.S. Department of Education—have come to be thought of as ideal institutions of choice, irresistible places to which ambitious students are drawn. Other schools are admonished to imitate these models, which is precisely what they try to do.

There is, however, a darker side to this magic of the magnet. A magnet school draws students to it, but it also draws them away from other schools. A tenth-grade girl once announced exuberantly in our tutoring room that she had just gotten word she had been accepted at one of the ed op schools. Congratulations were extended, and we held a party for her accomplishment. But to our lower-tier school, which she was leaving, this move represented one more defeat: she was not only moving up the pyramid, she was also fleeing the bottom. What we were really celebrating was her move to a safer school, her escape from the possibility of violence. In our small festivity, we discovered ourselves dramatizing Gramscian hegemony, in the sense that we had unwittingly reenacted the values of the dominant society, had suddenly become aware that this small transfer was emblematic of the entire hierarchical structure. "Magnet school," therefore, has become a phrase whose most important subtextual connotation is that rarity, the much sought-after nonviolent school.

Often the lower-tier principals, sensitive to having their schools singled out so notoriously, will point out that these days even prestigious schools have their violent incidents and suburban schools their shootings and major disruptions. Indeed, who would want to defend the proposition that American middle-class youth are not getting involved in a range of destructive and self-destructive behaviors?

It is clear that the issue of school violence is no longer just an inner-city phenomenon, if it ever was just that. And, just as obvious, it is also clear that the constant threat of violence currently saturates American and international life. Posters of missing or kidnapped children disrupt the charm and grace of quiet country towns. I am often struck, when speaking with colleagues from upstate New York, how closely their stories about rural schools can match those of troubled inner-city ones. Even suburban schools are beginning to get rid of student lockers for fear they may be the repositories of weapons. Is our conventional judgment that violence exists in its pure form in ghetto schools based on fact or on our own perceptions? Is it the case that, as one descends the social scale, outrageous human behavior is just not as well concealed as at the upper echelons? Or, like child abuse, does violence cut across all social classes and ethnicities but affect the poor and the marginalized far more than it does the middle and upper classes? Does the fact that middle-class vice is simply better hidden give one a license to study the phenomenon among the poor where it is just more exposed? I avoid giving statistical answers to all these questions, since my exposure to bureaucracies has led me to question all reporting systems, especially those that have bearing on violence.[8]

Still, one cannot ignore the fact that almost all of the forty-seven high schools that are equipped with metal detectors and large squads of guards are usually thought of as belonging to this lower tier; if that "fact" needs interpretation, then perhaps that is in itself justification enough for this study. Should our liberal scruples about stigmatizing prevent us from examining the conditions of schools that are the only option for the poor?

Beginning with premises of this sort inevitably leads to fruitless debates about whether one school is as violent as another, whether a particular school is the second or the third most violent school in the city, and whether one is exaggerating, finding something that does not exist, misinterpreting data, or believing that schools of the 1990s are more violent than those of the 1920s.

One way around this epistemological impasse is to view our entire reality as being in a "chronic state of emergency," as Michael Taussig does (1992, 13), citing Walter Benjamin's statement that "the tradition of the oppressed teaches us that the 'state of emergency' in which we live is not the exception but the rule" (1968, 257). To view violence as the norm rather than as the exception in late modernity is not a way of trivializing or sidestepping the issue; rather, it is a way of jolting ourselves out of the "dream world" of contemporary perception, referred to earlier, in which, Benjamin was convinced, we were all living. Before reflecting on Benjamin's advice to awaken ourselves, it is crucial that we not shrink from looking as clearly as we can at the nightmare itself.

Freshman Orientation

What does the entering ninth grader encounter on the first day of class in one of these lower-tier high schools? Almost all of these schools, as already indicated, are situated in marginalized—and sometimes deadly—neighborhoods through which the students and their teachers must travel each morning and afternoon. In some of them, students pass lots filled with ten-foot high mounds of garbage that has spilled onto the sidewalks and into the street. Crack houses may be sighted within a block of the school; certain corners near the school are permanently inhabited by drug dealers. Graffiti is ubiquitous.

Entering the building, students will normally[9] be diverted away from the main lobby and shunted to a side entrance (for better crowd control), where they will wait (outside, even in the most inclement weather), hundreds at a time, to meet the security guards who introduce them to the first *rites de passage* of a New York City high school in the 1990s: the wizardry of identity card machines, metal detectors, X-ray machines (for inspecting knapsacks), walkie-talkies, magnetic door locks, and a host of other forms of "security" technology. Students sometimes arrive at their first class half an hour late because they are waiting to be scanned.[10] Less obvious are the verbal exchanges and demeanors that introduce students to police culture and introduce the language of the street into the school environment. No one adverts to this subtle daily introduction of the criminal justice system lexicon onto the educational scene: "scanning," "holding areas," "corridor sweeps," and, as we shall see, the street vernacular that guards and teachers sometimes use in addressing students.

It is inaccurate to maintain, as some authors do (e.g., Alves 1993, citing Coon 1971), that American youth are not guided through initiation rites by adults. In the chapters that follow, I will suggest that, although teachers have progressively withdrawn from any meaningful role in this regard by detaching themselves from close emotional and social involvement with youth, these rituals have not become exclusively peer centered. The performance of these initiation rites, at least in the context of the schools, has been abdicated by the teachers and delegated to the low-status guards, who are ill equipped for the task of socializing youth into productive roles in Western society.

The students—even the ones who carry weapons—share the same hopes as the authorities, that all these devices will keep the school safe. But these jointly held hopes are obscured by the basic semiotics of the hand-held scanner as it traces the contours of the student's clothing. The scanner is more than a technological marker of radical suspicion, inimical in every way to the school's historic and humanistic aim of fostering mutual trust, respect, and courtesy; it represents the first radical and direct reorganization of the student's body space, now no longer sheltered within a cloistered pedagogical universe, by the technological power of the state. One African American girl who had participated in our program told me that she transferred out of the school to the safety of an ed op school because one of the guards had made suggestive remarks as he moved the scanner in the vicinity of her legs.[11] This police-power intrusion is happening within school space, which was previously conceived as a sanctuary. But it is important not to conceptualize the lobby as a space for the reproduction of violence independent of other sites in contemporary America. The dominant society's demand for immediate results and success stories, its obsession with test scores, "back to basics," and Japanese competition, and its retrenchment on funding for all poverty programs reminiscent of the days of the Great Society have all contributed to this deterioration of public space.

In June 1995, this convergence of school space and state-sponsored containment of street terror moved from esoteric theory to explicit news release when Mayor Giuliani moved to place disciplinary control of the school system under the direct supervision of the police (Newman 1995c). One tenth grader, commenting on the mayor's proposal, remarked that the mayor was apparently unaware that the police were already in his school, striding daily down the corridors, two by two, with weapons visible!

The formative and performative aspects of these first school lessons, then, pertain to the body, not to the mind. The ritual performance of daily scanning takes on a totally different aura in school lobbies than it does in airport entrances. Guard and student perform a duet of mutual mistrust while the students' peers stand or sit,[12] watching this first lesson of the day: frisking. Reconstruction of the student body has begun.

A PLACE TO AVOID

But even before they walk through the front door, these students have absorbed the rumors—from siblings, junior high school friends, and influential adults—about the school's reputation. Their junior high school guidance counselors have repeatedly reminded them that the local high school is a place to be avoided at all costs because of its history of violence. Their pastors have preached sermons exhorting their parents not to send them there. Groups of local ministers and priests have set up organizations opposed to the very existence of these schools.[13] Some of their classmates go off to the more prestigious specialized schools and specialized programs. Not being accepted into these highly selective schools at the end of junior high school and being forced, as a result, to enter the local lower-tier school is widely interpreted as failure.

The students who are not accepted into the ed op high schools or who cannot afford a private or parochial school therefore have no choice but to attend these neighborhood schools. High school officials take it as a given that these "list notice students" (board jargon for students coming directly from neighborhood junior high schools) come to their first day of high school with chips on their shoulders, because they know they have been assigned to this lower-tier school rather than having freely chosen it. They represent the bottom quartile of their class—the students who were "passed along" just to get them out of the junior high school building—and they know it. The core of a typical incoming freshman class, then, is drawn from this "list notice" group of poor academic performers from the "feeder" schools. In one school, for example, a full 66 percent of the entering ninth-grade class was reading below grade level; 63 percent had scored below 50 on a basic math test whose scale was 0–100.

To this basic group are added the "over the counters" (OTCs) or "walk-ins" (board jargon for students who arrive from overseas after the start of the academic year), recent immigrants who may be provided with ESL and bilingual courses if they are from China, Haiti, or Spanish-language countries. Walk-ins account for as many as 800 students annually in one of our schools with a total population of 4000. Finally, there might be as many as 300 to 400 students who have been held back to repeat ninth grade; up to a third of a typical ninth-grade class may consist of these "holdovers" or "retreads." One principal stated the situation quite plainly: "The desirable students get siphoned off before they ever reach the [lower-tier] neighborhood high schools."

Everyone in the system is aware of this pernicious effect of magnetism. And the process repeats itself every fall, despite the best efforts of the bureaucracy to provide "choice."[14] Most lower-tier schools find it impossible to attract the most educationally able youth and are forced to take those who do not make it to the other schools. Although the issue of choice has, in the early 1990s, received considerable public attention, several dimensions relating to inner-city schools have been left unexplored. The president of the New York City Principals' Association, for instance, stated that the choice issue is compounded by the fact that "we [in the neighborhood schools] get a number of youngsters who have failed in private or parochial schools and [have been] dumped by them. When these youngsters return to the public high schools they wind up in the neighborhood high schools; they don't wind up in the specialized or educational options high schools" (quoted in Lockwood 1988, 7). Lower-tier principals constantly complain about this "dumping" not just from the private sector but from all of the more desirable public schools. Even more infuriating is the fact that some lower-tier schools are often forced to admit students whom another lower-tier principal—one with more political clout—does not want in his school (Richardson 1993).

Put bluntly, the lower-tier schools do not have the luxury that the more prestigious or more powerful schools have of turning away students. Put even more bluntly, the issue of choice cannot be divorced from the issue of violence. The first serious result of all these factors for schools at the very bottom of the pyramid is overcrowding. The schools in which we operate are sometimes filled to 125 to 150 percent of capacity, and this overcrowding is alleviated only by low attendance patterns: on a typical day, up to a third of the students may be absent. These schools would not know what to do if all the students showed up on a given day. One of our schools currently has an enrollment of 2600, but only about 1800 attend on a given day; the principal admits quite openly that he is not unhappy about the low attendance pattern, since it alleviates overcrowding. In the next breath, however, he talks of the need for a more aggressive outreach program to attract the long-term absentees. Add to this picture the continuous movement of students in and out of the school: students coming and going due to family moves, disciplinary actions and suspensions, visits back and forth to the Caribbean, and absences due to fear of retaliation after a violent incident. Coming to school does not mean coming to class; cutting classes and walking the halls are two of the chief features of this novel school culture I will attempt to define. And all of these schools have high rates of teacher absenteeism.

Thus, incoming ninth graders find themselves in a school neither they nor their parents chose, a school to which they were assigned because of where they live, and a school they were probably counseled to avoid. As one teacher told me: "The students come in from junior high school disgruntled. Their academic advisement is lousy. They don't get any of their choices [of other high schools]. Therefore they get sent to a neighborhood zoned high school. They make 10 or 12 choices [of specialized ed op schools and programs] and end up getting none of them." Another school administrator put it this way: "The kids . . . perceive the school as having a bad reputation. Kids get involved in fights. Of course they go home and they tell stories to their parents and their parents want to transfer them as soon as they can. Many of them just drop—drop out of school."

Those who stay, and who set the tone of the school for new arrivals from overseas, are more than just "disgruntled." Realizing they have no alternative but to attend, they often enter with more than belligerent attitudes. They may enter with weapons in their pockets, armed to protect themselves, fearful of all they have heard about the school. Others, most of them recent immigrants, enter slightly dazed by all this and just seek a friendly face. It is for this reason that principals routinely ask us to work with the incoming ninth graders: they are indeed the most in need of academical, social, and emotional support. School officials feel that if students can make it to the eleventh grade, the last two years will most likely be more or less unproblematical. There is a good deal of evidence to justify their sentiments.

A SCHOOL IDENTITY CRISIS: LOWER TIER OR ED OP?

Faced with such an impossible set of circumstances, what does an energetic and dynamic principal of a lower-tier school do? The most natural instinct is to attempt to move the school up the pyramid from the third stratum to the second stratum, from lower tier to ed op. But the principal, with the practical wisdom that comes from everyday dealings with the board,[15] also knows that certain options are closed. The superintendent to whom the principal reports, although sympathetic to the plight of the school, is unable to honor a principal's request to assign fewer students to the school the following September; the waves of immigrants continue to pour into the city, and each one has the right to a free public education. The principal knows that the timid reforms of the 1980s and early 1990s (e.g., dividing the school into "houses") have not made a serious dent in these problems. Truly radical reform (breaking these large schools of 2500 to 4000 students into three, four, or five smaller and more manageable schools) is deemed to be out of the question due to the considerable expense, architectural and legal constraints, and bureaucratic red tape.[16]

From the perspective of the principal, then, she or he has only one realistic option left: to attempt to transform the school into one of the ed op schools that, after the magnet analogy, will attract the better students. "Better students," one principal put it plainly, are "kids who can read and write," and the ed op schools, with their achievement tests for admission, currently get these students. The schools at the bottom suffer not only because the students constantly *want* to get out of them but because some of the abler students actually *do* leave them.[17] The contrast between these two types of schools is startling: in 1991, one lower-tier school had a graduation rate of only 18.1 percent; one of the ed op schools in the same borough had a graduation rate of 73.4 percent. The contrast between a lower-tier school and the top four is even more startling: routinely, 98 percent of the graduating class of one of the top four schools obtain the more prestigious "Regent's diploma," while less than 1 percent of a lower-tier school's graduating class obtain one!

Since the skimming process clearly works so well (for the school that does the skimming), the name of the game for an enterprising lower-tier principal is to join in the skimming process.[18] With the board now proclaiming that it is moving toward smaller (approximately sixty to 180 students) Vision schools, this task becomes even more urgent, since most high school principals are convinced that the creation of Vision schools will skim students from their schools, just as the creation of an ed op school would have. "Whenever you create a small Vision school, you further hurt a neighborhood school," one principal said to me. All the principals I know would concur in this rather harsh judgment about the way in which the "small school movement" has been implemented in New York. I did not find a single lower-tier school official who did not see these latest initiatives (e.g., the creation of fifty "small, personalized settings," announced with much fanfare and received by the press with such enthusiasm) as anything other than calculated payoffs to pesky local community groups—as so much "political patronage" or as "sinecures" for certain school officials—who then lectured beleaguered big school administrators on how to duplicate their small-school "models."

INSIDE THE LOWER-TIER PRINCIPAL'S OFFICE

Let us eavesdrop at a not-so-imaginary staff meeting inside a principal's office in one of these lower-tier schools. He has brought together his key staff and union representatives. He tells them the school must move quickly to avoid further deterioration; the Vision schools will be proliferating soon, with several brand new schools opening in the next two or three years. He presents this recent move as a clear threat: "Our better students are going to be skimmed off to go to those new schools; that has been the history of the board of education." But he also gives them a model for attracting students to the school. He reminds them that the school is getting only the bottom group from the local junior high schools and that the overwhelming majority of them—close to 75 percent—do not graduate from high school. He proposes to inaugurate a program (usually some variant of an English-as-a-second-language or a bilingual program) that will result in admitting more recent immigrants into the school.

If this plan takes hold, he explains to them, the number of list-notice students will be greatly decreased, perhaps even cut in half. And he reminds them of what they are all aware of: "most of our discipline problems are incoming ninth graders from the junior high schools," whereas in the case of most of the immigrant students coming in from other countries, "I'm not gonna say they're angels . . . but generally speaking, they do fine, in comparison." The blame is not put on the list-notice students themselves, but on the training they have received in junior high school: "Not that they're bad kids, but they just have the junior high school mentality." The junior high schools that feed these lower-tier high schools *also* have bad reputations. They are said to allow the students to "do nothing except play." As stated above, many students do not actually graduate from these schools but are passed on, because they "aged out" and are not permitted to remain in junior high school past age fifteen. Some students, it is said, know in September of their eighth-grade year that they have already aged out and that they will be passed on to a senior high school, so they do nothing but play around, if they bother to come to school at all. These students are not portrayed explicitly as "bad" but simply as arriving at the senior high school lacking the necessary qualifications. But the implications of the proposed policy that the system forces the industrious principal to make are clear: decrease the numbers of list-notice students (most of them African American), and increase the numbers of over-the-counter students (most of whom are West Indian).

The school's strategy for survival, he explains, consists of trying to attract the more academically able students from around the city. He would happily settle for even 10 percent to 20 percent of students whose scores were at grade level or above. "The main problem," he continues, "is that 88 percent of the youngsters coming in to the ninth grade this year were remedial in math." That means that the math department has to spend the entire first year, and sometimes two whole years, teaching junior high school math, and then, by eleventh grade, the students are just up to the eighth-grade level. They cannot begin algebra until their junior year. "The same thing is true in reading. We're not talking about bad kids, we're talking about kids who can't read." In concluding, our principal sums up his concept and his hope: by bringing in a new group, the school will have the opportunity to improve the discipline as well as the scholarship and to become a "viable high school where teachers can teach, principals can principal."

If this strategy is adopted, the school solves its problem by increasing its reputation throughout the system and by excluding many African American students (and even the lower-achieving Caribbean students), who, in turn, will have to be assigned to other lower-tier schools. Proposals of this nature are considered to be commonsensical; many African American teachers and Caribbean teachers assent to it as outlined. The relative success and preferred behavior of one ethnic group in comparison to native-born African Americans are accepted as a matter of course. These black students are not seen as excluded because of their race or ethnicity, and their futures are left in the hands of the board's processes. The hierarchy of the system thus stands the conventional positivistic research on its head and renders irrelevant questions such as whether black, white, or Hispanic students create the most violent incidents. These strategies for importing and exporting populations and the consequences they entail force us to ask the question of whether ethnicity constructs violence or is constructed by it. If the ejected students end up on the streets, that is not considered to be the problem of this particular school, which feels it cannot take on the whole world's problems.

This scenario may never get beyond the planning stage; the only point in portraying it here is to illustrate the effect that the creation of ed op or Vision schools has on the ideology of those in the lower tier and to portray the way the system's constant skimming processes tend to worsen and segregate the schools at the bottom of the pyramid. Because these processes of creating "effective schools" or magnet schools or ed op programs under the guise of reform have been taking place since the mid–1970s (usually in well-integrated neighborhoods), the effect on lower-tier high schools in ghetto areas has been devastating. One junior high school principal whose school feeds one of our high schools told me that the high school "could reform itself til it's blue in the face," but parents still would not want to send their children to it because of the dangerous neighborhood surrounding it and because of the school's historical reputation in the community.

"THINGS HAVE QUIETED DOWN"

Such are the dreams that a school and its principal can dream; but to cope with the reality of everyday life the school administration must employ a different kind of discourse. To bolster staff morale as well as their own, lower-tier principals attempt to maintain a doctrine of progress, a conviction that things are getting better and better each year.[19] One principal said to me: "That [violent atmosphere] was in 1981. . . . The school was worse at that point because the kids were really in control of the building." From month to month, teacher conversation in the school varies between whether "things have quieted down and the kids are behaving much better" or "things have totally gotten out of hand." In one such discussion, two teachers informed me that there had been no incidents in the past couple of weeks "except for some of the usual fights, and, oh, the knifing incident." I asked if the student was hurt badly. "Yes," they both said, "very badly." One student had used a pair of scissors and stabbed the other student in the arm. "But just that one incident wasn't too bad for this school," one said, as they both laughed. Conversations easily slide from one side of this ambivalent discourse to the other: things are "getting better" or things are "chaotic."

The perception of progress is combined with quiet resignation that the school's life is permeated with violence and weapons. Thus, the perception of progress is constantly being threatened by an opposite perception of student disorder, chaotic corridors, and a school out of control. At the teacher orientation session in early September, the text of a principal's speech attempted both to reassure and to remotivate the returning teachers: "This year we are going to be in control of the school and the corridors; we are going to take control and be in control." But the clear subtext understood by all was that control had long since been lost and had little chance of being regained. Many teachers and almost all administrators share a common assumption: that the cause of the disarray is to be placed squarely on the shoulders of the students, especially on a small core of troublemakers. "All it takes is 50 kids out of 2500 who want to turn the place upside down, and they can do a very good job of it," one official said to me. Regardless of where the blame was to be placed, or the stated reasons for violence, there was the everyday presence of weapons in the school. One principal told me, "Kids carry weapons for a variety of reasons. A number of them, when they get up in the morning, they brush their teeth, they put the pants on, put your knife in your pocket, you put your shoes on, its another part of what you do in the morning."

The cynical acceptance of violence and threatened violence as a part of the daily life of the school had reached the point where it was quite explicit in discussions. One principal told me that he had a large gym bag at home filled with the collection of knives, chains, box cutters, chukker sticks, Chinese stars, and even two razor-sharp machetes which he had collected from students over the past two and a half years.

Survey assessments vary on the extent of students carrying weapons.[20] Officials in our schools estimate that "about half" of the students are equipped with some kind of weapon. Students' own estimates ranged from "about half" to "everyone":

> JD: Do a lot of kids carry knives and weapons here?
> KAREN: Of course, maybe even guns!
> JD: How many would you say?
> KAREN: I'd say about 50 percent of the school.

A school secretary told me that there were "an awful lot of kids carrying weapons, guns, razors." She said the place was "like a battle zone." A woman tutor, beginning the day's work with a group of Haitian girls, asked one girl to get out her pen. The girl opened her purse and a straight-edged razor fell out. The tutor froze; the other girls laughed. The girl said, "Oh, I carry it to protect myself. Everyone carries one; all my friends carry them." Reliance on force as an acceptable way to protect oneself or to achieve one's objectives becomes so accepted that no one even thinks to challenge the tenth-grade girl who sends a threatening letter to the principal (claiming she will have her male relatives come and "mess him up" if he doesn't transfer her quickly to a better computer class). Instead, she is treated deferentially and apologetically. Another woman tutor wrote: "Tasha came down and we had a long discussion on violence in and out of school. I told her about one of my students from the period three class who has been permanently suspended because she was carrying a knife with greater than a 3-inch blade. Tasha told me about her knife that she carries. She says she is as afraid of women as men hurting her and keeps it for protection—she has never used it though."

"IT'S A WAR ZONE"

These unrecognized rites of passage, buried in the everyday routines of school life, are the means by which students are socialized into a world in which violence is considered part of the normal order of things. These rites involve more than the enactment of violent episodes; they also involve students' narratives—revealed in their dialogues with one another or with trusted adults—of their own experiences as well as their commentaries about the experiences of others. One of our students told me that "kids bring in a lot of pen knives that no one could detect . . . razor blades . . . they have knives in their lockers in the gym; there are cracks in the walls where they can hide them." I asked one Haitian boy, a recent graduate, how he survived. "I gave them the impression I was somewhat dumb. . . . I set my own trend. . . . Some people would mock me and I would ignore them. Then they would look at me funny. . . . I would act eccentric."

The anthropology of the body draws our attention to how the body functions both as a transmitter and as a receiver of information (Lock 1993, 136). To interrogate current understandings of school violence, which harbor an unexamined mind-body duality, to understand how student knowledge is constructed, one must shift from the purely cerebral world of language and focus instead on materiality: the exchange of looks between peers, the slow strides in hall walking, the "hanging" in the halls, the rumpled cuffs down near the shoes, a group leaning silently against the wall, the sudden explosion of energy when something really starts to "go down." The space of the student's body is not discontinuous from the physical body of the school edifice or the surrounding neighborhood.

CLAUDE: You live in [the area]—it's like a war zone, right?
COREEN: Yeah.
FARLEY: It *is* a war zone.
CLAUDE: I told you I know every area.

Disorder unremittingly breaks through the routine, becomes part of it, and keeps the newcomer confused and off guard. One hears crashing glass falling from upper windows, but school staff proceed as if nothing has happened. Ear-piercing fire alarms go off and no one responds. Tutors doubt whether they should leave the tutoring room to go search for a student because there are gangs roaming a particular corridor or stairwell. From my fieldnotes: "Yesterday, K, a student,[21] was apprehended with an Uzi submachine gun and several rounds of ammunition in the students' cafeteria. He was trying to hide the weapon in his girlfriend's knapsack when the guard arrived. He said he was going to 'waste' two students who had insulted him the day before. Word of this incident spread quickly throughout the teachers' cafeteria today. A disaster was averted."

The violence is camouflaged by a discourse of denial, since surfacing these issues to the level of consciousness of the entire school community—with no hope of changing the underlying conditions—would only make apparent the painful and ineradicable admixture of street culture and policing technology that had permeated the terrain of the school. I once suggested to a recently retired teacher that it might prove beneficial for teachers to get together and reflect on why and how some of the disturbing events were occurring so habitually in the school. She reacted: "As a teacher I didn't hear half of what was going on. . . . I would hear about it two weeks later. I would hear only about kids who got knifed on my floor. . . . When you are there, you get used to it. Why should we disabuse people and tell them what a culture of violence they are living in? What would you gain by pointing out to them how disastrous the place is? If they are adapted to it, why make them miserable? Why give them awareness, if they will have to stay there and work?"

These incidents, more disorderly than normally acceptable, now recognized, now shrouded by silence, spark the suggestion that one is dealing with a homogeneous culture of school violence, a suggestion that further implies that the public areas of the school, prior to the advent of these disorders, were privileged spaces, historically devoid of any implication of violence. It is tempting to posit a culture of school violence hermetically sealed off from the larger society and to forget about what is happening in the larger community: the inadequate public assistance for families in need, the almost complete marginalization of these populations, the reality of the gun lobby in Washington, and the television industry.

Before attempting to transcend such a narrow and restricted notion of school violence, let us feel its full weight in the following excerpts, all taken from my fieldnotes:

> Last week a student shot a rubber band at a girl in the cafeteria. The boy and the girl's boyfriend came to blows over it. Both swore revenge and then met yesterday on the 4th floor hallway, the scene of many such showdowns, between classes. The first student pulled a knife. The other brandished a .38 caliber gun and shot the first boy in the back as he tried to flee. Today, one of the women security guards, standing on the spot where it had occurred, described the incident for me. She said that the hall was filled with students and that, as usually occurs in such incidents, the crowd gathered round to see what was happening to such a point that none of the guards or deans could get through. One male guard told me that he had to put his head down and push his way through the crowd. Then, he said, the dean, who had made his way to the center of the fray, handed him the knife after he took it away from the boy who had been shot and he took the knife back through the crowd. At this writing the bullet is still lodged in the boy's lower back as the operation to remove it is considered too dangerous to perform. The boy who did the shooting was placed in jail.

> Mr. . . . [a teacher who worked closely with our program] told me that yesterday he heard 3 shots ring out at the park right next to the school. Later, a dead drug dealer was found in the park. Another teacher, going home, got caught in the cross fire of a shooting between the cops and drug dealers on his way to the subway.

> Last Monday we [the thirty-five graduate students and I] spent the entire two-hour seminar discussing violence in the schools, Jesse Jackson's prescription for ending violence, and the *New York Times* editorial on the same topic. Afterwards I was beginning to wonder if I had not overdone it—after all, there is more to education than endless discussions about violence. But on Tuesday morning, S [a tutor] called from the school to say that yesterday Ms. A's [an ESL teacher] purse had been stolen from the ESL office, and with it her money, credit cards, and car keys. The students then went down and stole her car and have not yet been apprehended! At the same time another group of students ran through the corridors spraying mace all over the school. Everyone had to be evacuated, especially the pregnant girls and the babies in the LYFE [parenting] center.

That same day, N [a woman tutor] heard that a friend of one of the students was shot outside the school. [Later the principal told me that, besides all of the above, the evening before some people broke into the school and vandalized an entire computer room, smashing all the terminals.] All this in less than 24 hours.

Yesterday I went to . . . school at lunchtime. I chatted with Mrs. S [our coordinator] and, at first, she said everything was going well. But as I hung around, several things emerged. The principal came to the lunch room, looking very preoccupied, not smiling at anyone. Mrs. S then told me that there had been a slashing that morning— one student cut another's face with a knife; and this was on top of the knifing that took place last Friday. Then, G [the head of a community organization] said that six youth had been shot the prior week within a block of the school and that none of this had made the papers. One boy, a former student whom we both knew, had been killed. G had to pay for the boy's funeral clothes because the mother could not afford it. He said how tired he was of going to funerals and that he has started another "Stop the Violence" campaign, asking parents to observe a voluntary curfew and to get rid of guns. Then, before leaving, R, a Haitian teacher, told me of how another teacher had been punched in the face by a student that week (his nose is broken) and is swearing he will not return to the school. Finally, a paraprofessional was injured when attacked by some students whom she surprised when they were in a classroom by themselves, gambling. R said that in this school, things get covered up as fast as they happen; no one wants to talk about it. He thinks the guards should be trained in psychology and said that they overidentify with the kids and that, since many of them have not graduated from high school themselves, they are closer to the student mentality than to that of mature adults. Yet most of the staff of this school would assert (and I myself have to admit) that the tone of this school has improved over the past five years.

Yesterday one of our women tutors helped a male teacher break up an intense struggle between two girls in his classroom. One girl had the other around the neck; the tutor ran over and separated them. One had a big scratch on her arm. The girl who is said to have started the fight had given her hoop earrings and a gold chain to a friend before the fight started. The tutor and the teacher had to deal with parents, suspension, and then discussed his chaotic classroom situation for a long time on the phone last night.

The problem with such ethnographer-generated observations about school violence is not that they are not "true" but that they force subsequent analysis into positing a suddenly intrusive and inert culture of violence that never strays far from the school perimeter or relates to contemporary political events outside that perimeter. A (male Hispanic) tutor's reflections on a (Hispanic) high school student's dream begins to nudge our analyses beyond the narrow confines of the school-seen-as-cloistered-sanctuary, albeit a violated one:

> The other day I also worked with Y. He is a bright student who has been with us since the beginning of his [high school] experience. Y was telling me of a dream he had the other night about the school. He dreamed that a school teacher and a security guard were shot in the hallway. He remembered seeing the teacher dead and the security guard bleeding. Violence is everywhere and the students see it as part of their everyday lives. What scares me most is that we have come to accept violence as part of our everyday lives instead of trying to solve the root of the problem. We try to leave the guns outside the school instead of taking them out of the streets.

In our attempts to understand how this sad state of affairs has come about, neither explanation—that violence evolved slowly and gradually became the norm or that it intruded suddenly from nowhere—seems adequate. We are left with a tension between these two polarities. One can neither affirm a homogeneity of violence within the school perimeter nor infer that the school has a monopoly on the reproduction of violence in the community. The school walls are porous, violence flowing in and out, between community and school.

On the temporal plane, only a naive historicist reading of history can trace an undisturbed line of development from a supposedly pristine nonviolent past (i.e., up to the 1950s) to a supposedly chaotic present. The contrary thesis, a more sophisticated revisionist history of New York, insinuates a violent past doomed to endlessly reproduce itself (Sante 1991). The emotionality of the service provider, faced each morning with the expectant faces of children forces one to reject this defeatist and hopeless position.

If we allow ourselves, however, to remain momentarily locked into an ethnography of the present, one is required to explain these sudden intrusions of the violent into the everyday. "It happens in bursts," said one teacher, referring to those few weeks out of a "normal" semester when the whole place erupts: the blood on the floor, kids beaten to a pulp, kids getting knifed, ethnic groups fighting, the Haitians versus the Panamanians, kids shaken down for guns in the hall, security guards luring them out of the classrooms in order to search them. Where does normality leave off and "abnormality" begin? Are "acceptable levels" of violence in inner-city schools now considered normal throughout American society? That youth carry weapons "in ghetto schools" seems to have become a generally accepted fact of life among the American populace today (DeWitt 1993).

Once again, emphasizing how the abnormal blots out the normal and modifies it easily slips into right-wing talk of totally chaotic schools. Yet the violent and the normal are reconciled and coexist in the everyday. On the same day in which a teacher talks quietly to a visitor about a curriculum project and students work productively in the context of a busy tutoring room, I write the following fieldnotes:

> A meeting in the principal's office broke up fast when word arrived that a "female teacher had just been beaten up by a female student." The police had to come into the building. The teacher had to be taken to the health clinic and then to the hospital. The fight got so vicious that the male security guards would not break it up: "We're not touchin' females . . . unless they are starting to kill us; the lawyers would have a field day." The fight raged on until a woman security guard could be summoned over the walkie-talkies. When classes begin to change, outside the cafeteria, the hall deans and guards enlist some paras and teachers to form a human wall to make sure that students do not congregate around the principal's office. The girl who started the fight is still in the principal's office and they are afraid of retaliation. Police and deans have entered the hallways and put up wooden horses as barricades. Parents and students are waiting in the principal's office for suspension hearings, the outcomes of previous incidents. The principal is running around trying to take care of all this at once. The previous day a bulletin board was burned. Meanwhile, in the cafeteria, a huge fight erupts even while two policemen are there—all the kids standing on the tables

cheering the fight. The principal, making his rounds, bursts into classrooms just to make his presence known. He orders kids to take off their hats, and teachers apologize to him for allowing the hats to remain on. There are a full 20 staff members (10 guards and 10 deans or paras) in the auditorium facilitating the scanning process. About 300 students sit in the auditorium watching their peers get scanned on the stage or mill about in the lobby; they are forced to wait in these areas (an improvement over a few years ago when they had to wait outside in the cold) until it is time to change classes. Ten additional guards and paras are working the lobby, so, all in all, 30 people are engaged in the process of getting the kids into the building. Three security guards are absent because they had to go downtown for a hearing about an earlier incident. This causes problems for the logistics of the guards, the chief topic of a late-in-the-day conversation behind the closed doors of the principal's office. Interrupting this conversation, the principal makes a phone call to another principal to try to convince him to allow a troublemaker to transfer to his school. (Before the call, the chief security guard advises the principal to downplay this student's problems and to stress the student's athletic abilities in making the case for the transfer.)

A "normal" school somehow keeps going on in the midst of all this, with our own students coming in and out of the tutoring room and attending their classes. How are teachers able to tolerate all this and sustain these two contradictory discourses? One stratagem is to relocate the abnormal to another space: one long-time teacher (now retired) related to me how frightened she was when her superintendent insisted that she visit a neighboring school with a very bad reputation, one in which three students had been killed the previous year:

> It's funny, about a year or so before I left, they had some kind of program where they wanted social studies APs [assistant principals] to visit their counterparts and the superintendent sent me to [another lower-tier school]. I was very unhappy, I didn't want to go. I called the AP, I said you want to pick me up? You want to take me to work? You want to take me home? I'm not coming by myself. I was very unhappy; once I got in the school, it wasn't bad but I really didn't want to go. . . . It wasn't my turf.

To most outside observers, there was not a great deal of difference between the two schools. The veteran teacher was "never afraid in her own building," on her "own turf," despite her frank acknowledgement of the daily presence of weapons, but was terrified at the thought of going to the neighboring school.

Schools or "Schools"?

What do these coexisting contradictory discourses suggest about contemporary schooling in the lower-tier high schools of New York's inner cities? What does it mean when the terms "normal" and "wild" can both be predicated of a school with equal veracity? The suggestion I am making here is that, in order to make a first approach at the phenomenon with which we are dealing, we might provisionally make a distinction between the traditional institutions everyone calls schools and the institutions we are discussing here, which might be thought of as "schools." It is equally important to understand that, in denying these lower-tier establishments the appellation "school," we are not lapsing into the right-wing camp, which advocates nothing more than closing down the public system. The point of the quotation marks is not to indicate a totally chaotic situation but rather to stress the coexistence of these two prevailing discourses, the serpentine ways in which the discourse of "normal schooling" has learned to live more or less comfortably, more or less anxiously, alongside the "discourse of violence," which also serves as a "normal" communicative strategy. The corollary of this cognitive shift is significant: even though the word *school* appears over the front door, and even though all the players (administration, teachers, and students) speak as if they are dealing with that familiar institution, such is not the case. The second corollary is that most of the educational literature—journal articles and school management manuals, even the most recent works on reform, written with the traditional school in mind—will not be of much help in dealing with this new entity, the "school." Contrary to the belief that a dedicated principal can turn such situations around, a hierarchical system, intent on fostering excellence at the top, can create a series of "schools" at the bottom of the pyramid. Part of my message, then, is a plea to debunk this "great man theory" of education, which always assumes that a "dynamic principal" can turn a bad school around, since all of these principals are essentially operating in truly unmanageable situations, as are their superintendents. The existence of "schools" is historically structured, and it will not yield to quick fixes.

Thus far, we have been considering how these competing discourses co-exist at the level of the school system and at the school site itself. We shall also examine how this same obfuscation takes place in the theoretical litera-ture. Before doing so, however, we must take up the recent history of how these marginalized inner-city institutions called schools become recon-structed into a new and scarcely recognizable category that I have hesitat-ingly dubbed "schools." But before dealing with either of these topics, it is necessary first to explain my own presence in these inner-city school corri-dors by describing how our program originated.

CHAPTER TWO

TUTORS, MENTORS, ETHNOGRAPHERS

A post-modern ethnography is fragmentary because it cannot be otherwise.
        —Stephen A. Tyler, in James Clifford and
        George E. Marcus, eds., *Writing Culture*

You catch it on the edge of a remark.
        —Harold Abrahams in *Chariots of Fire*

DROPOUT PREVENTION

To explain my presence in the New York City public high schools more fully, I will describe the role I played in initiating a collaborative program that focused on assisting those students the schools considered potential dropouts. One snowy weekend in February 1985, I went to Long Island on a group retreat with ten New York City high school principals and some officials from the central board's high school division. I had been contacted by the official at the board responsible for "dropout prevention," since it was known that I was heading a group of New York University professors and graduate students who were interested in providing whatever help they could to the school system. The principals had been selected to attend a kind of think-tank weekend because their schools had been singled out from the 126 high schools in the city as having the highest dropout rates.

It was a very relaxed setting, and, despite the implications concerning their leadership abilities, the principals were far from being on the defensive. A kind of gallows humor prevailed. "With dropout rates like this, we must be doing something wrong," one principal said. As the weekend progressed, their humor became easier to understand, since it became clear that they all recognized the discouraging tasks they had to face. Every fall, the large majority—up to 75 to 80 percent—of the students entering the ninth-grade classes in these huge schools possessed math and reading scores appropriate for the third- or fourth-grade levels. One third of the freshman classes in these schools was composed of holdovers, students who were repeating ninth grade for a second or even a third time. These principals were reminded every day, by multiple sources, that their schools were "the worst in the city." But the use of the word *worst* in this case had a euphemistic connotation that went far beyond low reading and math scores and was, in fact, a code word for another, rarely spoken, word: *violence.*

I was unsure of what I or others at the university would be able to contribute to alleviate the situation; the principals, in turn, were not sure what to make of me. But by the end of the weekend several principals had invited me to pay exploratory visits to their schools. I decided to begin with a school (henceforth referred to as Alpha School) that was ranked, on standardized tests, as 125th out of the 126. My choice of this school was due largely to the extreme willingness of the Hispanic principal to become involved in the collaboration.

A few weeks later, I attended a meeting in the principal's office at Alpha School; present were his key advisers and lead teachers. We agreed to begin our effort in the most uncomplicated way possible: to design a strategy based on the school's most significant features: (a) it was approximately 75 percent Hispanic and 25 percent African American;[1] (b) it had the second worst dropout rate among all of the city's high schools; and (c) its students were dropping out mostly at the ninth- and tenth-grade levels. Since a large proportion of these students were recent immigrants, our initial approach consisted in identifying graduate students[2] as potential tutors with three distinct sets of skills: those who had been trained to teach English to non-native speakers (ESL); those who had some experience in Hispanic bilingual and bicultural education; and those who were studying to become bilingual counselors. For the tutoring space, the school put at our disposal a fairly large, unused recreation room in the basement. Soon the head of the ESL department, a woman who was delighted with our presence in the school, was referring recently migrated ninth and tenth graders to us. Our nine graduate student tutors (two as paid research assistants, seven as volunteers) began working in the tutoring room, as a team, three days each week, five periods per day.

With the support of the president of the university, we were able to obtain state funding for the project the following fall.[3] Thanks to this subsidy, we began again at Alpha School the following September (1985) and expanded the program into three additional inner-city high schools. The grant paid for the assistantships (full university tuition remission plus a small stipend) for the graduate students who would work with me and for field trips for the high school students. Since 1986, through a combination of private, federal, state, and board of education funds, the program has been expanded to support the work of seven teams of graduate students working in seven large high schools, two small alternative schools, and a large elementary school. All in all, about forty graduate students work in the program each year.

From the beginning, we were aware of the warnings about "band-aid approaches" to urban educational reform, about inadequately evaluated dropout-prevention efforts, and about the need to get on with the serious business of restructuring schools rather than simply bringing in "outside intervention programs." And we were sensitive to the problem that identifying students as potential dropouts was itself a not-so-covert form of labeling.

But by the mid–1980s, all of the schools with which we began to collaborate already had in place various kinds of "reform" efforts: "houses," collaborations with businesses and banks, mini-academies, and similar initiatives—most of them mandated by 110 Livingston Street, the central headquarters of the board of education. The last thing they wanted from us was another restructuring project that would promise total "school reform." Their felt need—which we elected to honor rather than to quarrel with— and specific request was that we organize a team of six to eight university tutors who would concentrate on working individually and intensively with about 125 to 150 students in each school. This represented only a small fraction of each school's population, which included from 2500 to 4000 students, but such an arrangement would give the school a resource for what it saw as some of its most problematic students. During a given period, a tutor might typically work alone with an individual student or with a small group of five to six students; during a whole semester we might see no more than sixty to seventy students. Academically, the goal would be simply to find stimulating ways to assist and motivate the students as they attempted to cope with their classwork and homework. We recognized the body of research that warned that, by focusing on the individual so-called at-risk student rather than on changing the whole school environment, we could be exacerbating the situation rather than helping to alleviate it. But the schools felt—and we ourselves began to see—that these students would be out on the streets if one waited for the long-range reform efforts to take hold. We forced ourselves to think small.

TUTORS

From these decisions regarding what we would *not* do (i.e., restructure the school), a positive profile of what we *would* attempt began to emerge. We would establish, within the confines of a literacy center and tutoring room, a milieu that would help create a supportive dialogic relationship between tutor and tutee. We would try to run a serious, challenging tutoring program for as many students as we could handle comfortably. At the same time, we did not want to restrict ourselves to individual relationships and thus prevent small groups of tutors and tutees from working together.

Having made these initial decisions, we soon learned that identifying and selecting students was tricky business. State and local funding sources have set up criteria for "at-risk-ness" that are reminiscent of, and in some ways overlap, the criteria set up for admission into special education pro-grams.[4] Even beyond these grant requirements, an individual student's entry into the program may require some sensitivity from the tutors. One hopes that a tutor will be able to find a link with a tutee: a bilingual Hispanic teacher refers a girl from her ESL class who is pregnant; a woman tutor notices a tough-looking boy leaning sullenly against a corridor wall, invites him into the tutoring room, and, miraculously, he smiles and accepts; a coach brings in his star soccer player, a recent immigrant from rural Jamaica, whose English, he says, the teachers cannot understand; a student takes it upon herself to bring two friends to the program; an Asian student sees his friends working with the tutors and wanders over out of curiosity; a hesitant fifteen-year-old girl is hooked on the program after noticing a tall, handsome boy come in and sit down to work with his tutor. ("*He* does tutoring wichu'-all?" she asks, as her friends burst out in giggles. "He sure does; I told you that you came to the right place," responds the woman tutor.)

Students usually come to see the tutors during their lunch period; tutors carry the lunches on trays from the cafeteria to the tutoring room to save time. This commensality is an aspect of our program that I have not yet fully explored, but it always amazes me to watch the rapport between the tutors and the adolescents when the graduate students go to the cafeteria, bring down the food, serve the high schoolers, and munch french fries with them while both pore over whatever academic subject. Occasionally, teachers will suggest that a student might even come for tutoring during class time—for example, during a large ESL class of thirty-five to forty students. Sometimes tutors go out into the halls or make classroom presentations to get students into the tutoring room. One woman tutor wrote in her log, "Since I spoke to you last many things have happened & I want to bring you up-to-date. As we discussed, I've been searching the classes & the halls for lost souls. I've caught up with a few and have been trying to bring them back."

Anyone unfamiliar with the amount of hallwalking that goes on in the corridors of lower-tier schools might mistake this log entry for evangelization. The challenge is to make the tutoring room more appealing than the corridors. Students forget appointments or may be only half-motivated to come. The tutor, especially at the beginning of the semester, often has to hustle around the school to remind a student about a tutoring appointment. A large group of obstreperous boys may arrive at the program and resist being split up among different tutors. A girl may arrive stating that she hates all men and will work only with a woman tutor. A student might not relate well to one member of the tutoring team. The team leader's task of switching the student from one tutor to another then involves the delicate balancing of personalities and workloads to avoid hurt feelings on all sides. At times, teachers may attempt to show support for the program by referring those who are chronically absent or who have had a history of failure in junior high school with the result that students may then assume the worst: "We are being put into special ed!" The principal may refer a roaming hallwalker one day and a more willing student struggling to pass the regents' biology exam the next. Students who have been segregated into low-achieving classes (which students realize are for low achievers, despite euphemistic terms such as "Star House," "Achievement House," and the like) may view referral to the tutoring program as a further sign of disrespect. A boys' dean may decide that the tutoring room is a perfect place for students who have been disrupting classes to come in and cool off. The challenge for the tutoring team is to work with these diverse motivations, to keep the tone of the room upbeat, relaxed, responsive, and welcoming—without appearing to be omniscient.

REFLECTING ON PRAXIS

In the early days of the program, as graduate students returned to the university by subway each day, they began to express a need to get together on a regular basis to reflect on what we were doing and where we were going. We decided to meet every Monday in seminar style for two hours—meetings that evolved into a six-credit graduate course. The impetus for creating the course had nothing in common with the usual graduate-school curricular requirements. These young adults sought a contemplative moment in a hectic week; they had a real need to discuss every angle of all the issues manifesting themselves in the adolescents' behavior and language. Henceforth, our program existed at two main sites—the tutoring room at the school and the seminar room at the university—with a range of sites in between: pizza parlors, museums, basketball courts, students' homes, clinics, and funeral parlors.

But what would be the content of such a course? The weekly discussions in the seminar room at the university were—and still are—patterned by the events and needs arising daily in the tutoring rooms of the schools. It became increasingly clear that our approach would have to be broadened beyond the concern for cognitive issues such as math education, literacy acquisition, ESL techniques, and study skills if we were to be adequately prepared for working directly and individually with at-risk students in these so-called troubled schools. Much more than the mere addition of a wider range of academic subjects was entailed.

We began to reflect on the new identity we were in the process of forging for our role as tutors. We had created a new persona that was neither classroom teacher nor guidance counselor nor special-ed expert. We had established who we were *not,* but who exactly were we? How were we to conceptualize ourselves and represent ourselves to others? We felt a close kinship to the school outreach workers, the paraprofessionals who went out to the housing projects or the streetcorners in an effort to retrieve truants for the school. But in the final analysis, we were still tutors—that is, teachers who happened to work with individual students rather than with entire classes. During one seminar, when we asked ourselves how our students perceived us, we came up with several different titles, with sister, older brother, friend, and even mother predominating. Clearly, "transference" was at work and new identities were being forged. No matter what identities tutors imagined for themselves, it was clear that the students were themselves engaged in constructing identities for the tutors:

> [White woman student's log]: There is always this attempt to bring me into some sort of acceptable grouping by the kids. The other day when I was helping some students, Juan looked at me and said, "You know, you look Hispanic." I was tickled. "What makes you say that?" "Oh, I dunno, it's just when you talk in Spanish, you look like you could be Spanish. When you talk in English, you don't talk like a white person, either. Like that other lady, she's definitely white, she talks it, too. But you could be Dominican."

SEARCHING FOR IDENTITY

The wide range of seminar topics gives some indication of the complexity of melding all these roles together, with the central thrust on encouraging techniques that begin with the students' interests rather than with where the curriculum is: using a "whole language" approach in teaching reading and writing to adolescents; keeping dialogue journals as a way of encouraging writing; tutoring math through student-generated rather than textbook-generated problems; presenting speakers who have clinical experience with contraception and with AIDS; establishing a respectful context in which the issues of race, homophobia, and other sensitive topics can be discussed; examining ideologies of immigration; sharing pertinent articles from the educational literature; discovering the proper procedures for referring cases of child abuse, suicide, and violence; establishing the climate in which tutors can speak frankly about the relationships students develop with them; finding room for aesthetic practices and possibilities; sharing stories of success—and failure—and, in general, learning from each other's approaches and styles.

Behind each item on this rather random and eclectic list of topics, of course, lie whole fields of specialization and bodies of literature. Graduate students always resonate better to authors such as Paulo Freire or Dick Hebdige than to articles from the standard educational research journals. But the basic texts of this course are drawn not only from the scholarly literature but from the graduate students' own logs, which represent their personal reflections on events in the schools, their feelings about the interactions they witness between teachers and students, their comments on school policies, even their dreams or those of their students—in short, anything they feel comfortable revealing to the group. These logs become the texts on which to reflect at the Monday seminar. Phone calls and personal consultations are crucial for particularly critical situations where someone is in danger or abuse can be prevented.

Tutors drop in at our office after school to talk about particular students, to report on bizarre events, or to arrange field trips or luncheons for their students. One important measure of the relevance of the course to the daily work of the graduate students in the schools is the vehemence with which they strive to take control of the seminar's curriculum and insert their own approaches, reading material, and points of view. I can hardly describe these seminars as stress free. At one point, the group decided to shut down the seminar for a week until we all had a chance to cool down and rethink our own most cherished positions on race, class, and disparate approaches to urban education.

Plurality and Heterogeneity

Each team is constructed so that it is as multiethnic, multilinguistic, and multidisciplinary as possible. We consciously assemble the teams in this way not because it is "politically correct" (although a recent version of political correctness would perhaps disapprove of such arrangements)[5] but because this heterogeneity corresponds to the diversity of the students we serve. A typical team consists of tutors from Trinidad, Puerto Rico, Canada, Mali, Brazil, China, and the United States, of artists and mathematicians, of jazz singers and athletes, men and women, gay and straight. In any given year, Alpha School, which has a preponderance of Hispanic students, may have three or four graduate students from Spain, Colombia, or Puerto Rico as part of an eight-member team; Beta School, which is largely West Indian and Haitian, might have a few Trinidadian women and French-speaking African men on its team; Gamma School, which is 48 percent Asian, might have tutors who speak Mandarin, Cantonese, Shanghai dialect, Bengali as well as Spanish. A tutoring team might have a mix of black Americans from Harlem, whites from suburban California, and international students from Europe or the Third World.

The high school students, sitting in the tutoring room and observing tutors with such diverse backgrounds interacting amicably, inevitably ask the tutors questions such as, "Are you guys friends? Do you guys hang out and party together on weekends?" (It is important to keep in mind that there are no white students in any of these schools; such questions may arise, since there is rarely an opportunity to observe white-black or white-Hispanic interracial friendships.[6]) Such questions lead us to reconceptualize ourselves not so much as conventional role models, a distinctly individualistic notion, but as a kind of corporate role model—a group of adults with diverse backgrounds working together, enjoying one another's company, conflicting with one another at times, but also attempting to resolve frictions in a harmonious way, searching, in brief, for what Victor Turner has referred to as "existential" or "spontaneous" *communitas* (1969, 132). The program ideal is to create among the tutors a small community in which the youth also feel comfortable and welcome. Here is how a West Indian woman graduate student, who had been in the program for three years, depicted the climate of the tutoring room:

> One of the many positive things about the tutoring program is its diversity in the ethnic and racial backgrounds of the tutors. We have our disagreements . . . but we are able to discuss them as issues—which they are—at our staff meetings. The [high school] students are able to see us agreeing and disagreeing and attempting to solve our disagreements by discussing them. Much more of this is needed in high schools like Beta School. Students need to be aware that people from different racial, ethnic, and religious backgrounds can get along, that there will always be disagreements and differences of opinion, but they are not always because of differences in race, religion, and ethnicity. This does not mean that we pretend that various kinds of prejudice do not exist, but merely that prejudice is based on a type of ignorance from which one can rise. I remember last year JK [a Jewish male tutor] was able to erase some rather disparaging assumptions some [Beta School] students had about Jews. Similarly, RL [an African male tutor] was able to inform some of my students from the mini-school that all of Africa is not like what is projected in the television news. About two weeks ago D [a Japanese-Canadian male tutor] had a similar experience with a student. The student's reply in a discussion that was taking place between him and D was that ". . . all of you look alike." His reference was to D's Asian features. Like JK and RL, he was amused at the display of ignorance and D asked him if all black people in the room looked the same. Since we cover an array of physical differ-

ences—R being from Africa and myself and others from various Caribbean Islands—the reference D made helped the student see the folly of his statement. It would be great if more of this type of discussion could take place. On none of these occasions was there anger which made it suitable for a discourse of this nature. Too often expressions of this nature take place in environments of anger so that assumptions and accusations based on ignorance are exchanged instead of dialogue.

MENTORS

Our "identity," then, merges two roles: that of a tutor who helps students cope with the demands of the curriculum and that of a mentor who takes time to turn away from academics to listen to whatever concerns, fears, or dreams students wish to share. Field trips to art and cultural centers and museums around the city are of great help in this regard and may produce the most unexpected results: "I had to pull him off the computer when it was time to go and he asked me if the public was allowed in the [IBM] museum because he was interested in going back to this museum on his own time. Even L asked about going to the Museum of Natural History once again on his own time. (We had visited the Museum of Natural History last semester, but as always were rushed for time.) I was glad to see these two normally apathetic students be inspired to visit museums on their own."

Straightforward requests for tutoring might easily mask a deeper, concealed issue. One of the graduate students, a woman from Central America, who was herself pregnant, found that a request for help in mathematics was coupled with a far more pressing issue:

> Another important thing that happened today was that while I was waiting for the elevator to come, a young female student asked me if I was a teacher. I explained to her the reason why we were there and she told me that she needed some help with math. Then she asked me if I was pregnant and how many months did I have. When I told her that I was four and a half months, she looked surprised. (I think that was the main reason why she wanted to talk to me, not her math problems.) She told me that she was pregnant too. She said that she had just found it out yesterday (with a home test kit). She is 16 years old and holds a part-time job as a cashier. She also told me that her family didn't know yet, and she believed her preg-

nancy would cause a great deal of problems at her home. She said that both she and her boyfriend work. But she is ambivalent; she said that she would still like to live with her mother. My impression is that she doesn't know many issues about pregnancy; she asked me such questions as: Can you walk upstairs? I am not sure she wants to keep her baby, if she is pregnant, nor do I know if the father knows or is going to help her. She is a potential risk for dropping out and I would hate to see her leave school. She is in 12th grade and said she wants to finish high school. She agreed to meet with me on a regular basis during her lunch hour. If she is pregnant and decides to keep her baby, I can be of real help in offering her parental training. If she isn't pregnant, I would also like to meet with her to talk about future non-planned pregnancies, the difficulties and realities of child rearing, etc.

If such descriptions of our daily activities sound suspiciously close to self-promotion, I can only reassure the reader that the grimmer, less edifying side of life in the tutoring room will surface in the following chapters. I am frequently asked what data I have to demonstrate that the program is "successful." Such inquiries usually imply an interpretation of success based on improved attendance and grades; in the everyday life of the tutoring room, success is often defined by something as ephemeral as receiving a smile from a previously depressed student, convincing a student to come to school the next day, or listening to a student relate the exciting news that she or he has finally passed the math competency test. In any case, one does not have long to savor success. The same day that a teacher reports that his students find our program to be "the highlight of their week" because they are getting real help is the day a university official tells me that the young man his office hired at my suggestion (and who I was convinced was "turning his life around") was just caught stealing. Given some of the unpleasant episodes that will be related in the course of this text, perhaps it is only fair to ourselves to begin with a couple of log excerpts that will give the "feel" of the tutoring room when the program is working at its best:

> [Beta School] The beauty of the program is that it eludes all labels. It is college prep and basic literacy, mentoring for troubled students and for over-achievers like EV. (Apologies to Professor R for using the term "over achiever." I'm always stumbling over somebody's ideology.) There is no stigma attached to tutoring with us and no being subjected to swift and fatal categorization. How else can you ex-

plain J [another woman tutor] working with FM and PG [two students with widely divergent personalities] at the same time? Or VR tutoring math and ESL simultaneously by having his ESL student explain a problem to the math student in Spanish and then having the math student tell her to say it in English? Or that SH will work with the kids on SAT preparation in the middle of the room while NR draws pictures of Bart Simpson on the board? I think it is this very diversity that enables us to have such a positive image throughout the school.

[Gamma School] There is a feeling of camaraderie in our room that is infectious. We have only been here two weeks and each of us [has] caseloads of at least twenty students. I had six new admits today alone. It is wonderful to see Harry and Thelma working with Chinese and Bengali kids. And I have my share of mainstream kids as well. Students will walk by our room daily and want to know what to do to get involved. There isn't an idle moment in the room, and everyone is cooperative and supportive of each other's needs. Hallelujah!!!

For most tutors, the greatest frustration is the realization that there are so many other students who need and want this kind of individualized help but are not receiving it. An awareness of one's own limitations becomes a crucial component of the program.

ETHNOGRAPHERS

It is the informality of the tutoring room that most especially opens the space for the third ingredient in the definition of our role, that of ethnographer. As a safe haven from the frenzy of the school corridors, a relaxed middle space somewhere between the institution and the street, the tutoring room becomes a place where students feel welcome enough to come in and hang out, to talk and joke—perhaps even, at times, to hide. It therefore becomes an ideal place from which the graduate students can learn the student perspective—a carton of fruit juice and a few cookies do wonders. As one Hispanic fifteen-year-old boy told me when I asked him why he liked coming down to the tutoring room: "We can be ourselves [here]. We don't have to be stuck up. We don't have to impress nobody, [pausing, with a smile] . . . only the girls, that's different!"

But if the tutoring room opens a space for ethnography, it is for an unconventional kind. The fact that the anthropologist and those she or he writes about both hail from the same society has not, of course, been considered an obstacle to doing ethnography for a long time. Roy Rappaport (1993) has recently suggested that domestic research should be more highly valued by anthropologists than it traditionally has been. Ethnographers from Jules Henry (1963) to Paul Willis (1977) have for several years been producing research on schools in their own cultures, and the field of school ethnography has burgeoned during the 1980s. There is even a sense in which our schools *are* "far off and exotic"—located as they are in marginal and troubled areas far from midtown Manhattan. The usual warning given to those seeking to do an ethnography in one's own culture—namely, to try to "make the familiar strange" (Erickson 1984)—was hardly necessary here: one graduate student from Australia told me he felt more culture shock in going from Manhattan to an isolated area of Brooklyn than he had in going from his hometown of Perth to Lebanon, where he had previously taught. Then too, the high school students are largely, though by no means exclusively, recent immigrants from many lands: from St. Lucia and Bangladesh, from Tobago and China, from the Dominican Republic and Liberia.

This great heterogeneity of students combined with the equally great diversity of graduate students at times brings about the most unlikely tutoring combinations: a young man, an M.B.A. candidate from Shanghai, working with a boy who recently immigrated from Port-au-Prince; a Jewish woman from Westchester County working with a group of young black Muslims from Brooklyn; a man from Zimbabwe tutoring three girls from Vietnam. Diverse combinations occur: a Brazilian graduate student artist tutoring recently immigrated Puerto Rican and Dominican youngsters in a Brooklyn neighborhood, brings them over to Manhattan to introduce them to the Metropolitan Museum of Art's collection of African masks. All of these examples amount to additional reasons to support Kirin Narayan's (1993, 671) argument against the traditional distinction between "native" and "non-native" anthropologists. Is a Barbadian graduate student doing tutoring and research in a Brooklyn high school among recent immigrants from Grenada, Trinidad, and Barbados a native or a non-native?

The issue of the identity of my graduate students mirrors the anomalies surrounding my own identity. Should I consider myself an "outside" ethnographer studying the cultural "other"—since the schools clearly consider me (and the tutors) to be guests? Or am I more comparable to a teacher doing a "self-study"—since the schools also often describe me (and the tutors) as regular "inside" members of the school staff?

The graduate students were, on the one hand, my coworkers in the program; on the other hand, they could be viewed as my fellow ethnographers, since these schools had often become the sites of their dissertations. Their roles shifted back and forth from "members of the community to be studied" to my "secondary informants" to colleague-researchers. Or was it perhaps the case that I was doing an ethnographic study of them and their interactions with the students? Even more undecidably, was I, writing about the tutor-student exchanges, being parasitical on their logs? In the end, I have chosen to regard them as key local informants, part of the complex scene to be studied.

As for the tutoring room itself, it would be false to view it as a kind of natural space that enables one to capture "pure student voice"—as if it were a politically neutral site. Such a naive reading would miss the constructed dimension of this ethnographic space. Its suitability as a place to dialogue with students can perhaps best be described through a conversation I had with Emile, a Haitian student who had been in the United States for five years, who spoke English with a decided Haitian accent in a mainstream (i.e., all-black American) class, and who emphatically did not like people laughing at his speech. In contrast to his feelings in the classroom, he felt free enough in the security of the tutoring room to confide to me: "I stay on my own; in class, I keep my mouth shut. When you are with friends on the outside of school, then you can talk freely. The problem is you shut up in class." The tutoring room is a relaxed and secure space precisely because it is under control, at least most of the time. We shall return to the theme to which this Haitian student alluded: the peer group's ability to take control of the classrooms and corridors, a control the school system has relinquished. Hence the paradox: a carnivalesque atmosphere in wild classrooms or an unruly corridor was not always the best for an ethnographer to capture true student voice, because the peer culture—through intimidation and violence—has the capacity to silence student voice when adults totally abandon it to itself.

The order in which we discovered the three component parts of our role was significant: first tutor, then mentor, then ethnographer. We did not perceive ethnographic research to be primary; the basic purpose of entering the schools was, and remains, the performance of a service. "Hanging out" ethnography certainly did not originate with us, but it was at this point that we parted company with most other forms of "hanging out" ethnography: we were not there just to "listen to the voices" of adolescents—we were there explicitly to engage those voices and even to redirect them, even though officials thought of us primarily as pure instruments to help raise the test scores.

But *qua* ethnographers, repugnant as this may sound to an older anthropological generation, we were in the field with a mission. Entering an institution with these complex sets of overt and covert understandings has both drawbacks and advantages. The "people from the university" may be seen as naive and inexperienced, even if some tutors are in fact more experienced than some of the teachers. On the other hand, the very process of collaborating in the work of the schools gave us an extraordinary vantage point from which to learn about urban schooling, to do research, and to reflect on our own praxis.

The prevailing sentiment in academia generally relegates service programs to an inferior status, something to be performed by social agencies or "activists" on the basis of knowledge arrived at through previously accumulated "hard data." Universities are seen as sites for the production of knowledge through research, not as places for the application of knowledge through service: service is viewed as the handmaiden of research, and not vice versa. Schools of social work never have the prestige of departments of anthropology. Even within the field of anthropology, the concept of "applied" anthropology, despite the creation of respectable journals such as *Human Organization,* has always been considered to take second rank to theory and to "pure" anthropological research. The very phrase *ethnographic research* has a ring of certitude about it: besides asserting "I was there," it contains the further implication of "and this is what I found out about *them.*"

When it comes to ethnographic research in education, doctoral committees share the common cultural anxiety that American taxpayers have about "outcomes": how many students (in this school, program, experiment) showed academic improvement? How many students remained in school as a result of your program? How many exhibited a changed attitude toward school? Legitimate questions all, and certainly quantifiable, but tinged with a quest for a certitude that is not available. The trace of uncertainty that I hope the reader will detect in the following pages stems not from a blind loyalty to a deconstructive approach but from the dialogic nature of the tutor-student relationship. The adolescents I write about—and, through my writing, pass judgment on—may so modify their behavior tomorrow as to negate the whole story. One Brooklyn teenager with whom we worked intensely—tutoring, organizing musical performances, providing summer employment—was, when last heard of, selling drugs on the streets of Boston. Is he therefore to be reported to some educational funding agency as a failure or a dropout, or should we wait and hope that at some point he will remember that some people cared?

COUNTERMETHODOLOGY

I have dwelt on this near-universal attitude that privileges research in order to stress the countermethodological approach of the present work. "Normal" social science—even critical ethnography—assumes and affirms the personage of the researcher, the activity of research, and the necessity of research results, whatever the methodology selected. Even ethnographers sensitive to the concept of reflexivity in research usually understand it as a way of reflecting on one's data, or on one's own biases, or as negotiating one's research outcomes with the participants (Anderson 1989, 254). My intention is not to dismiss these methods in an offhand way but to stress that these concerns, including the issues of validity and reliability, arise from positivistic scientific research paradigms.

What is being attempted here is a reflection on one's own real-world work, on the daily practice of teaching and tutoring, on services provided. It is this self-reflection that I am defining as research. The central point is that we are *not* in the schools primarily or exclusively to study students. My contention is that our daily involvement with the learning process of the students—our attempts to motivate them, to teach study skills, to communicate values, to help them critique the school's curriculum but still pass the exams—should not disqualify us from this self-reflexive moment and the ability to write about it. Stephen Tyler (1986, 134) calls postmodern ethnography an "object of meditation that provokes a rupture with the commonsense world and evokes an aesthetic integration whose therapeutic effect is worked out in the restoration of the commonsense world." In referencing Tyler, I am certainly not presuming to assert in advance that my product will be a postmodern ethnography, only that the goal of the writing is to reflect as nearly as possible the realities of our postmodern culture, one cutting and revealing edge of which, I will maintain, is the inner-city school corridor.

In employing an approach that attempts nothing more than a contemplation of the work of my tutors and myself in the daily exercise of our collaborative program in the schools, I am also attempting to effect a critique of the ethics and the epistemology of the way school research is normally carried out: the university professor or, more often, the graduate student entering the schools for the sole purpose of collecting data. This book attempts to respect students' and teachers' resentments about being made subjects of study or even ethnographic informants; it attempts to take seriously the epistemological *bouleversement* that dialogical anthropology has effected in emphasizing the process of knowledge production (read here as daily tutor-student interactions) over the accumulation of the end products of research. In short, the participants' (tutors' and students') "culture"— even, and especially, when that culture turns out to be a yet-to-be-defined culture of violence—is conceptualized as being constructed in the process of dialogue and not as a preexisting antecedent to it (see Maranhao 1990). At the same time, I attempt to avoid the pretense that, in writing about these experiences, somehow all representation is excluded.

DECONSTRUCTING THE RESEARCH-SERVICE BINARY

My distinction between research and service may be thought of as a kind of Derridean binary opposition such as that which exists between speech and writing. Christopher Norris makes the point that, for Derrida, a deconstructive reading that subverts the established priority of speech over writing is not simply a question of "inverting the received order of priorities, so that henceforth 'writing' will somehow take precedence over 'speech' and its various associated values" (1987, 35). Analogously, by challenging the preeminence of research over service, I do not then intend to place service (i.e., teaching or tutoring) upon the pedestal from which research has presumably just been knocked.[7] The essential trait of research— the generation of new knowledge—is always already present in the dialogic teaching encounter if one assumes that the ideal teacher remains open not only to learning new "data" from the student but also to the continuing modification of her or his identity. Many of the self-critiques with which anthropology is currently reproaching itself (e.g., countering the illusion that it can adequately represent the cultural "other") also apply *a fortiori,* to all the direct service encounters, from social work to psychotherapy to teaching. So esoteric has social science research become that ordinary teachers (or, in our case, tutors), like Molière's bourgeois gentleman—who was amazed to discover that he had been speaking prose his whole life without knowing it—cannot be convinced that they have been "always already" engaged in performing a kind of inchoate research in the very act of teaching.

Whenever any of the tutors or I articulated in the seminars what we had been experiencing in the schools, the other tutors were ready to give their own interpretations, sometimes adding powerful emotional support, sometimes providing a powerful antidote. The complexity resulted not just from the mixture of sexes, ethnicities, classes, and sexual preferences in the seminar room, a mixture that matched the heterogeneity of the tutoring room; it resulted also from the fact that tutors resisted allowing their charges—or themselves—to be placed in categories determined by others. Most important, some tutors insisted that their own subjectivity not be defined by a single characteristic, be it race or religion. With such a polyphony—at times, cacophony—of interpretations, no one could go away convinced that he or she had captured an adequate representation of urban youth culture. What did emerge, however, was the realization that violence had the elusive ability to rearrange all the categories of race, ethnicity, culture, and class. That university students of color represent inner-city life differently from other students is by now a well-accepted fact of academia in the 1990s. These highly sensitive issues were grist for the mill of the Monday seminar room and had to be dealt with head on for the sake of the tutoring room.

True, we were and are seeking, as Geertz (1973, 9) might have put it, to understand the adolescents' understanding of what they and their peers were up to as they encountered these "toughest" of inner-city schools and neighborhoods, and, yes, we feel that the tutoring room is a privileged perch from which to do this. Most of the teachers in these schools were forced to work with 130–150 students each day while we had the luxury of providing individual instruction. But the daily surprises from the students themselves are our best corrective for any illusions we might harbor that we have nailed down their lives, attitudes, and feelings. Here is a woman tutor reporting on her own interaction with a sixteen-year-old Jamaican girl: "Student:

'You knew I was crying and you never came over to say anything!' Tutor: 'I thought you wanted to be alone.' Student: 'I wanted to be comforted.'"

It will be clear, then, that this ethnography makes no claims to scientific objectivity. Educational researchers' concerns over the importance of empirical facts, data collection, dependent and independent variables, regression analysis, and the other claptrap of scientific inquiry finish by conspiring with the very ills that plague the educational system itself: performance outcomes, measurable results, and evaluation indicators. The problem with such research is not just that the conclusions are usually so obvious;[8] the real problem is that even the educational ethnographies get so caught up in this quest for provable facts and hard data that the complexities, conflicts, and disorder of everyday life get factored out, as does the personality, demeanor, and temperament of the ethnographer whose invisibility is directly proportional to his enhanced prestige. The quest for scientificity is as ubiquitous as it is understandable: the various governmental agencies that fund our programs equate ethnography with merely anecdotal information; they want hard evidence and measurable outcomes set out in neat data bases in exchange for public funds. This is the same positivist language the schools use.

"Hanging-out" Ethnography

During the first year of the program, I tutored alongside the other tutors in one school; the tutoring provided me with direct daily access to the students. I still tutor from time to time, but, as the program grew and developed during the late 1980s and early 1990s, my main task changed to keep track of what everyone else was doing. My associate (a former tutor who became my assistant while he, too, was engaged in writing a school ethnography for his dissertation) and I visit the ten schools on a regular basis, react to the graduate student logs, conduct the weekly seminars, and talk to anyone and everyone in the schools—principals, teachers, students, security guards, custodians, parents, and local community members—about whatever topic emerges as most important on a given day.

Structured interviews were not attempted. In listening to students, I have tried rather to be guided by Charles Briggs's (1986) reappraisal of the interview process. Briggs stresses the importance of learning the natives' *means* of acquiring information if one would get at the *content* of their point of view. Imposing our own Western communicative devices (such as the interview) on students leads to stereotypical answers. The tutoring room affords an opportunity to participate in the students' ordinary conversations and to listen to their narratives about their lives in and out of the school at the same time that we are engaged in working with them.

It may go without saying that the adolescents with whom we work manifest an intense desire to be understood and to be listened to. But many educational researchers still do not understand that formal or informal interviews chill this warm atmosphere and stifle casual and spontaneous comments about items of interest to the student. For the ethnographer trying to understand the world view of the adolescent, nuances get lost. As the character Harold Abraham says (referring to the way one picks up anti-Semitic prejudice) in the movie *Chariots of Fire:* "You catch it on the edge of a remark."

SNIPPETS AND SITES

As the program expanded from 1985's handful of tutors to today's thirty-five to forty per year, from one school to ten, and from fifty students to almost a thousand each year, certain consistent patterns emerged across all of the neighborhood schools. Certainly each school could be said to have its own distinctive individual school "culture" (Erickson 1987), but I was most interested in identifying those themes that emerged as common patterns across all the large schools.

Much that has been stated about our collaboration with the schools assumes ideal circumstances. School officials, like all human beings, sometimes confuse the ways they believe they *should* behave (normative behavior) with the way they see themselves as *actually* behaving (their "emic" view of their own behavior); others, viewing that behavior from afar, may see it quite differently (e.g., my "etic take" on the officials' behavior). Principals would no doubt be shocked if they could hear the tutors complain in the seminars,[9] or in their logs, of the cavalier way in which tutors sometimes feel they are treated:

> [Woman tutor's log in an alternative, small school]: It is very difficult to feel attached to a school when you don't really have any person from the hierarchy coming up and asking you how is it going and so on. It always feels like we are going it alone. However, for me I have sufficient experience in a school situation to know that

students get a lot from someone simply coming up and saying hello and asking how is it going. I do it all the time—definitely the students are getting to know my face at this stage. . . . Today I had planned a little party for N, B [students] and myself so I brought in fruit and nuts and we had a great time dancing in between fruit and nut binges!

[Same tutor, the following week]: His [the principal's] attitude is so offhand that I honestly feel like we are working in a vacuum. He [is] totally unaware of the efforts we are making and even though they may not mean to be offhand and disinterested, that is what we are seeing. There is a lot of cosmetic stuff going on in this school. . . . Do they want our help or not? Do they have any commitment to the program? I do suspect however that my writing and feelings are a bit extreme today.

I present the above not to suggest that tutors always felt unsupported in these schools (this particular school was one of the smaller schools, and we normally associated small schools with caring atmospheres) but to open the question of (a) the whole domain of the tutors' feelings, incarnated in a school setting, as well as (b) my ethnographic relationship with this embodied presence of the tutors and with my reading of their feelings, of their writings, and of *their* readings of the journals and poetry of their tutees. Teasing out all of these levels of interpretation is clearly not possible in each excerpt. In the above examples, do I react by speculating that the tutor was particularly depressed that day or that this is a more generalized situation? If the latter, do I judge that it is time for the principal, the team, and me to sit down and discuss the predicament? Or do I conclude that she has put her finger on a constant of the board of education? I present this brief textual negotiation to intimate a process that may or may not take place in everyday life but that cannot always be made explicit in the chapters that follow.

I have already indicated that the tutors are a highly diverse group, but I want to stress that on any given team one is likely to find women and men, gays, lesbians, and heterosexuals, young married people (sometimes even to each other!), Muslims, Jews, and Christians, "upscale" people and people struggling to pay the rent on their apartment. It is therefore impossible to describe a set of cultural values for which one should be on the lookout in the reading of the logs. Suffice it to say that they partake of the same fallacious views and genuine wisdom that all of us do who live in late twentieth-century America; we spend a good deal of our seminar time trying to reflect on those views.

In selecting narratives about episodes and incidents, I have attempted to focus on the conflicting borders between discourses rather than on consensus. Many frictions have, indeed, been omitted as too complicated, painful, or threatening to relate here; but an informed reader will be able to read between the lines. I employ pseudonyms when referring to these schools because each of them is struggling—with our modest help and the help of many other groups—to improve its own self-image within the local community and within the school system as a whole. Adolescents' self-images are closely bound up with the self-image of their school. Pseudonyms provide one way of talking frankly about what is really happening without offending many valiant efforts. The superintendents, principals, and teachers are striving, according to their own best lights, to find a way to improve the schools and to help students assume some of the responsibility for what is happening in the schools. The fact that I finish by disagreeing with many of the directions these efforts are taking does not mean that I do not have a profound respect for these educators, most of whom find themselves in impossible managerial situations.

The material for this book will be drawn mainly from the three largest inner-city high schools in our program. The poverty indices of all three neighborhoods surrounding these schools are among the highest in the city of New York. It hardly needs to be said that in all these schools the vast majority of students are poor enough to be eligible for the federal free lunch program. But such statistics cloak the embodied concreteness of poverty in the projects:

> [Woman tutor, Gamma School] Ignacio missed school the other day. When I asked why, he [said he] had been to the hospital because a cockroach had crawled into his ear and they had to take it out with surgical equipment, he described the amplified sound it made crawling around in his eardrum and said his head has ached so bad the last couple of days and he hasn't been able to concentrate on school nor has he slept, for bad dreams and the fact that it crawled in his ear while he was sleeping.

Socioeconomic data are usually greatly underestimated, since the government counts only those who actually submit the school lunch forms;

many students are reluctant to do so because of the stigma attached. All three schools have dynamic, energetic, and extremely hard-working principals (Alpha's is Spanish, Beta's is Italo-American, and Gamma's is Jewish) and have undergone complete metamorphoses since their origins in the early part of this century: Alpha was originally a vocational school; Beta was an all-girls commercial school; and Gamma catered to a Jewish immigrant population.

We think of Alpha School as our "flagship" school, since that is where we began. Each year we send the largest contingent of tutors there (seven or eight) to work with the 75 percent Hispanic, 25 percent African American student population of 2600. The school is located in what is one of the city's most violent neighborhoods. Its "chop shops" cater to the stolen car industry, and its decaying piles of trash and garbage are heaped high on surrounding lots. The *New York Times* referred to this neighborhood in 1986 as "a no man's land of abandoned buildings, empty lots, drugs and arson."[10] The houses and apartments that formerly occupied these lots were burned out during the riots of the 1960s and during a blackout in the late 1970s in response to discriminatory redlining and other illegal and corrupt housing practices. Other lots have been leveled to get rid of the crack houses of the 1980s. At an evening parent meeting, I listened to parents' concerns about how they were going to get home safely from the meeting, not to talk of student achievement. Alpha School prides itself on its business course, its ESL/foreign-language program, its swimming team, its current attempts to restructure, its struggle—together with the surrounding community[11]—to become a safer place, and its record of involving local community organizations. But it frankly admits that it is frustrated in figuring out what to do to improve scholarship. In a typical year, Alpha may have a ninth-grade class of 900, of whom only 200 will graduate.

Beta School is located on the borderline between an area whose gentrification was halted when the real estate market bottomed out in the late 1980s and a neighborhood that has in recent years seen violent, nationally televised, clashes between local black and Hasidic Jewish groups. When the borough superintendent first invited me into this school in 1985, he informed me that it was one of the most troubled, overcrowded, and dangerous high schools in the city. I counted thirty-five different countries, including almost every island of the West Indies, represented among its student population of 2400. The school had five principals during the 1980s, and two chancellors threatened to close it down because of the violence. Under the current principal, the school considers itself a safer, more orderly place than it was in 1990 but is concerned about losing its better students to more prestigious high schools and about the large number of students (up to 75 percent) who enter unprepared from the junior high schools and stand little chance of graduating. It prides itself on some outstanding Caribbean graduates, its Saturday Learning Center, its PM school (with late afternoon classes), its collaboration with community-based organizations, and some excellent counselors and teachers, many of whom are African American or from the Caribbean.

Gamma School has a long history of serving immigrant students; approximately 85 percent of the student body come from homes in which a language other than English is spoken. Its total population is over 3200—about 48 percent Asian, 42 percent Hispanic, 9 percent black, and the remainder from a wide variety of ethnicities. As in all of these schools, the term *Asian* includes a variety of cultures and nationalities—specifically, Chinese, Vietnamese, Burmese, and Indian; "Hispanic" includes Dominicans, Puerto Ricans, and natives of many Latin American countries; "black" includes students from many of the Caribbean countries as well as African Americans. It has an enviable record among neighborhood schools (e.g., 92 percent of the Chinese students pass the prestigious math regents exam) but is concerned about the disparity between these statistics and those of other groups (e.g., only 17 percent of Hispanics pass the same exam). The school believes these disparities are due to "home background," but local Hispanic politicians complain that the school is not trying hard enough with the Hispanic students. It feels it is always being compared unfavorably with the city's top school, which has the advantage of selecting the best students yet graduates only 82 percent of them on time. This top school also sends some of its students to Gamma School, which is then charged with the failure if the student drops out again. It hosts an annual "Asia Night," which brings together the entire surrounding Chinese community to enjoy student performances. It contains a large annex, a separate building for about 800 ninth- and tenth-grade Spanish- and Chinese-speaking recent immigrants. Unlike Alpha and Beta Schools, Gamma does not have metal detectors. I think of it as higher up the pyramid—closer to the ed op schools.

If an evening meeting takes place at any of these schools, the respective principals automatically call the local precinct in order to have a few officers on hand to prevent intruders from entering the building. After an evening meeting at a Brooklyn school, before heading back to the relative safety of Manhattan and my doorman-guarded apartment building, I observe the police putting on their bulletproof vests ("guaranteed for up to 9 mm.; not guaranteed against shotguns") to go out into the night and routinely face the possibility of encountering weapons incidents. "Nobody's usin' a .22 or a .28 anymore—9 mm. is all they're usin'," one young officer tells me matter-of-factly. No one would think of bringing up the topic of gun control lest the officers roll their eyes and look at you as if you are as "out of it." While this ethnography is situated within the walls of Alpha, Beta, and Gamma School and other schools like them in Brooklyn, lower Manhattan, and the Bronx, the focus is on the porosity of the boundary between school and street, between the institution and the larger society. Each of these schools has a symbiotic relationship with the local "projects" (the low-income housing projects) and is embedded societally within a neighborhood, precisely the kind of neighborhood that Greg Donaldson has captured in *The Ville: Cops and Kids in Urban America* (1993). In his depiction of the shootings at one high school (which are the incidents referred to at the beginning of chapter 1), he has demonstrated the impact of the street on the school. What remains to be sketched is a fuller diagram of the two-way nature of this porosity—how violence is imported into the school from the community as well as how it is exported back into the street from the school.

These short thumbnail sketches of the schools could be greatly expanded to include their unique histories, their individual school cultures, and their separate records of achievement. In refraining from doing so, I am willfully blurring the distinctions between them precisely in order to stress their commonalities as lower-tier inner-city schools. It is my intention merely to fix their identities in the reader's mind so that some of the allusions in the text will make sense. But I am also trying to stress that I have no intention of doing a comparative study of the degree of aggression and violence in all three schools. Even mentioning the word *violence* in the same breath with *ethnicity* immediately implies an interest in comparing the magnitude of aggression amongst groups: which ethnic group, which school, is more vio-

lent than the other? Such a stance also presupposes that the students themselves are the prime vehicles for the introduction of violence into the
schools. In the pages that follow, I question this common assumption, since
it omits the complicity of the school system itself in the construction of
violence.

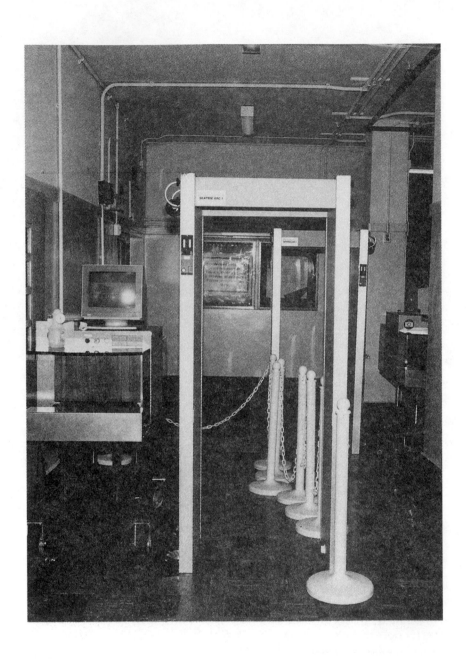

CHAPTER THREE

FOUCAULT, SECURITY GUARDS, AND INDOCILE BODIES

Thus discipline produces subjected and practiced bodies, "docile" bodies.
—Michel Foucault, *Discipline and Punish*

They don't hassle you.
—fifteen-year-old girl (recent immigrant from the Caribbean)

EMERGENCE OF A DOMINANT DISCOURSE

Following the murders of three students and the critical wounding of a teacher in one lower-tier high school—the incidents referred to in chapter 1—the response of the New York City Board of Education was to allocate more funds ($38 million) for weapons scanners, extra police officers, and security guards. With every electrifying incident, the teachers' union, attempting to reassure frightened teachers, has called for a strengthening of the guard apparatus. The guards' union, in turn, has been only too willing to comply with this escalation of "security."

There are also the obligatory reassurances to parents and the public that most schools are calm from day to day, that even the most troubled schools are havens of safety compared to the surrounding troubled streets, and that serious incidents are declining. The rest of the response has also become predictable: the chancellor and the union lament the lack of federal gun-control legislation and routinely call for more specialized counseling and conflict-resolution training for teachers. School board members like to stress the idea that students use weapons for protection in order to get to school safely, placing the burden of blame on the larger society, *outside* the school. In fact, there is a good deal of truth in this assertion: some of our schools have begun "Home Safe" programs, organizing students to walk in small groups for self-protection against gangs as they make their way home from school in the afternoon. Our graduate students often accompany students from the school to the subway at 3 P.M. for the same reason. But it has become increasingly difficult for the board to pretend that most of the violence students encounter is on the way to and from school.

The fundamental response to escalations of violence, in hard dollars, is an expansion of the numbers of security guards and their technological apparatus.[1] Although violent student acts (corridor knifings, shootings, murders) are perceived as abnormal and rare, and as interruptive of the daily pedagogical scene, the techno-response is seen as normal, as natural, as the only possible solution. Thus, the police-state counteraction becomes entrenched in the normal architectural setting of the school as space is re-arranged to accommodate metal detectors and the auxiliary technologies they spawn. Funds are appropriated for more and better trained guards, metal detectors, X-ray scanning machines, electromagnetic door locks, alarm systems, emergency telephones, and other security equipment. I am told by officials responsible for security that all these devices are in the primitive stage compared with the technology that is planned for the near future. Incidents happen, and when they do, even in tight budget years, money for high-tech expenditures and guards somehow materializes. As one boys' dean told me, "If I have a rape in the school this year, I'll get two extra security guards next year."

Educators not familiar with U.S. urban schools find this escalation of security hard to understand. Once when I accompanied a visiting principal of a Swedish high school on a tour of one of our schools, she refused to believe me when I told her there were seventeen security guards on regular duty and insisted on checking with the school authorities to make sure I was not exaggerating. Her school in Sweden, like the one she was visiting in New York, contained a number of immigrant groups yet had no security guards—only the principal and teachers. I get the same puzzled reaction from graduate students arriving from overseas—from China to Mali. Today there are over 3200 uniformed school safety officers in the Division of School Safety of the New York City Board of Education, a contingent larger than the entire Boston Police Department;[2] this number does not include regular police officers assigned to the more troubled schools (both plainclothes and uniformed) or all the ancillary personnel ("paras") as-signed to security. In size, this security force would rank as the ninth largest police department in the country, falling between those of Baltimore and Dade County, Florida.

SECURITY GUARDS: AN ETHNOGRAPHIC ESSAY

In New York City schools, too, there was a time when the only adult presence in schools was that of the principal and teachers. When did the build-up of these large security forces begin and, more important, how and why? Older teachers cannot remember the presence of any security guards (who prefer to be called school safety officers or SSOs) until about 1968–69. Even then, it was merely a question of hiring a single guard (usually a retired policeman) to protect the main school entrance from intruders at the time of boroughwide demonstrations during the teacher strikes and decentralization debates then occurring. In most schools, even the lower-tier ones, large concentrations of SSOs began appearing only during the late 1970s or early 1980s. Today, each of the schools we work in has a squad of from twelve to eighteen SSOs on regular duty,[3] not counting one or two regular police officers assigned from the local precinct, and undercover officers to deal with specific problems. When the scanning devices (used to check for weapons at the front door) were first introduced, I counted as many as forty additional guards (over and above the basic seventeen) arriving in five or six vans on a given day at Alpha School; now that weapons scanning has become routine, the regular guard group is supplemented only by a smaller scanning troop with specialized training in the body- and knapsack-scanning processes.

The school safety officers, like the custodians and the cafeteria workers, have a chain of command independent of the principal. Like tenants in a landlord-owned apartment building, principals are at the mercy of those who control the material dimensions of the school. Custodians control the heat, light, electricity, water, and cleaning; cafeteria workers, the food; school safety officers, the security and access. Each of these groups has its own chain of command extending outside the school to a borough office. "I have no control over the security guards; they don't report to me," one principal told me. Most principals would probably bristle at that remark: they like to present the image that they and the security organization have reached an understanding that enables the principals to direct guards whenever and wherever they wish. But all uniformed security officers report to and are managed by the central board's Division of School Safety, which has a mandate to "ensure the safety of the entire system" (Travis, Lynch, and Schall 1993, 8.). It is also true that in most schools there is an assistant principal whose main function it is to supervise the SSO force within the school—but indirectly.

In reality, principals do *not* manage or control the squadron of guards in their schools, despite their protests to the contrary. If they want to make a special request (e.g., for extra guards for a basketball game), they must do it in writing to the leader of the guards, who can reply that such a request is impossible. New security equipment (e.g., X-ray machines) is constantly introduced into the schools, and the principal and the teachers are usually informed about it only after it has appeared. This arrangement of keeping the principal only indirectly involved in the supervision of the guards is, by all accounts, the direction the board will follow in the future. The hottest political issue on the New York City educational scene has become the future training and "strengthening" of the SSOs and the Division of School Safety. Will the New York City police have direct supervision over the guards or will they only be involved in training them at the police academy? Either way, this will mean a further weakening of the managerial control that principals have over the guards.

Currently, the "AP" (assistant principal), who carries a walkie-talkie all day long to maintain contact with the guards, and the uniformed (blue blazers, white shirts and ties, gray slacks or skirts) guards are assisted by men and women "deans," former teaching staff, who are assigned to full-time disciplinary work. In 1994 a new player was added to the team: a "security coordinator" (usually a retired police officer) who, under the AP, is responsible for organizing this disciplinary team. In Beta School, for example, the total internal school security force, besides the seventeen guards, is composed of five hall deans (including a girls' dean), eighteen paraprofessional assistants, and several teachers "on building assignment." One city policeman is also on permanent assignment to the building, and another policeman is assigned to teach classes on safety. The AP has a total of no fewer than 110 "security personnel" to supervise, the bulk of whom are the guards, paraprofessionals, and the deans. By comparison, the size of the teaching staff is 150. There are specializations of many types: hall deans, girls' deans, cafeteria deans, special-ed deans, roving deans, girls' bathroom paras, scanners, and regular guards. The AP's day begins with a trip to the basement, where he picks up the security guards' and deans' twenty-seven walkie-talkies, whose batteries have been recharging overnight. The constant chatter and static of the walkie-talkies ("This is unit 14, at stairwell 12, 10–4, over and out") dominates the acoustical space of the school: in the lobby, where the visitors' sign-in desk is run by several guards, throughout the upstairs corridors and stairs, and even into the classrooms, where these distracting noises constantly drift in.

> 9 A.M. in the lobby of Alpha School: There are seven guards and paras in the lobby, working the card access machine, the scanners, and the X-ray machine. Others sit at the sign-in desk, or stand around and chat. Students are being scanned, or checked through the card machine. . . . Four tall boys pick up the white plastic stanchions and bang them down on the floor, creating loud explosive noises. The guards freeze for a second but no one reacts or does anything. The boys walk on, clearly in control of the situation. The woman at the sign-in desk looks at me with an expressionless face.

Despite the fact that the guards report directly to the central board, the principals have the right to rate their performance. But it is difficult for a principal to get rid of a poorly performing guard. In one school, it took almost two years for the principal to get the chief security officer transferred, despite the fact that everyone quietly acknowledged that he had a drug problem. Like unsatisfactory teachers, these problematic guards tend to be shifted from school to school due to union safeguards. Negative ratings of guards do not result in their removal or in a reprimand unless they commit an egregious crime. "They get a low rating, they do less," said a former principal. I asked him to imagine a solution; his response:

> Do me a favor. Get rid of the New York City school safety officers. I could bring in a private group [of guards], not one that's going to bust heads, but one that's going to be paid a little bit more, not under all the board of ed. mandates, guidelines. They could probably do with half their number if they would get their rear ends off the wall and just keep moving around the building. That's what works: if kids see you, they are not going to be up to anything. If you plant yourself up against the wall, or if they know they're gonna see you and all you're gonna do is either wave or turn your head the other way, then, you know, what good are you?

Although most lower-tier principals would probably be reluctant to support the idea of employing a private security agency, the management of the guards ends up being one of their major concerns. The procedures guards are expected to carry out each day are highly detailed. In an effort to keep out unwanted intruders (drug dealers, students from other schools), the guards screen visitors at the front desk. Every visitor must present identification, sign in, and receive a pass for a specific room destination. After fresh trouble, these interactions are tense: "If you go anywhere other than room 310 you will be escorted out of the building!" a guard once told a student's mother (who also had a younger child in tow).

Students must insert their ID cards into a guard-operated computerized machine whose green light permits them to enter; the machine also records attendance, produces records of absences, and accumulates disciplinary data on each student. Attendance is taken again during "official class," and comparisons are made with the machines to determine students who are in the school but cutting classes.

At this point, the student steps on a rug that is programmmed to switch on a red light for every third, fourth, or fifth student, the frequency depending on the density of the crowd at a given moment. A red light signals that this particular student must be scanned; a green light, that she or he may proceed directly to class. After that, students are searched for weapons with a magnetic scanner, and knapsacks and bookbags are run through an X-ray machine. "Archway" or airport-type detectors are also currently being introduced. Guards permit students to enter school only at specific times so they will not loiter in the lobby or in corridors before class; groups of students who arrive too early are kept waiting outside, even on cold and rainy days unless special arrangements are made to "hold them" in the auditorium, a procedure requiring a supervisory teacher. In some schools, the logistics of channeling three shifts of students through a ten-period day, with each student attending for eight periods, including lunch, become exceedingly complex. Lobbies, auditoriums, and some classrooms are transformed into holding areas, disciplinary arenas theoretically under the control of the guards, where students wait to go to class.

CORRIDORS AND STAIRWAYS:
THE SPACE OF THE GUARDS

When classes are in session, the hallwalker is the main target of concern for principals of lower-tier schools. It is specifically forbidden for students in lower-tier schools to hang out in the corridors during class time for fear they will make noise, bang on doors, open doors, or otherwise disrupt classes already in session. (Students in the ed op schools, by contrast, are allowed the privilege of lounging in the corridors, since they are deemed to be better behaved.) The mission of the security guards is to patrol the corridors and stairwells, to look for students who are cutting classes, to challenge students who just like to roam, to keep students moving briskly along the corridors, to prevent loitering, and to handle confrontations, fights, or mischief of any sort. As for the period between classes, it is impossible to describe the maelstrom in a lower-tier school corridor: a mass of moving bodies pushing, yelping, grabbing, shadow-boxing, embracing, and perhaps even threatening, followed by guards shouting, "OK, let's move it!" Yelling at students in groups is the surest sign that authorities have lost control and that the unacceptable behaviors—whatever they are—will resume as soon as the authority's back is turned. Some principals, showing visitors around the school, will make a point of reprimanding students or of telling them to take off their hats; as soon as the principal leaves, the hats go back on and the behavior resumes. Students ignore the principal altogether and walk on.

The students have their own perceptions about the radical differences between corridor policies in the lower-tier school and those of ed op or parochial schools. One tutor reported the following conversation that took place during a Sunday outing with a group of boys and girls from our tutoring room:

> "They [i.e., students in ed op or parochial schools] don't have guards or nothin'."—"Anyone can just walk in there."—"They look real nice."—"You go there and the bell rings and the kids who don't got class, they just sittin' there in the hall and they don't got no guard to tell 'em to get to class."—"That's cause they trust them. They don't need guards 'cause they do their homework in the halls, and they don't cause no trouble. You do that at [our own school] and we'd have a riot or somethin'."

The guards also keep gate at the cafeteria and gym areas at the beginning and end of assigned periods; they do not allow students who do not have their computerized program card (daily schedule) to enter, and they allow no one to leave before the appointed time. For fear that students might loiter in the cafeterias beyond their assigned lunch periods, cafeteria doors are the subject of intense control, with another set of ID card machines attended by the guards. If a student "hangs" in the cafeteria and does not come to class for several periods, it is assumed he is selling drugs or is a potential troublemaker. The school safety officers are expected to govern the building's strategic space: the lobby, the corridors, the cafeteria, the auditorium, any public area, and any isolated area in the school where large numbers of students are gathered and where trouble could conceivably break out.

Opinions about the effectiveness of this low-paid[4] security guard force in maintaining school discipline usually reflect one's philosophy about school discipline in general. Almost all of these jobs are filled by young black and Hispanic men, and some women, from the local communities. What is certain is that, in the lower-tier schools, this novel assembly has become a paramilitary force that has taken on an independent existence with its own organization and procedures, language, rules, equipment, dressing rooms, uniforms, vans, and lines of authority. What has never been studied is its pedagogical impact on the institution of the school. Through the mediation of these units, the language, gestures, outlook (or world view), and tactics of police interaction with street criminals have gradually been introduced into the everyday discourse of the schools. The guards' interactive styles and demeanors are relayed to the students and become formative of student identity—an area heretofore ignored by educational researchers, despite the now constant association between guards and students.

DISTANCING THE BODY

Essentially, the entire guard apparatus was a creature of the teacher's union, which forced the board to establish it as teachers refused to be responsible for directly disciplining students. The United Federation of Teachers handbook entitled *Security in the Schools: Tips for Guarding the Safety of Faculty Members and Students,* is explicit on this point: "Teachers . . . have an obligation to break up fights and prevent injury—but that obligation does not require physical intervention. There have been too many tragic injuries to faculty members and court decisions have held that a teacher who was disabled while breaking up a fight was not entitled to 'special protection'—that is, no more protection than is owed to someone who wanders in off the streets."

As one teacher put it, "The union tells teachers 'Hands off! Hands off students! Stay away from conflict! Don't get in the middle! Don't get involved!'" Where a teacher has been hurt trying to break up a fight, or getting between students, the insurance industry has refused to pay for medical care, and the union has lost such cases in court. Police also tell the teachers they should not attempt to break up fights between students. They are encouraged to act the way the police themselves sometimes act—to avoid going near the students, not get physically involved, and, in general, walk around the combatants and leave them alone until the fighting stops. The police even recommend getting other students to pull the combatants apart, but they state explicitly that teachers should not get in the middle. The union-chapter chairperson also tells teachers explicitly not to get involved, certainly not when there are knives. In one school, the union told the teachers that when fights break out, they should leave their classrooms, close the door, and call the security guards. Most of the schools have installed "emergency" telephone systems in the classrooms so teachers can call the security guards directly and more rapidly. Some of the planned technologies (e.g., wrist radios for teachers) will speed communications even more.

Teachers are thus encouraged to avoid physical interaction with students and are advised to notify security immediately in the event of a fight. The body of the student becomes the province of the security guards while teachers abdicate this responsibility. Who could quarrel with the wisdom of such a policy? In an age when the weapon, or at the very least the threat of the hidden weapon, is ubiquitous, who would be so foolish as to recommend that a teacher, young or experienced, intervene when students are engaged in intense combat? Is it not common sense to summon the security guards, who, although not armed themselves, are trained to intervene in such crises and have direct access to police and emergency medical help? If a male teacher, for example, attempts to separate two girls who are so angry that they are choking one another, and one of them gets injured in the melee, the consequences may be devastating for his career. He may find himself sued, charged with sexual abuse, and ultimately suspended or transferred to another school.

   This commonsensical policy, however, also has the effect of decentering and fragmenting students' identities by establishing a sharp boundary between their bodies and the intellectual, spiritual, and cognitive "side" of their subjectivities. By managing student bodies as separate entities, the school renders them more visible, more real.[5] It therefore becomes important to understand the consequences that ensue when the guards' commonplace gatekeeping function changes to a paramilitary task of mingling with students when their bodies are at their most highly charged and emotional peak—during intense physical combat with peers. This shift in function, in turn, raises questions about the effects the permanent presence of the guards, the police, and their technological security devices have had on the familiar and traditional interactions between teacher and student, both inside and outside the classroom. What have been the effects of these occurrences on the relationship of the teacher to the corporeality of the student? Have such developments deepened the Cartesian mind-body bifurcation so that supervision of the student's mind has become the province of the teacher whereas supervision of the body is consigned exclusively to the guards? Have teachers now become distanced from the bodies of students in ways that go beyond the distancing caused by the legal fallout from sexual abuse cases, because of which teachers are now understandably reluctant to lay hands on students, even in the most benign fashion? To answer these questions, we must first explore both how the guards visualize their own roles and the ideological configurations into which the policing arm of the state would fashion them within these troubled schools.

   Their strategic location at the front door of the building, their ability to challenge the comings and goings of students or visitors, and their immediate access to important information about everything going on in the school lend an aura of excitement to the SSOs firmly stationed in the school lobby and seemingly in control. The corps of guards takes on a certain centrality as they communicate to the unseen distant corners of the school or are asked by the principal, "What's happening?" Through the crackle of the walkie-talkie, they are the first to know when some "action" is "going down" anywhere in the school. The "really important" knowledge in the school becomes not the binomial theorem but the report about the latest fight on the fourth floor. The guard is the first and last person a student sees at school; on many days, the guard is the only person to interact with a student in the corridors. A smile from a guard or a friendly chat on the front steps often breaks the sense of anonymity and alienation students feel.

The official proclamations conceptualize the SSOs as the first line of defense against the violence of the streets; hence their pivotal role at the front doors. Despite all the precautions, however, intruders, including drug dealers, students on suspension, or someone who "has a beef" and wants to threaten a student, still manage to get into school buildings. Intruders, however, are not the main problem on a daily basis, and, in all fairness, it must be said that the schools we worked in over the 1985–94 period did appear to improve in their capacity to keep them out. But this problem has not disappeared, and the technological response is understandable if viewed from an administrative perspective. One principal told me the story of how Jose, a boy who had been discharged from the school after he was apprehended having sex with a girl in a stairwell and who was known to be armed much of the time, kept getting back into the building despite the guards' efforts. The story is instructive not for the purpose of evaluating the guards' efficiency but for illustrating the security process itself:

> PRINCIPAL: Jose, after he was discharged, didn't attend where he was discharged to, and was in fact back in the building a number of times. On one occasion, we caught him and had him arrested. But he still got back in. All the security people knew him, but Jose kept getting back into the building.
> JD: How so?
> PRINCIPAL: Sometimes you end up with a security officer replacing another on the door. If [the student] comes in with a batch of kids and has an ID card, no matter whose ID card it is and the green light goes off, sometimes they just don't know you. They're watching the lights and not the faces.

The schools we are discussing occupy enormous buildings with multiple exits[6] and complicated gate systems to gyms and swimming pool areas. Until 1992, the exterior doors in some schools were sometimes locked to keep out trespassers. Cafeteria doors were bolted to prevent students from leaving and wandering the halls, fire regulations notwithstanding (trusted staff members were given keys so these doors could be opened quickly in case of an emergency). Due to the protests of fire marshals—who threatened to shut the schools down—magnetic lock systems, which can control all doors from a central location, were being installed in forty-one high schools in 1995. These high-tech systems are so complicated that only the chief custodian in each school appears to know how they operate; loud door alarms sound off constantly as students exit remote doors at whim. The students who came to our tutoring program were aware of how intruders could slip through the network of security guards and technology:

> CLAUDE: I was in the gym that day. Yeah. I was like, "I know them [the nonstudent intruders]. They're hustlers." I'm like, "Whatcha doin' here? They don't belong here; I know them." They're from. . . . I'm like sayin', "I know they don't belong in the school." They came in. They was lookin'. I knew they was lookin' for gold. 'Cause I know how they act. They lookin', lookin'. They saw one kid with a big cable. He was scared. They just took him. I just backed up because I knew what they gonna do. An' one just pull out [a gun]. "Give me the gold." That's it!
>
> SYDNEY: The fellow didn't even wanna give it to him.
>
> CLAUDE: He didn't give it to him. He thought. . . . Everybody just say, "Are you crazy?" and he like this: [gestures that the boy finally handed over the gold necklace].
>
> SYDNEY: He don't afraid of nothin'. He wasn't scared at all.
>
> CLAUDE: He ran in back o' him.
>
> SYDNEY: He ran behind him after that—an' they got guns! Now another day a nigger tried to do that to me once. Couldn't get shit.

In this brief student dialogue, one can detect several of the elements of a culture of school violence beginning to take shape. Although the boys exhibit some surprise that hoodlums can freely enter the school and steal from students at gunpoint, there is no real expectation that authorities will be in control of the school space. It is taken for granted that the security force will not be doing its job, that the supposed barrier of technology is completely porous, and that the traditional school structure has broken down. No one is shocked that the sanctuary has been violated.

At the same time, Sydney and Claude socialize one another into the mores of the street culture, which has now transplanted itself within the boundaries of the school. The language, too, is important, not just because of the lack of familiarity with standard English, but because the use of the lowest possible prestige idiom ("nigger," "shit") is a way of demonstrating affinity with the values of the street culture—toughness, bravado, and the ability to keep one's courage when faced with the reality of a gun. What is suppressed is the issue of death or at least the suffering and pain the gun could have caused.

GUARDING THE BODY

In the everyday life of inner-city schools, it is difficult to imagine the tension under which the unarmed guards[7] operate, given the school system's expectation that they react to corridor or cafeteria fights that sometimes involve weapons. Such incidents have a way of drawing all students from the surrounding area into a transfixed mass. Word quickly spreads that a fight is in progress, and soon hundreds of students are crowded around the combatants, whooping and cheering. Security guards radio downstairs for reinforcements, and hall deans race to the scene to break through the knots of students anxious to witness the fight. The guards and the hall deans, not the teachers, are expected to make contact (i.e., grab, push, separate, touch, disarm, restrain) with the body of the student and its extensions in space (weapons, clothing, knapsacks):

> MR. E [Jamaican hall dean, addressing me]: It's rough, it's rough! These people [two black American security guards, a man and a woman, who were present] have a rough job. Yesterday they took a gun from a guy.
> JD: Not again! We just went through that three weeks ago! What happened?
> MALE SECURITY GUARD: Yeah, and he had a bullet in it. He was ready to shoot!
> JD: To shoot another student?
> FEMALE SECURITY GUARD: Yes, but it don't make no difference. Anybody who got in his way. A bullet doesn't have to have your name on it. It was terrible.

The female guard described how all the students in the corridor crowded around the boy with the gun, thus preventing any one from getting the weapon from him. On such occasions, the policeman assigned full-time to the school usually radios for reinforcements, and the corridors swarm with police for several hours afterwards. The street and sidewalk in front of the school fill with police cars, guards' vans, and ambulances.

> FEMALE SECURITY GUARD: Yeah, and if there is trouble, they [the students] don't run away from it. They run towards it.
> MALE SECURITY GUARD: I don't understand it. They all form a knot, so it's impossible to see what is going on or to get through to break up a fight. This behavior is crazy.

This behavior, this fascination with the conflict, is far from crazy from the point of view of those involved and needs to be understood on its own terms. Philippe Bourgois (1989, 8)—who worked with drug entrepreneurs on the streets of East Harlem—points out that such conduct, which may appear irrational to the outside observer, can be reinterpreted as being essential in maintaining credibility with one's peers, who are looking to see how "soft" another participant is. This rushing to observe the violent fights in which one's own peers are the combatants creates a kind of anticommunity, the polar opposite of the unified and harmonious community schools have traditionally striven to create. But the street culture dictates that one only has oneself to rely on for survival, and the lessons learned at these spectacles may be more important than those of the classroom of the auditorium stage. The tutoring room, again:

> [Two students are telling a woman tutor about a riot that occurred at a neighboring school]: On Thursday all the students came wanting to discuss violent topics. . . . They said that [at the other school] a student was stabbed with a broomstick, another was shot, and another was sliced around the back of his head from ear to ear. One said his brother went to school there. Another group of students began telling me about what the . . . section was really like. The picture wasn't very pretty. One student lives there and deals drugs with his brother. He also claimed that when he is at home he carries a gun. He also talked about beating "crack heads" and how he chased one with a baseball bat and beat him in his own home. The way that they laughed about it was very unnerving. He just couldn't see the moral wrong in beating another human being. So I then asked if he worried that someday someone would come for him. He stated that he was untouchable. That because of his friends, cousins, and his brother he had "too much props, and too much juice." But if someone did they would be dead. It was so shocking to hear this fourteen-year-old kid talk about all this death and violence so casually. I really wonder if he will see the ripe old age of eighteen. I hope

I can have some influence, but with the strong environment that he
is surrounded by, what can I really say?

Since the border between street culture and school culture is so porous,
the stress under which the guards live is constant. Following major incidents, such as break-ins or fires,[8] the guards are expected to perform "corridor sweeps" (again, New York City Police language has surreptitiously invaded the academic halls), in which they stop every student in the building
and check their ID cards. Guards are called into classrooms to break up
fights, or they enter classrooms when the noise becomes extremely high
because a substitute teacher is unable to keep control. Sometimes two or
three guards are required to stop fights or to settle a class down. Whether
restraining students at cafeteria doors or breaking up fights, guards do, in
fact, come into physical contact with, and sometimes grapple with, students' bodies every day. One security guard told me that he is so exhausted
when he goes home that he just plops in front of a TV set with his friends
and drinks beer. It is not surprising that guards are often absent on Mon-
days or that authorities assume they are "hung over" from the weekend.
One security guard said to me on graduation day, "I just thank God I got
through the year without being injured."

EXCEEDING THE BODY

Teachers often complain that the guards can never be found when they
really need them or that they just joke with the students instead of disciplining them. Sometimes teachers cannot hear students in class because of loud
noises coming in from the walkie-talkies in the corridors. Undesirable inti-
macies can develop between student and guard. A Caribbean woman tutor
wrote in her log: "It upsets me tremendously to hear a security guard who
is considerably older than the students telling a female student that she
looks cute." One of our African male tutors, hurrying down a deserted stairwell late one afternoon, reported seeing a male security guard passionately
kissing one of the female students. A guard in another school was fired for
getting a girl pregnant. A guard at one high school was charged with rape
and endangering the welfare of a fifteen-year-old girl, prompting the resignation of the director of the School Safety Division (Newman 1995c). It is
difficult to say how exceptional these cases are.

> JD: Do some of the guards date the girls?
>
> Principal: Yeah, in a number of cases.

Such overfamiliarities occur between students and teachers (and college professors!); the point of relating these aberrations is to establish the fact that close relationships develop between students and guards because of their daily contact. The fact that students do not truly expect the guards to keep the corridors safe and secure does not mean that they do not look to them for other fundamental human needs: recognition, approval, and friendship. Students develop playful relationships with the guards and some of the hall deans, horsing around with them, giggling, playing tricks. Hugging of guards is a common sight. One woman tutor, referring to the way a girl related to an approachable hall dean, said, "She has a look of unbelievable joy on her face every time someone is kind to her." However, the hall deans—quasi-supervisors of the guards—were the only faculty members specifically assigned to interact with the students in the school's public spaces; and, like the guards, their role, even if they were former teachers, was confined to the purely disciplinary side of student life.

The guards' role, however conceptualized at an ideal level, may be evaded (by doing only the minimal, and then only when being observed by a supervisor) or exceeded (by taking on functions that were never contemplated). On one occasion, I saw a couple of hall-roaming boys going down the corridors, banging their fists on the doors of classrooms, and waving through the door windows to distract their friends and the classes inside. New to the school, I was unsure whether to ignore the whole incident or to intervene. When the female security guard approached them, they playfully threw their arms around her and gave her a big hug and a kiss. No action was taken. The corridor becomes more than just a disciplinary space, even for the guards. In short, students often hang out with the guards and develop personal relationships.

The guards, although conceptualized by the system as extensions of the technology, as pure disciplinary machines, are, in fact, human beings with goals and desires. Several of the guards have asked me how they could escape this very stressful work, so lacking in prestige, by continuing their education at the college level. One Haitian paraprofessional (a role deemed even lower than that of the guards), who was assigned to patrolling the cafeteria during lunch hour and accompanying the students to the hospital and the police station after fights, wanted to continue his education so he could get a teaching job. Some guards easily picture themselves doing a better job than the classroom teachers even now. One female guard, highly critical of the teaching, recalled how she was called in to quiet down a class and ended by going to the board and doing a math problem because no one else could do it: "[speaking to a male security guard] Remember the other day when we went into that classroom? Kids in this school are in 10th and 11th grade and they are doing math at the junior high school level. When I was in 10th or 11th grade we were doing geometry and trigonometry."

Guards also had their views of the moral dangers and failures of the school, one of which was the presence of older students, who, they felt, were streetwise and could introduce negative behavior: "[female security guard] I wouldn't want no son or daughter of mine who was 15 to be going to school with 21 and 22 year olds, would you? Some of them have had two babies already, and the older men. . . . They used to have special schools for them to go to, at night. Now they just put them here, and now the board allows students up to age 22."[9]

VOICE OF THE GUARDS

But the most emotional issue, one I believe is at the heart of conflicting ideologies of contemporary urban education, concerns the clashing roles of teachers and guards vis-à-vis student behavior. Its roots are in the gradual withdrawal of teachers, over the past several decades, from the responsibility for schoolwide discipline, when the union contract removed this function from their job descriptions or reduced it. Despite the fact that some principals are now trying to involve teachers once again in patrolling the halls by giving them more "building assignments," and despite the fact that some principals even find their local union chapter chairpersons to be reasonable about the issue, teachers and the union itself are still resistant to the move.[10] One union official told me that the central role of the security guards was to see to it that students should "behave as students should be behaving." Teachers, on the other hand, are thought to be totally absolved from this role.

But one principal frankly admitted that not all guards saw the matter so simply: "The school security officers," he said, "ask why do they have to be the bad guys?" The guards feel not only that the teachers are not helpful but that they exacerbate the situation by ignoring blatant student infractions of rules in the corridors and public areas. This same principal indicated that the guards "don't want to discipline kids" when they see the teachers' lack of involvement. Both teachers and guards, he said, are acutely aware that when they tell a student "Take your hat off! Take your Walkman off!" they can be the target of violence. Guards tend to avoid those hidden spaces (usually remote stairwells) where they know that students hang out, smoke, have sex, or have loud parties (often with radios at the end of the school-day). In one of our schools, the remote stairwell used as a trysting place was known as "the hotel." When teachers complained, the guards act as if they were receiving new information, and when they began to patrol those areas, the students moved on to other unpatrolled places.

The resentment, anger, and fear on the part of the guards clearly surface in casual conversations with them. Here are my fieldnotes on a conversation with two African American male SSOs held just outside our tutoring room in Beta School:

> I stop to chat with one of the security guards (Mr. R) standing in the corridor as I'm leaving the 3rd-floor tutoring room. The other guard (Mr. K) comes over and comments on how well dressed I am. I respond by telling them that *they,* the SSOs, are the best-dressed people in the school, with their white shirts, pressed uniforms, gray trousers and navy blue blazers. K says, "Thank you for the compliment." They both complain about how sloppily the teachers dress most of the time. R says (trying to imagine the thought process of a student who has a teacher who doesn't dress neatly): "Well, why should I go to four years of college to come out dressed the way you are?" I asked both guards if they thought the students saw them, the guards, as role models. R said he wasn't sure, he would have to ask some of the kids that question, but from his smile I thought I could detect that he felt they did perceive him that way. He said, "Hey, if you can only make a difference in the lives of a few of these kids, that's what it's all about." He lamented about how colorless and drab the neighborhood was that these kids lived in and, pointing to the institutional green paint on the walls, how drab the school itself was, how the school should represent a little lightness in the students' lives.
>
> I asked to what extent the teachers involved themselves in issues regarding student behavior. They both complained about how the

teachers called them into the classroom for the least little thing. A kid is talking too loud, or a kid is playing his radio in a corner and refuses to turn it off. They complained that they are only supposed to enter the classrooms for major altercations, but in fact the teachers call them in for the slightest thing. They made the point that many teachers cannot control a class, that teachers do not know how to manage a classroom, that teachers have a fear of the kids. I responded that maybe some of this fear is justified—that kids sometimes carry weapons. They said, yes that is true, but you are going to get attacked or killed on the outside anyway so while they are here, inside the school, the teachers should try to change things while they have a chance to. When I asked if teachers ever acted as disciplinarians in the hallway, they said it would be wonderful if each teacher would do just that, that it would make their jobs infinitely easier and that the *kids* would really notice the difference. I asked them if they actually did any teaching. They said that I would be surprised how much—that they are constantly trying to motivate kids—to tell them that studying and doing academic work is to their advantage. They saw themselves more as guidance counselors than as teachers. But they said that their immediate supervisors discouraged this role because they saw it as "fraternizing." They talked about how this particular corridor is where "all the action is" in the school and how they deal with the kids with a tough demeanor in the corridors and how tough a kid has to appear on the street in order to survive. R said that in his neighborhood you even hear little 5- and 6-year-old kids saying, "Don't mess with me or I'll kill you!" He felt that the mother was too often alone in raising the children and that her role was "character development" whereas the father normally "sets the rules," and since many of these kids have no fathers, they reject anyone—SSO or teacher—who imposes a rule on them. Watching some of the boys pass by with the new fashion of letting the top part of their pants hang down loose over their hips, R said he understood that this fad had started in the prisons where, if the prisoner's rear end was clad in tight pants, he was the target of sexual remarks and attacks. Hence the loose, sloppy look was a way of avoiding such sexually loaded remarks. Similarly, he said, the bandannas were a way of avoiding remarks about one's hair-do. After I tell them about my background and experience as a former Jesuit priest working in Jesuit schools, they both begin telling me that the main reason for the kids' poor behavior is basically religious. K said that the kids "have not accepted Jesus Christ in their lives." When I let a four-letter word slip, R asked me, with due apologies, how I, as a former clergyman, felt about using such language. A bit nonplussed, I replied that I was not perfect and that I sometimes just slipped. He smiled a forgiving smile before I gave them both the double handshake and departed.

By the end of the conversation, I found myself musing over how closely the guards' corridor comportment resembled, in important respects, the friendly teacher-student contacts that might have taken place many years earlier: chatting informally with students, challenging self-destructive behaviors, receiving student confidences, being in touch with the youth subculture. It might be stretching a point to call these SSOs teachers or spiritual guides, but they clearly had taken over aspects of the teacher's mentoring and disciplinary roles. An ex-teacher: "The security guards are the kids' buddies. They fool around with them. They knew the kids so much better than I did. If I had a problem, they would say, 'I'll keep an eye on him.' I had a kid who threatened me and the guard told me exactly what to do. He said to send a letter to his parents, certified mail—he told me a series of things to do. They know the individual kids, who their friends are—they are like camp counselors—another important adult in their environment."

This former teacher also recalled how much the guards had helped her, counseling her in how to handle a girl who had threatened to knife her and to "get her" after school. She felt that the guards, with their established relationship with the community and the students, could do much more of this kind of thing if they had better schooling. I think of the guard with whom I walked around the Alpha School neighborhood one afternoon about 3 P.M.—"Hey!" he said to a boy roaming the streets, "I didn't see you in school today!" But officially, this more humanistic presence on the part of the guards was strongly discouraged. The SSOs blurred the boundaries not only between their own role and that of the teacher but even between themselves and the guidance counselors:

[Fieldnotes]: George [a security guard at Alpha School] told me about a girl who tells him her step-father is beating her with a walking stick but that she doesn't want to see a guidance counselor about it so she talks to him. Then he told me another story of the girl he claims to have saved from committing suicide and who is now graduating this June. The School Safety Division frowns on such "fraternization" and would restrict the guard-student contacts to supervision and movement of the physical body in space.

But human beings will not be so restricted:

> [Female tutor's log]: Harold came down [to the tutoring room] to say howdy. He's so funny. He comes into the room with a "school safety officer" on his tail. The guard was asking him whether or not he was giving him a hard time. Harold was explaining to him jokingly that he just wanted to make sure that he was paying attention. The officer was laughing and so was I at Harold's creative approach to staying out of trouble.

> [African American student]: The guards are like big kids; they ask us to go out and buy them a Big Mac, even though kids are not supposed to leave the school grounds.

As indicated above, not all guard-student contacts are so benign. Students often see the guards as the enemy and bitterly complain in the tutoring room of the treatment they receive from them. These are, after all, authority figures onto whom large masses of students transfer their feelings every day. One student, who was stopped by a guard in the corridor and who tried to show the guard his pass to get into the tutoring room, said, "It don't matter, even with this thing, they still treat you like garbage."

What is certain is that a whole new language of the corridors has arisen, from police terms (*scan days, access cards, holding pens, corridor sweeps*), to labels for students (*hallwalkers*), to forms of address ("Yo," "Hey, my man") and behaviors and dress styles (swaggers, jeans crumpled around the ankles, hoods over the head) borrowed from the streets and the jails. As one Caribbean woman tutor put it, discussing the school halls: "The last thing in your mind is that it is a learning environment. In a private school the vocabulary is totally different."

The simple inference that can be made is that a wholly new phenomenon, unanticipated by the board of education when it introduced the guards—and completely ignored by the field of educational psychology—has occurred on the educational scene: a bonding between students and security guards. Students can now aspire to become guards, and some, in fact, do so. But insofar as the security force serves as one (but not the only) mechanism for the introduction of street culture, the school becomes a site for the reproduction of violence, beyond anything else.

DOCILE BODIES?

At this point, we might turn from the ethnography of the corridors and ask ourselves what messages these public spaces contain for pedagogical theory. It would be easy to conclude that the presence of the SSOs, the police, and the hall deans, with their panoply of electronic surveillance machines, represents a higher-order expansion of the old panopticism, but dressed up and greatly intensified in hi-tech clothing. Does it not appear self-evident that we are witnessing a heightened kind of surveillance—one infinitely more detailed and pervasive than even the "fussy" seventeenth-century military inspections Michel Foucault refers to in *Discipline and Punish* (1979, 140)? At first blush, this would seem so, but before answering definitively we should review Foucault's decipherment of panopticism as the constitutive code of modernity.

Most fundamentally, Foucault viewed the Panopticon, Jeremy Bentham's ideal prison, as one of the many new modes of social control that were developing in the seventeenth and eighteenth centuries and that professed to be more emancipatory than their predecessors but in reality were not. The progression from the confessional box to the psychiatric couch and the evolution from public executions, torture, and dungeons to modern prisons were, for Foucault, steps toward far more efficient and pervasive techniques of social domination. Whereas previously the mutilated body of a regicide who had been hanged, drawn, and quartered could be paraded to instill a lasting message in the minds of onlookers, now—in the classical age—the body was being converted into a "useful machine" through the mediation of a whole set of methods and rules for controlling and correcting its operations. A "docile body" (Foucault 1979, 138) was being created, one that could be "subjected, used, transformed, and improved" (136), especially in the context of the boarding school or the military camp. Within the space of the barracks or the dormitory, "no detail was unimportant" (140), and the body was subjected to uninterrupted surveillance—the "gaze" (171)—eventuating in human subjects mastering, managing, repressing, and ultimately supervising themselves.

But for Foucault, the effects of this "supervision of the smallest fragment of life and of the body" went far beyond seventeenth-century secondary education and prisons: concentration on the "meticulous observation of detail" spilled out of these particular institutions and into modern society as a whole. Panopticism and surveillance were "destined to spread throughout the social body" (207), to penetrate it "through and through with disciplinary mechanisms" (209), resulting in the formation of "what might be called in general the disciplinary society" (209). As a result of this successful dissemination of panopticism, societal surveillance became permanent and complete—precisely because modern society was in a permanent state of fragmentation. Under the regime of modernity, we incorporate into ourselves the role of both supervisor and supervised—we become "the principle of our own subjection" (203), and pedagogy rests on the basic assumption of an unremitting concern for "character assessment." In the hands of Foucault, the Panopticon thus becomes a metaphor for all of modernity. "The man [*sic*] of modern humanism was born" (141).

But the school was not the only instrument of domination: it took its place alongside the prison and, most especially, the industrial factory. Recall the 1913 glass-ceilinged school auditorium reminiscent of the "arcades" and the Benjaminian reading of the same (see the introduction). When all of these large schools were designed at the beginning of this century—(and not just the "vocational" ones)—they were seen as correlates to, and as prep schools for, an industrialized working class that could sit there, look through the glass ceiling at the heavens, and dream the dreams of an expanding commercial economy—an economy that no longer exists. New York City school discipline of the early days of this century—whose restoration will occur, it is now almost unanimously agreed,[11] only through a "strengthening" of the security guard apparatus—must be understood as having been, even then, when it seemed to work so well, a response to an already-fractured school system functioning within a constantly fissuring factory economy, which is precisely why the discipline had to be applied in the first place.[12]

What, then, are we to make of the whole Foucauldian thesis in the light of corridor life today? Can we really say that "docile bodies," capable of responding to the exigencies of the world of work, are being produced?[13] Can anyone seriously contend that meticulous attention to detail occurs when the guards' chief concern is to check for large weapons at the front door? How can the model of "continuous surveillance" continue to function when the "network of gazes" has totally collapsed? Teachers, as we shall see in the next chapter, far from being all-seeing monitors, are unswerving in their efforts *not* to see student misbehavior, much less minor impolitenesses, in public places. The teachers' supervisory gaze is conspicuous by its absence, not its presence. Even the most flagrant violations and inappropriate behaviors are studiously avoided. Teachers walk from their classrooms to their cafeteria as if they had blinders on. Meticulous observation of detail has given way to a willful determination *not* to see misbehavior or even outright crime. In this climate, the guards, far from representing the all-seeing surveillance contemplated by Foucault, feel constrained only to enforce the majority of the rules when they themselves are being observed, and even then they resent having to be responsible for student behavior when the teachers and other "professionals" have all but abandoned it. What has happened to the internalization of supervision, which the Panopticon is supposed to promote? Can it be that this new panopticism of technology and security might better be thought of as the total absence of panopticism?

THE ANTI-PANOPTICON

Is it credible, then, to speak any longer of Foucault's panopticism in the context of contemporary urban education? Is not the whole enterprise that attempted to construct "the disciplinary individual" in the process of a massive shutdown comparable to the departure of the manufacturing industries in these same neighborhoods? One might argue that panopticism is still very much with us, at least in the cognitive realm, with its standardized testing and emphasis on grades, SAT scores, and the like, but is the hyperinsistence on these vestiges of the enterprise of modernity itself not a symptom of its imminent demise? To answer these questions, does a reading of the extraacademic architecture not tell us far more than "life in classrooms" does? Two public areas—the cafeteria and the bathroom—are very revealing in this respect.

High school cafeterias, far from being laboratories for the observation of student conduct Foucault unearthed ("In the dining rooms was 'a slightly raised platform for the tables of the inspectors of studies, so that they may see all the tables of the pupils of their divisions during meals.'"), are places to be sedulously avoided by teachers who would never think of eating with students. Cafeterias are thought of as the prime spaces for the generation of student conflicts and have become the exclusive province of the guards, except when the principal can twist the arm of the union chapter chairperson to permit a few teachers to assist the guards. Coincidentally, in Alpha School, teachers, sitting well removed from students in their own dining area, refer to the students' cafeteria as the "dungeon," the form of imprisonment the Panopticon was supposed to replace.

Extreme images sometimes need to be countered with extreme images: in contrast to Foucault's example of surveillance in eighteenth-century toilets ("latrines had been installed with half-doors, so that the supervisor on duty could see the head and legs of the pupils, and also with side walls sufficiently high 'that those inside cannot see one another.' This infinitely scrupulous concern with surveillance is expressed in the architecture by innumerable petty mechanisms" [1979, 173]), our students complain that in order to avoid these fearsome, filthy, vandalized, and sometimes violent places, they try to use the bathroom at home before they come to school or they rely on a friendly guard allowing them to leave for home. Bathrooms are places for hanging out, smoking a joint, setting fire to the toilet paper (if there is any), flooding the sink and toilet bowls, and harassing weaker-looking peers. Guards refuse to remain inside the bathrooms as supervisors, but the lowest-ranking guard is stationed outside the door, full-time.

One custodian verified that of the twenty-four original bathrooms in his school of 2600 students, only two were now available for student use—one for boys, one for girls—and six for teachers. All the rest were now used as storerooms for textbooks. Throughout these "schools," boys' bathrooms never get toilet paper, soap, or paper towels and only rarely have doors on the stalls. In one school, students must go to the dean's office to pick up a few sheets of toilet paper. This humiliating lack of amenities and privacy exists not because students are subjected to the "supervisory gaze" but because completely unsupervised students are abandoned to one another's gazes. It is no wonder that students often have to urinate in stairwells. On one occasion, I have witnessed the results of defecation in the stairwells or in secluded spots in remote areas; the mess was not cleaned up for several days due to a dispute between the custodian and the principal. Tutors have reported similar incidents.

We leave the matter of the guards with many unanswered questions. Are they pure disciplinarians, teachers, guidance counselors, role models, friends, parent substitutes, or all of the above? Do they represent a new elevated level of panopticism or the total abdication of panopticism? To pursue these questions more fully, we must consider the role of the teacher. But already we have some hints: partly through the figure of the guards, charged with the oversight of the body, it appears that the role of the teacher has transformed and concerns only the care of the mind. The educational establishment has moved far to institutionalize the mind-body cleavage inaugurated by Descartes in the seventeenth century. It is this changed role of the teacher, now quite distanced from interactions with the body of the student, that we shall examine in the next chapter.

CHAPTER FOUR

TEACHERS AND THE "MARSHMALLOW EFFECT"

For power is in its fraudulent as in its legitimate forms always based on distance from the body.

—Elaine Scarry, *The Body in Pain*

JD: Do you ever discuss the difference in school climate—the difference between the 1950s and the way things are now?
Retired teacher: This is the major topic of conversation at every teachers' reunion and retirement party.

DEFINING STREET CULTURE

School space is frequently conceived of as a pristine sanctuary that has been invaded by a culture of street violence; the 1960s are usually cited as the years when the sacred precinct started to become defiled. This conceptualization assumes that the present chaotic state evolved directly from a previous ideal state and that the evolution was precipitated by a sudden intrusion of street culture. This mélange of school and street ignores the fragmentation in social sites outside the school system: community-police interactions, the criminal justice system, the welfare system, the homeless shelter system, to say nothing of the economic forces that have affected family life. In our quest to explain the presence of school violence, the notion that a culture of violence suddenly intrudes, *ab extra,* into a placid school space seems ruled out for at least two reasons. First, the Benjaminian perspective alluded to in the introduction causes us to wonder if the modernist school of the early nineteenth century did not already have the seeds of violence within itself. Second, Foucault's treatment of panopticism reveals that the need for a disciplinary mechanism came from the sense that the modern institution was "always already" falling apart. However, the ethnography of the corridors presents us with some clear analogies to what has come to be thought of as the primary analog of violence—the street, especially as it is defined by Philippe Bourgois (1989), who sharply delineated the components of street culture in his ethnography of crack dealers in East Harlem.

In his fieldwork with drug-dealing inner-city residents, Bourgois (1989, 6) identified an "inner-city street culture" penetrated with ideologies, values, and symbols "completely excluded from the mainstream economy but ultimately derived from it." He represents street-level inner-city residents not simply as victims of oppressive economic forces but as active agents struggling vigorously for dignity, meaning, and survival. Their concerns for providing a living for themselves and their families, however, ultimately translates into intracommunity violence. Rejecting both reductionist economic explanations of inner-city poverty (because they represent a passive and weak interpretation of human agency) as well as the now-debunked concept of the culture of poverty (which, from its middle-class vantage point, tended to blame the victim rather than the oppressor), Bourgois is nevertheless explicit and graphic in his descriptions of muggings, gratuitous beatings, and other forms of ruthless assault carried out by these inner-city inhabitants.

The drug dealers he worked with, refusing to accept low-wage jobs and the racism of insensitive employers, opted for the fleeting dignity and the "prestige" of the streets, resulting in violence, further marginalization, and aggressive behaviors that were ultimately self-destructive for the dealers and their community. This culture of terror that ends up dominating and oppressing the inner-city resident is most often self-inflicted, "even if the root cause is generated or imposed externally"—that is, by the dominant society. Bourgois graphically depicts the internal logic requiring this "culture of terror" to permeate the underground economy:

> Violence is essential for maintaining credibility and for preventing rip-off by colleagues, customers, and hold-up artists. Indeed, upward mobility in the underground economy requires a systematic and effective use of violence against one's colleagues, one's neighbors and, to a certain extent, against oneself. Behavior that appears irrationally violent and self-destructive to the middle class (or working class) observer, can be reinterpreted according to the logic of the underground economy, as a judicious case of public relations, advertising, rapport building and long-term investment in one's "human capital development." (1989, 8)

Bourgois's own risky participation in street life disclosed how violent public behavior must be cultivated in the underground economy if one is to survive and gain respect. One cannot appear soft or weak (a "pussy"); one must demonstrate a capacity for effective violence and terror, the nerve to hold up under gunpoint, and a reputation for ruthlessness in order to get hired by drug bosses. The ruling ethos is to trust no one, to demonstrate that one is "tough enough" to command respect, and to be entirely self-sufficient. Bourgois shows how these behaviors serve the dealers' immediate business purposes in the short term and are, in fact, quite similar to some aspects of the morality and ideology of the mainstream American business community, whence they are ultimately derived.[1] But in the long run, the culture of terror ultimately "has a traumatic impact" (1989, 9) on the majority of community residents who work at regular jobs, on the participants themselves, and on their women associates.

STREET CULTURE IN THE CORRIDORS

The parallels between Bourgois's descriptions of street styles and activity and the day-to-day practices within an inner-city school are compelling, even though he was dealing with a population older than the school-age groups described here. Whether the focus is on inner-city streets or on inner-city school corridors, the basic cultural assumption is the same: no commanding force, or at least no legitimate authority, is in total and effective control. Like the drug dealers, who are more afraid of one another than of the police, the students fear one another far more than they fear the teachers or the guards. It is this fear that dictates the carrying of weapons. It is not just that power has become fragmented; it is incumbent upon each student to establish her or his own individualistic controls, because the basic legally sanctioned protection is lacking.

This prime characteristic of the street culture, a need to appear tough, to be one's own police force, to incarnate one's own agency of violence, is evident to tutors on a daily basis: "[Tutor's log] S got himself in some kind of trouble. It had to do with a remark he made to some other guys who thought another kid made the remark and went after him. The other kid swore vengeance against S who seemed genuinely frightened for his life. He was having his brother-in-law meet him at the train station with a gun and he kept saying, 'One phone call, that's all I gotta make is one phone call

105

and my homeboys be down there to mess them up.'" One of our students, on his arrival at Kennedy airport, was met by an older cousin, who gave him a gun, as reported by a tutor from his home country:

> His cousin gave him a .44 which he returned because it scared him. It was some two weeks later when he was witness to a murder on the steps of his building that he changed his mind. As S reported, "The guy looked right at me." Since then he has become well versed in the area of weapons. In this, he is encouraged by a brother-in-law who is a loan officer in a bank but whose second job is drug dealing. . . . It seems as though the "posse" consists of several relatives, most of them older, whose influence is overwhelming. S seems very resigned to this lifestyle.

Traditional educational research, faced with such an occurrence, would disdain intervention and would seek only to understand or interpret. I mentioned in chapter 2 that our own interactions begin with explicit intervention as the primary goal; ethnography is secondary. In this particular incident, two of our tutors were able to get both boys together and "resolve" the dispute, but in this ambience everything is by nature unpredictable and all "resolutions" can be undone: students may or may not "code-switch" behaviors from "street" to "polite." Bravado and machismo language may or may not result in an ill-fated event: a stare, a toe stepped on inadvertently, a cultural style that is misinterpreted, a joking remark about someone's girlfriend may or may not lead to a decidedly nontrivial outcome: a knifing, a shooting, a death.

This is not hypothetical: since 1992, students associated with just three of the schools in which we work have been either the victims or the alleged perpetrators in ten murders. I am counting only actual deaths, not gunshot wounds, knifings, guns shot into ceilings, or gun sprayings in front of schools and similar lethal scenes.

A YOUTH CULTURE ANTINOMY

The student world view contains an apparent contradiction: on the one hand, students feel required to demonstrate "tough" behaviors; on the other hand, they signal in numerous ways that they are appalled that authorities are so lax as to permit such disrespect, ill manners, and outright violence within the confines of an academic institution. Although this paradox is true of student discourse in general, it can best be followed by listening to the reactions of students recently arrived from overseas, because their fresh insights illuminate a set of features that have become taken for granted.

My focus on recent immigrants, however, reveals what they have in common with African American students rather than what sets them apart, as the work of Ogbu (1978) tends to do. Educators tend to think of recent immigrants as cooperative, eager, and attractive until they become "Americanized," a code word that further stigmatizes American-born youth of color who may be more inured to the looser school practices than are their Caribbean fellow students. African American youth *also* find these practices disconcerting once the issues have been consciously raised and discussed with them. I rely mostly on illustrations from Caribbean students, since they form a large segment of our caseload in all schools, but comparable arguments could be made from the experiences of other international groups (e.g., Chinese, Africans). My spotlight is on the social and behavioral aspects of student life, abstracted from that from which, in the real world, they cannot be separated—namely, academics.[2]

To state the matter simply, recent immigrant students, whether from the Caribbean or from elsewhere, are highly critical of the ineffective and weak attempts at control in New York City high schools and of the general breakdown of order. These recent arrivals—many come here between the ages of thirteen and sixteen—exhibit great irritation with their native-born classmates who go beyond the bounds, disrupt classes, and threaten others and with the educators who allow this to happen. In brief, these new arrivals crave for structure and discipline but rarely find either. A group of Bengali-speaking students come to the tutoring room appalled that their math teacher cannot maintain order: one side of the classroom, filled with African American and Hispanic students, spends its time taunting the Bengali students, making insulting remarks about the teacher's sexual orientation (to his face), and generally acting disruptive. The Bengali students complain that they cannot learn and they cannot understand why a teacher would allow a class to spin out of control in this way. Yet the African American and Hispanic American students with whom we work, far from opposing the recent migrants concerning the desire for structure and the need to develop the toughness to survive, are in total harmony with them. If less vocal about their expectations for structure than those born overseas, they have been conditioned during the lower grades and junior high school not to

107

expect anything different from the ethos of the New York City system. In some ways even more proletarianized than their Caribbean counterparts, the American students have usually not had the benefits of their peers' more orderly schooling experiences in other countries.[3]

Putting aside other distinctions for the moment, then, the primary and shocking first impression the immigrant student receives is the unwilling-ness of the school staff to enforce behavioral standards that would have been routinely enforced in the home country. The fifteen-year-old just arriv-ing from St. Lucia does not immediately discern differences in academic standards; but nuances of dress codes, execution of norms of politeness, and enforcement of rules of conduct transmit latent values—prelinguisti-cally, and through the body, as it were—from day one. The message the high schools are sending to these recently migrated adolescents is that, while there are regulations forbidding students to bring radios, personal stereos, earphones, and beepers (to say nothing of weapons) into the school, in reality, teachers would prefer not to see or deal with infractions of these rules. The most disruptive students are rarely or ineffectually chastised. As growing adolescents, inclined to test rules and expecting to find a system that upholds standards, such as they might have encountered in the more traditional schools of the Caribbean, they find instead that the system yields to their youthful pressure at every turn. As one African American woman counselor—one to whom we were most comfortable referring pregnant girls—told me: "The Caribbean kids are constantly complaining that teach-ers do not get respect." She continued: "Teachers have ceased saying 'You can't do that anymore.' Kids become aware of this situation and they realize that the teachers are powerless in matters of behavior. The result is they can 'act up' and the teachers can't do very much." The space of the school be-comes a locus of terror for the immigrant student, who suddenly realizes that the school is a presocietal state where anything goes and where the strong may prey upon the weak more or less at will.

THE "MARSHMALLOW EFFECT"

[A fifteen-year-old Hispanic girl, explaining to her female tutor the difference between the Catholic school she attended for seven years and the lower-tier public high school she was now attending]: "It's like here, the teachers . . . don' say anythin' when you miss their class or mess up your homework; the nuns, they make you look stupid and feel bad kind of like my mom treats me."

As I became acquainted with lower-tier schools, I began to think of this phenomenon as the "marshmallow effect" of the New York City high school system—wherever students pushed a rule, the system, like a marshmallow, gave way. Personal stereos, beepers, hats, bandannas, hoods, and jewelry are all officially forbidden but unofficially tolerated. If students were challenged, they usually cast scornful looks at the challenger and strolled on, continuing with exactly the same behavior. Boys' hats are the most visible and flagrant symbol of the control students wield. Everywhere promulgated but not really enforced, the no-hat rule and its constant infraction represent more than youth resistance to the traditional school. The ubiquitous hat, perceived by teachers as a mere trifle over which the principal is obsessed, is read by the incoming migrant as a sign that the traditional school no longer exists, that both faces of the street culture are now present: legitimate authority makes ineffectual stabs at control while the peer group exercises almost complete—but imperfectly complete—control. The frightening message for the newcomer is that the adults have handed over the school not to some democratic process (e.g., a student senate) but to the aimless, anarchic, and often unpredictable whims of the adolescent peer group. The peer group now essentially controls the inner-city school but is itself essentially out of control; the ineffective external controls of the technological security apparatus are perhaps the exception.

At issue here is the existence of behavioral rules that are almost never enforced by teachers and only inconsistently enforced by administrators. At class assemblies in the auditorium, students sit, hats on, with clusters of friends and chat or talk out loud, only half-listening to whatever the speaker is saying. Teachers are rarely present. If they are, they rarely monitor the students, and speakers on stage have to get used to speaking over the noise of constant conversation. Behaviors of this type, officially proscribed but actually allowed, are now so commonly accepted that it would be hard to define them as deviant. In fact, an all-school assembly has become a thing of the past: principals fear to bring the whole school together.[4] Small "assemblies" are organized for partial, more manageable groups such as the senior class. When questioned, school officials interpret the school system's methods of enforcement not as laxity but as part of the "freedom" inherent in American society, a freedom to which immigrants would have to adjust:

> The other difficulty in adjusting comes from kids who come from places like Barbados where you don't open your mouth in class unless the teacher tells you to open your mouth in class. And if the teacher comes down on you for something and the parent finds out about it, you get double, because your parent gives it to you also. And they [the parents] don't even ask if you were right or wrong. If the teacher says you're wrong, then you're wrong. Then they come into a system where they suddenly find they have their rights, and rights different from their home country. And that they maybe don't want to go to their 5th-period class and nobody's gonna know about it. A kid goes home and starts talking about rights to the parent and the parent looks at the kid like, are you crazy? Until they begin to realize that New York City is different from Barbados. But I think the main problem in adjustment is the difference in the freedom. The fact that there is so much freedom in the school as far as what the kid can get away with.

Immigrant students' own experiences lead them to a different interpretation of the processes they are experiencing. But adjustment, freedom, and cultural adaptation were typical of the explanatory concepts used by school staff. This discourse tends to justify and normalize the lack of disciplinary effectiveness by hiding under slogans about students' rights in the United States while it silences the sensitive topics immigrants raise about violence and teachers' responsibilities for supervising student behavior. The irony of all this is that the student-rights advocacy groups that are most vocal about these freedoms look on such officials as the enemy.

"Becoming Americanized"

A student from overseas begins to become "Americanized" when she or he, under pressure from friends, begins to cut classes:

> [Tutor's log]: Today I was struck by how much the Bengali boys have become "American," or is it just that they have lost the initial fear and discomfort of being in a new place and are allowing their teenage exuberance to shine through? Though it is exciting to see the shift of these students and their linkages with other students it is also disturbing because as these boys become acclimatized they are also beginning to cut classes, take homework and studies less

seriously. M has been here for almost two years and has become over the past two semesters quite insolent toward teachers and really works at the hip image. . . . R was a high achiever last semester but now he's not even passing math and his English homework is often not done.

The tutors will sit down with students such as these and counsel them about how self-destructive such patterns are; teachers, involved with 150 students a day, do not have the time or inclination. Before undergoing this "Americanization" process, recent arrivals are perceived as identifying with the school's highest aspirations: they still get involved in ethnic and cultural activities, form the core of the Honor Society, and work on all the extracurricular activities. "The extracurricular groups are filled with Trinidadians and Barbadians, but the American kids are not to be found," one teacher told me. The standard interpretation by staff—irrespective of their own ethnic and racial background—was that the American students were the ones who were indifferent to school functions and who introduced the negative behaviors. Since the only "Americans" in the school were black, the conclusions were inescapable. In this regard, the speech of the Caribbean students, or adults, often echoes that of the native born: one West Indian, speaking of a student who was bullying other students, said, "T. would not act that way at home. He's behaving as though he's an American." Such statements, made in a school devoid of whites, has obvious negative undertones regarding black Americans and further disparages an already disenfranchised group.

A contrary discourse, which blamed the Caribbean students for disruptive behaviors, was evident in statements such as "Years ago all of the Jamaicans were high achievers, go-getters, with strong family stability and strong family traditions." (In this statement, "Jamaicans" refers to all West Indians, a usage common among many teachers.) Now, so this line of reasoning went, the present generation of migrants is "not as striving a group" because "they have become Americanized," presumably prior to migration from the Caribbean.

Such language also conjures up images of West Indian students going to school in neatly pressed uniforms, coming from neighborhoods where one was known by name, and entering a "traditional" school where teaching and discipline were taken seriously. West Indian teachers often discussed these issues of student behavior and had their own theories and ways to analyze the problem. In one such discussion with two teachers, the one from Barbados told me of his relief on learning that he would no longer be teaching a class of all West Indian students as he had done the previous semester:

> BT: In a way I feel a little bit relieved, because I was getting more behavior problems than anything else, you know.
> JD: Really?
> BT: Yeah. Big kids 18 years old, you know, 17 to 18, tough. I be getting some real behavior problems.

When asked about the issue of the "Americanization" of Caribbean students, his response was:

> BT: I am not one who believes that. I think that system . . . that . . . we left behind, we think it's still in place. A lot of it is gone, you know. A lot of the kids that come in are already rebels and already pretty tough characters.
> JD: Before they get here?
> BT: I think so. I mean some people tend to blame it on here but I tend not to, because I feel that already the seeds of rebellion are in a lot of these kids, and they just maybe get a little more latitude to let it come out.

The other teacher, from Guyana, then added: "They [Caribbean students] adapt very quickly to this situation here. Very quickly they learn the same bad things." The Barbadian teacher, however, took exception to this language because "it makes it look like these are little angels coming here and being corrupted, and they're not." Finally, the Guyanese teacher agreed with him: "No, they're not, they're not; I don't think they are. No, because they're coming here and very quickly they sort of pick up the bad part." Asked about how quickly such a transition takes place, the Guyanese teacher responded: "Well, I'd say very quickly—by the time students are in first semester in school here. They tend to learn all of the little tricks, you know." But the Barbadian teacher continued to insist that one should avoid giving the impression that the students here are "bad kids" and the ones that come from the Caribbean are good and that "these bad apples make these good kids bad." He felt that this kind of a definition caused a lot of conflict. He said he clearly saw the danger in West Indian teachers making statements like "Oh, you becomin' like the American kids." If the students had had more latitude in the West Indies, he felt, "there would be more troublemakers right there." In the Caribbean, he believed, the society is so much smaller, adults can monitor and see students more regularly, and, as he put it, "a lot of people know people." But in Brooklyn, "the minute they walk outta their apartment buildings, nobody knows them," with the result that "they can be rebels without even botherin' to look around twice." His analysis, then, centered on the idea that New York urban society gives West Indian students "just that little more latitude to do wrong things" than they had in the islands, but he felt that the seeds of rebellion were already there. He strongly denied that they "just come here and see an American kid and become like that." The Guyanese teacher persisted in his belief that "the good kids continue to be good." But the other students, the ones being discussed, he felt, were "basically not bad kids" but "have to put on this act" in order to survive in this city environment.

It is important to note the central thesis in this discussion: that immigrant students, soon after they arrive, are persuaded by their friends that to survive in New York they must "act tough." Both teachers talked about the influence of American movies in the Caribbean and how the violent movies prepare students even before they arrive here. The Barbadian teacher felt that under this influence, those who are not better educated "can't wait to get some of the action" when they do arrive. When they come here, he added, they become negative, skip classes, become very tough and just "hang out." "I see some little kids here, man. This short fellow, real tough, street-tough, hardened already. Little fellow, you know, it's unbelievable."

Such speculation about whether students have become Americanized in the Caribbean or only after they arrive here may indeed mask class prejudices regarding others from their own country. These prejudices are traceable to the colonial period, but the interlocutors themselves possessed them unwittingly. The implication of such discourse is that, after migration, the "weak" ones do not keep up with social expectations. For students, those expectations include conforming to school standards; for parents, they include cooking for their families and taking care of their children. These expectations were taken for granted at home in the midst of a loving and caring community. Without this, in the isolation of New York apartment living, so this line of reasoning goes, "the weak don't do it."

Recent non-Eurocentric models of migration (e.g., transnationalism) that focus on losing or retaining one's sense of ethnic difference in a society imbued with racism are extremely enlightening but are generally based on interviews with adults and sorely need to incorporate the perceptions of adolescents. If, for example, in Beta School, Jamaican youth are perceived to be ruthless, it follows that nobody will bother you if you become a Jamaican; the obvious choice for a Haitian youth is to incorporate a Jamaican identity, even though the school has an active Haitian Club with dynamic Haitian teachers who are attempting to foster pride in Haitian culture. The two particular ethnic groups employed here could just as easily be reversed or other groups (immigrant or nonimmigrant) substituted, depending on the neighborhood or school in question. Thus, the agency of violence, uninhibited at the school or at any of the sites these students might encounter outside of school, is revealed not as the product of a particular ethnicity but as constructive of ethnicity itself.

SEARCHING FOR STRUCTURE

Beyond all these theories about how Caribbean (or other) adolescents become Americanized, two paradoxical factors emerge, then, from the youths' discourse as they try to make sense of and cope with the migration experience. The first is the pressing need to act tough in order to survive the world of inner-city school and street culture; the second is an equally compelling, though sometimes disguised, search for some of the structure and order they left behind.

It remains for us to examine more closely this developing demand on all inner-city youth, migrant or native, to act tough. As mentioned earlier, it is obvious that a broader linguistic[5] and cultural phenomenon, not at all limited to marginalized communities, is at work in American society as a whole. Clearly, inner-city poverty and its sequelae (among which is violent behavior) do not have their foundations in the ghetto alone but are directly related to the overall American economic structures (W. J. Wilson 1987). But the question I am raising here is whether or not the worst deprivation that we as a society inflict on inner-city youth is an unwillingness to confront their unacceptable behaviors, to supervise them and to interact with their bodies (as well as with their minds) in ways that were previously reserved for the elites in Western society—and to do this while simultaneously deconstructing that same Western culture. The basic phenomenon of school life, as the students experience it, is that teachers no longer challenge them as they walk the halls, threaten other students, disrupt classes, or otherwise act inappropriately.

In chapter 3, we saw how the overwhelming presence of guards and technology has, since the late 1960s, resulted in the almost complete withdrawal of teachers from supervising, touching, and interacting with the body of the student in school corridors and public spaces. But in distancing themselves from the physicality of the students, teachers have yielded more than just the "hands on" responsibility for separating adolescents who are scuffling with one another in corridor fights. To the extent to which the body of the student (conceptualized here not just as a physical organism but as a constructed entity on whose surface conflicting signifiers of dress styles, demeanors, textbooks, and weapons struggle for dominance) has been taken away from educators and handed over to specialized functionaries, the problems this move was designed to solve (i.e., conflict and aggression) have been exacerbated rather than alleviated:

> [Tutor log] N (a girl) also described a fight she witnessed, where young men were fighting in the hall. One, who was at a disadvantage (basically fighting on his own—the other had friends around), pulled a knife out of his sock and slashed the other boy's face. N said, "Yeah, the teachers all stayed in their classes. And the security guards always take their time responding to calls because they're afraid to break up the fights." L [a boy] responded about the incident, "Can you believe [the student who drew the knife] came back the next day. What a fool! They could have shot him on his way into school!"

As these "schools," zones of convergence of contradictory social forces (but by no means the *only* such zones on the political landscape), have spun more and more out of control, the response always escalates in a techno-security direction, thereby further distancing the professional educators from the student. "We have thrown out 200 troublemakers since September," one principal told me. With each new cycle of escalation, the body of the student is either literally exported from the school scene (through "safety" transfers, suspensions, dropouts, injuries, jail, or, in the extreme, death) or becomes the isolated solitary hallwalker, safe only to the extent that she or he acts tough and uses "street smarts."

Let us return abruptly to the Benjaminian imagery: Susan Buck-Morss

(1989, 312) refers to the sandwichman, hawking the wares of consumer capitalism along the Parisian arcades with advertisements hanging from his neck,[6] as the "last degraded incarnation of the flaneur." Today's adolescent flaneur of the urban school corridors, wearing this year's fashionable jacket and shoes, with his pants' crotch somewhere down around his knees, is our own latest incarnation of the flaneur, now reduced to the small monadic entity of his own body space, which is all he has left for protection. The space of the corridor finds itself locked into the cycle of violence followed by technocratic response followed by continued violence.

REMNANTS OF MODERNITY

This sea-change in the historical concept of the teacher's role, originally intended as the delegation of vexing disciplinary responsibilities, has resulted in the transformation of the school from the familiar institution of the nineteenth and early twentieth centuries to a pastiche of (1) remnants of some of the academic controls of modernity and, dialectically opposed, (2) an absence of almost all other controls, indicating a modernity in decay. In dispensing with or parceling out several of the teacher's traditional functions (disciplinarian, mentor, and spiritual guide) and in retaining the purely cognitive and academic functions, educators have simplified their lives but have radically changed the established relationship to the student, ultimately affecting the likelihood of conducting a viable school. A decade or so before the arrival of the guards, other functions that had been part of the teacher's traditional role (e.g., guidance, counseling, college advisement, working with the handicapped) were handed over to the guidance counselors, school psychologists, and other "special ed" experts.[7] Today, even more functions are rapidly disappearing due to the introduction of outside social agencies designed to cope with dropout prevention, conflict resolution, drug abuse, and other social ills.

Precisely because the teacher's and the principal's identities are fragmented, this delegation of responsibilities does not "work" in any pragmatic organizational sense: no one is really in control of the building. In the face of this power vacuum, it is sometimes said that "the kids are in control."

One way of investigating whether this notion is correct is by tapping into the memories of older teachers, those who have been working for the system for twenty-five to thirty years or who are recently retired. Their recollections about school life in the 1950s and early 1960s are not too dissimilar, *mutatis mutandis,* from the "Jesuit fantasy" I indulge in later (see the epilogue). In their versions of disciplinary tales, New York City high schools were once orderly, even quiet places where disruptive students used to be referred immediately and directly to the principal, who took corrective action. One black alumnus of one of the lower-tier schools recalled, with relish, how "one little Jewish lady, Mrs. . . . . " had controlled a whole corridor with its six classrooms singlehandedly back in the late 1950s. One teacher who had taught in Beta School since the 1950s recalled wistfully how the "problem" in those days, when it was an all girls' school, was that the place was "too quiet." "Detention" took the form of an after-school period in which students did useless work. These teachers now talk about how "society" has taken away these and other constraints. I asked one retired teacher, who was also a former dean, to elaborate. She remembered how, in 1968, there was still a dress code for students. Although she believed that "some of it was unrealistic," she related, with some regret, how, after one girl was sent home for coming to school in slacks, the courts decreed that there should be "no dress code as long as you are not disruptive." She continued: "The teachers began to say: 'If there is no dress code for students, why should there be one for me?' Some teachers dressed as if they were cleaning the basement. There was a loosening up of attitudes towards the schools."

She recalled being shocked when, during the early 1970s, on the first day of class in September, students started running through the corridors, as if they had been pent up all summer and were just waiting to run amok. Something had happened, she felt, in the way they began to view school in those days. A serious academician herself, and one who instinctively tried to "talk to students" rather than "to discipline them," she had come to the conclusion that "learning can't go on when [the school] is that disruptive." She profoundly disagreed with the tactics of her former principal:

> I don't think—I don't really believe—I ever got used to the idea of having security guards in the school, actually. I won't mention names, the former principal, OK, he would say in the morning sometimes, "I'm holding the school with 9 guards . . . or 12 or 15." Look, he was *holding* the school with 9 guards? You hold it with the teachers. . . . That's their job. Their job is not only to teach but to be part of the atmosphere that creates a community in the school . . . and the security guards (whatever their positive relationship with the students) makes the place a penal institution. And I don't

> like penal institutions. I was never able to accept it . . . from the day
> I came back from maternity leave in 1978, when the guards were
> there and I had never seen them before in that number.

Although she was never hostile to the guards, she went on to describe
how the guards had taken away "that community role" that she expected
teachers to play: "the teachers became more and more isolated in their
classrooms." Most teachers now, she felt, take the attitude that their domain
is the classroom, that "the security guards have the halls" and, "as long as
I can maintain the classroom," please do not disturb me. She went on to
recall some of the teachers' humor inside her social studies department:
"'They [the guerrillas in Vietnam] may have the highways, but we have the
cities.' People said that. As long as you keep the cities, like the way we had
in Vietnam. . . . We used to laugh, especially in social studies, we'd say,
'Well, they [the students] got the halls today, you know, whatever . . . they've
got the halls, but they haven't got the classrooms.'"

WHO'S IN CONTROL?

Classroom behaviors of the most edifying type do occur. Contrary to
conservative discourse, the contemporary inner-city school should not be
represented as chaotic. It is simultaneously both better and worse than
right-wing discourse allows; it is a mélange of contradictory behaviors and
values: in any one of these schools, one may glance through classroom
doors and observe orderly scenes reminiscent of the 1940s or 1950s, while
on some other corridor a bloody episode is taking place. Teachers may not
know until the end of the day about a serious disturbance on a remote
corridor. In such a blend, such traditional judgments as "things are getting
better" and "things are getting worse" may both be correct and truthful
statements.

Even more surprising, one is constantly struck by the dedication and
competence of the women and men, principals and teachers, who work in
these schools year after year: the English teacher who counsels with her
students on the telephone late at night, treating them as if they were her own
children; the Haitian science teacher who manages to keep the attention of
thirty-four students while conducting class in a mixture of Haitian Creole,
French, and English; the principal who arrives at 7 A.M. and leaves for home
at 11 P.M., after an exhausting school day and an evening spent with parents,
police, and community leaders; teachers who resolutely refuse to focus on

the violence because they are intent on seeing to it that their students progress, pass their exams, and graduate; principals who try to keep their spirits up even after supervisory visits by central board-of-education personnel who lecture them on how well someone else is doing at another school; borough superintendents, responsible for twenty to twenty-five such inner-city schools and for all that goes on in them, who somehow manage to keep their wits about them and attempt to focus on reform.

At the outset, then, it is important not to categorize all school staff members as "burnouts" or "good guys" or to glamorize one teacher to the disparagement of the rest.[8] Inner-city schools are justly proud that they can and do perform, in some ways equal to, and in some ways superior to, the highly specialized ones. I have heard principals present convincing data that their math, science, or English departments are equal to the "top four" schools in the city. They are trying to bridge the huge gap between the expectations placed upon them by state and city standards and the low levels of preparedness in the students they receive each year. The marvel, then, is that school staff and students are able to function in the face of such negative conditions and formidable obstacles. If a teacher's behavior or principal's response to a student appears to be "fascistic" or totally improper, one must constantly remind oneself that these educators are functioning in a fundamentally impossible managerial environment. None of these considerations can negate the fact that when competent teachers drop out of the system, less well-trained or even completely ill-equipped people are sometimes hired to take their places; but an understanding of the issues will not emerge if we focus only on the individual teacher or principal behaviors rather than on the discourses and policies that ultimately construct them.

CLASSROOM VIGNETTES

With these caveats behind us, and taking as a given that the students dominate school corridors, we are now in a position to examine a few vignettes of classroom life to answer the question, Are the students *also* in control of classrooms? In distinguishing between classroom and corridor spaces, an obvious distinction on the face of it, I am also making an implicit (and provisional) distinction between "private" and "public." That is, the classroom still represents a society where one may be known by a proper name and where the occurrence of a distinctly human event—the smile—

is still possible. The corridor, by contrast, stands for alienation and estrangement. Standard textbooks on school management proclaim that these two spaces should ideally complement one another. In lower-tier schools, however, a spatial as well as an ideological mutation has taken place. Just as the traditional "general" department store, under the impact of conspicuous consumerism, has slowly dissolved its main public area and evolved into an assemblage of private boutiques (e.g., Gucci, Elizabeth Arden), so, too, the traditional school has withdrawn from the public space of the corridors and has dispersed into privatized classrooms. Every teacher must work alone to establish norms of governance, set disciplinary guidelines, clean and prepare the space—and all these are in addition to normal teaching duties. In other words, each classroom is almost a self-contained unit operating in many respects free from the others and from the rest of the school, since the communal aspects of school life have been converted into an anticommunity.

The following excerpt is taken from my fieldnotes after a conversation with a young white woman, Y, who was just completing her first year of teaching at Beta School, a school she specifically sought out in order to work with inner-city youth:

> I asked Y how things were going. She replied that the first thing I
> had to understand was that "it was a total fraud to think of this
> school as an educational institution," that if she adhered to her
> standards in a social studies class, only three students out of 36
> would be literate enough to pass legitimately. What happens is that
> the students "are not doing the work, I know they are not, they
> know they are not," and as a result, they know they are not going
> to pass, so they become "totally disruptive in class both academi-
> cally and behaviorally." She finishes, she said, by compromising and
> telling them that if they will do "such and such make-up work," she
> will pass them. But she stressed that she was doing this as a disci-
> plinary device so that they will not be disruptive when the principal
> comes in to audit her. She therefore passes them on to the next
> grade, even though they have not done the work. She now under-
> stands, she said, how these kids have gotten where they are, by be-
> ing "passed along" in the lower grades. Her classroom, she said, is
> one continuous distraction, with constant disciplinary problems
> and even the unproblematic students tugging at her for different
> things. She was describing here her "worst" class; these students,

she said, were all "retreads," who had failed once before—some of them twice before. She learned that one student had been at Rikers Island for attempted murder.

Teachers such as Y have three class preparations each night and teach five classes per day to 160–170 students. With "do nows" and homework to correct, Y works at her job virtually all the time, with no time to reflect, either at school or at home. Y says she "only works and sleeps." She has despaired of the prospect of transferring any knowledge at all; she feels that neither she nor her colleagues have abandoned their principles of what is right and what is wrong; rather, she feels, she has been forced to "suspend her principles" while teaching at Beta School until such time as she is able to get out of "that crazy school." If all this sounds slightly reminiscent of *Horace's Compromise,*[9] there is a good reason: it *is,* except that here—in contrast to middle-class schools—the teacher's "compromise" is also motivated by intimidation, fear, threats, and violence. Y told me that she had asked a teacher what he would say if a student threatened to kill him. His response was, "I'm here 8–3 Monday through Friday. Come and get me!" Y is hoping to transfer to an alternative school next year.

Another teacher, L, a Chinese man who had lived and suffered through the Cultural Revolution and who was just completing his first year of teaching at Gamma School, had previously been a tutor. My fieldnotes reflect our conversation:

> L said that an article was circulated among the teachers entitled "Learning from Asian Schools." L felt that the U.S. *should* learn from Asian schools. When he began the semester, he said, he took over from another teacher. She told him, "I'm glad you're taking over—I can't control this class." But, he said, she had given even the worst students 80s, 90s, and 100s. He said he gave them what they deserved—30s and 40s. The teachers, he said, do this to flatter the students, "to make them happy. They give them grades as gifts." "There is no quality-control mechanism. In China, you have to pass the national standards. A teacher is judged by how many of her or his students can meet the required standards." "The Hispanic students here ask him," he said, "'Why are you so unkind to us? Why can't I pass your class?'" We have to create social pressure, he felt, on crime and on criminals. There is no sense of shame in the U.S., he said. No pressure. Yesterday a girl was involved in a mugging; today she is in the classroom laughing. When he asked some teach-

ers what had happened (after a violent incident), they responded that they didn't want to talk about it. Over the school loudspeaker every day, he said, the announcements "say that everything is good. There are never any reprimands. They don't let the teachers know about the violence. They don't discuss it."

Violence is the subtext in every conversation; rarely does it become the text. One Trinidadian tutor described the scene as she went to a classroom to meet some students:

> Ms. E has been assigning V and M to me once per week. They put on such a show when I go to pick them up, but once we get to the tutoring room, all is well. One day I went to pick them up and there was a "spitting" match going on in the class. Ms. E is my size but shorter and I feel sorry for her. The students scream awful words to each other, male students in the hall yell things to students in the classroom. . . . Ms. E does her best. . . . I could never handle a class like this. . . . I'd go insane. I asked V why do male students treat the women students so disrespectfully . . . swearing and grabbing them. . . . The young women do the same to the young men. He shrugged. He said that is how his mother talks to him. I think this is the basis for the continuance of abuse in the home.

Tutors' logs routinely recorded students' complaints and perceptions about the lack of order in certain classrooms:

> A is shy; I'm trying to make her feel more comfortable but I'm not sure how well it worked. She's from Barbados (three months here) so I tried to get her to think of the differences between Barbados and here, then to look at the cultural ideas being discussed in the Caribbean and see how they are similar or different from here. Her mother is still in Barbados; she is here with her father. She said for her science class she received a failing grade because "everyone else in the class was noisy." Her story was that she could understand the material but that the class was so noisy and ill-behaved that she, and everyone else, got poor marks. When I asked her if she wanted to speak to the guidance counselor about it, she just said, "No, that's OK." Will speak with her about it again next week.

Students' own ideologies of teaching and learning had no room for out-of-control and disorderly classrooms; on the contrary, their conversations with me were laced with complaints about how other students did not respect teachers, did not listen to them, and came in late without reprimands or penalties:

> T (Black fifteen-year-old female student): I like this class. She don't take nothing. And I like reading and I like looking for answers.
>
> N (Hispanic fifteen-year-old female student): She don't joke around, that's what I like. She serious.
>
> MALE TUTOR: She knows how to joke around, too.
>
> T: She take her class serious. I don't like these other teachers. They . . .
>
> JD: Why? Because they let the students fool around too much?
>
> N: Yeah. They let you joke around, and that's not right.
>
> JD: Is this just in these [dropout prevention] classes?
>
> N AND T (in unison): The whole school!!
>
> N: I think if you come to school, it's to learn, it's not to . . . It's work, work, you know, think. You know, school time is to think about school. That's what I think. You go to school to run a school, to learn.
>
> JD: And you are saying that doesn't always happen?
>
> N: No. See, if we don't try hard enough the teacher goes, "O.K. I don't have to teach. I still get a check."
>
> T: That's what my math teacher used to say.
>
> JD: Your math teacher used to say that?
>
> T: Not only my math, my social studies. "O.K., I don't care, I still get my check. I get paid for doin' nothing."

But maintaining control, in the context of these "schools," is not for the teacher just a question of following consistent patterns that have been set down by school administrators. A corridor completely peaceful one minute and in total disarray the next has a direct impact on classrooms. On one occasion, six intruders entered the classroom of a Jamaican teacher, approached him, put a pistol to his head in front of the entire class, and pulled the trigger twice. The gun was empty and the boys ran away, but the teacher was so shaken that he was unable to return to school for the next few days. One Trinidadian tutor wrote in her log: "I met L and a friend in the cafeteria. They joined me and we discussed their irritation at the problem in Room 600. It appears that the class is run by three students: H and F the violent, and C, the vociferous, loquacious tyrant. The latter I've personally experienced. They told of the swearing the three direct at both teacher and class, the violent acts directed towards themselves and M (a female student), and their attempts to cope. It was very revealing and sad."

The combination of out-of-control classrooms, substitute teachers, and unsupervised youth melts the boundaries between classroom, corridor, and street. In the following instance, the classroom turmoil was frightening for a girl, brand new to the school, in which initiation rites included sexual harassment unchecked by a passive adult: "[tutor's log] All of the boys in room 248 were written up yesterday because they 'jumped' a new girl. This girl was brought up to 248 for the first time and, unfortunately, Mr. D, the teacher, was out. The substitute teacher was an older man who could not cope and the boys started touching the girl in 'private' areas and trying to kiss her. The boys were upset that they were written up for things they claim they took no part in."

The treatment of this girl as a sex object, a single incident torn out of a single day in a single school, makes clear the extent to which the ethos of the school has been transformed. The impact is seen most dramatically when a student whose earlier experiences have been shaped by traditional cultural and educational systems, even highly colonized ones—be they Caribbean, Chinese, African, Indian—enters a New York City lower-tier school. If migration is stressful and conflictual for adults, it can be harrowing for adolescents,[10] as reflected in this tutor's log:

> P recently arrived from Jamaica and is having difficulty understanding her teachers. Their accents are foreign to her . . . she has difficulty understanding me sometimes, even though I grew up in the Caribbean—Trinidad. I think there should be classes where P and students with her problem can engage in conversation with American teachers. ESL is supposed to help these students, but I question ESL. . . . Conversation does not seem to have a role in the [ESL] class. I subscribe to the belief that language is culture and understand the need for P and other immigrants—of which I'm one—to retain something of the "homeland." But one has to acknowledge that for P and others to participate on a national/global perspective, they would have to know how to use the globally accepted structure of the English language. This does not mean that P has to lose her identity; she can operate on both levels. I try to engage P in as much conversation as I could. Beta School was a shock to her. As I've

pointed out in previous logs, many students from the Caribbean, and I suspect other countries, have a television/movie image of American high schools. She was most shocked at the manner and dress and behavior of the students, particularly since almost all of the students at Beta are from the Caribbean. How and why, as well as from whom, did they acquire these mannerisms? I could not tell her. Beta School does not get students who excelled—in say, Trinidad, for example. These parents prefer to send their students elsewhere. If they do attend Beta, it is for a short period of time. N is an example; she arrived from Trinidad last semester and is now attending school elsewhere. The students at Beta arrive there with attitudes to education they acquired from wherever "home" might have been. The freedom that American high schools like Beta allow reinforces and almost encourages these attitudes. The respect for teachers that might have been—in the Caribbean—is lost at Beta, as students walk out of classes when they please, even though they are not supposed to, and are quite rude to teachers as well. I question the role of the guards and the function they play in the school. I don't think their presence helps this discipline problem.

The question, How and why, as well as from whom, did they acquire these mannerisms? refers to the shock of both tutor and tutee at seeing their fellow islanders able to engage in behaviors that would not have been tolerated in their native countries. This is a variation on the same question we are pursuing: how did these "schools" get so far out of control? In the following exchange, J, another talented and caring tutor from Trinidad, is pushing S, who had arrived eighteen months earlier from Trinidad and was beginning to sell drugs, to let her know if he gets into trouble, while A, a girl who recently came from Barbados, listens and interrupts.

> J: I hope you will open up your trap and tell me. Part of caring about someone is caring whether they get into trouble and if you can keep them out of trouble.
> S: The only reason I do that [selling drugs] is for the money. I don't take the money and buy clothes, sell my soul for a mess of jewelry and this. That's not my style. All I want [laughs] is my little beeper. See, I don't bring it to school anymore.
> J: You better not.
> S: I bring it to school sometimes.

> J: Which reminds me. The Walkman—don't bring it to school no
> more.
> S: The Walkman?
> J: Don't bring it to school no more.
> A: Why not?
> J: It's not supposed to be in school in the first place.
> A: They don't hassle you about it. You can listen to it in your free
> time.
> J: They're being very nice about it. It should not be here.

ABSENCE OF THE "GAZE"

This fifteen-year-old Barbadian girl's offhand comment on school discipline can be taken as a kind of preliminary axiom that sums up the ethic of the lower-tier high schools, immediately obvious to anyone coming fresh into the system: "They don't hassle you." It is this recognition that teachers are not performing surveillance, that the previously ubiquitous Foucauldian "gaze" of adult teachers has now been transmuted to eye contact—or avoidance of eye contact—with the peer group that convinces the student from overseas that there are no disciplinary boundaries and that almost any behavior goes, something the native born recognize much earlier in their scholastic careers. This phenomenon also helps to explain the curious fact that migrant students sometimes even exceed their American counterparts in indulging in aggressive behavior. When boundaries for behavior are so loose, they can be read as nonexistent by a newcomer while natives recognize that ambiguous limits do, in fact, exist.

These conclusions should not be taken to imply that the students are the sole, or even the primary, carriers of the street-culture virus into the schools. Unlikely mutations and role reversals take place in rapid succession: the class bully suddenly takes over and imposes order on an unruly class on perceiving the embarrassment of the teacher, known to be an alcoholic, in the presence of two visitors. Breaches of etiquette by school staff (a secretary habitually speaking brusquely to students, a teacher who speaks disparagingly about a student to one of our tutors, even in the student's presence) are ways in which adults act to import the culture of violence, transform it, and export it back to the streets. I know of situations in which teachers have brought weapons, including guns, to the school. One student interpreted a teacher's behavior in precisely this way:

[Woman tutor's log] In speaking with N [a girl] and L [a boy], . . . both appeared to be impressed with the large amount of fighting that had been occurring in the school since the beginning of the year. N, who appeared to become quite animated and enthused, described many fights she was privy to. One fight she was impressed with involved a teacher and a student—"Yeah well Mr. X should never have jumped S [a boy]." It seemed S had more friends than Mr. X could deal with, because soon after he allegedly started with S, S's friends came to his rescue, 10 of them jumped Mr. X—and as L said, "Did you see Mr. X's two black eyes—yeah, they were swollen!"

As this incident makes clear, a teacher's disengagement from the ideology of physical surveillance is not necessarily inconsistent with the teacher's actual physical contact with the body of the individual student. Teachers, like students, are aware that inside the building, as on the streets, they have no protection but themselves. "Having respect" (i.e., being known as tough) translates into having a reputation for aggression, while "chilling" (i.e., retreating into hiding) is recommended for those without it. There are no other alternatives, no other imaginable future: "You got nobody to back you up." Flamboyant anticipatory exhibition of violence by students or by staff, the scholastic equivalent of a preemptive strike, is the only meaningful practice in the construction of an identity. "I'm gonna live because I got respect in this school," as one student put it. Some teachers withdraw into almost complete passivity. A fifteen-year-old Haitian boy: "Some teachers did nothing. . . . One of my math teachers . . . I'm going to class everyday, 8th period. . . . The kids know that he will just pass you with an 85. . . . He gave me a 90. . . . I never did any homework. If kids were smoking in the class he never did anything. He would read a few pages from the textbook, give some old tests, and that was it. I just stayed in the room and let everyone go by." If trying to uphold academic standards, a teacher might suffer consequences: "[the same student] I heard of a teacher being cut in the face because the student received a failing grade. . . . He never came to class . . . he was suspended, taken to jail, and the teacher stayed. The teacher can't really do anything. . . . If the student gives the teacher a problem in class, they just call up the security guards. [Acting up] makes the kid feel like he's someone big. . . . I'm a fool, you know I'll be back tomorrow so why do you bother to harass me?"

Other teachers develop a reputation for employing a tough street style as a mechanism of control. One black social studies teacher was held up by her department as a model for how to maintain an orderly class—she never had any discipline problems. When asked how she did it she told her fellow teachers: "I'm just a real bitch!!" A student described his "respect" for her as follows: "VS is a no b. s. person. She will tell you 'fuck you' back—she will diss you so hard. . . . She would tell you how stupid you are . . . how we as black people, people have worked hard to get where we are and now you come up here and make a fool of yourself, using words that a student never heard in his life, she would use it if it comes down to it. She is very down, she is mad-cool." Here the etiquette of the street has been substituted for rational, humanistic methods of control. Her colleagues are impressed and her supervisor even holds her up as a model for maintaining order, but only because her method works.

A Culture of School Violence

In the "school," then, moral instruction has become separated from discipline and pedagogy, and students are socialized into a culture of street violence. The school is, of course, only one of a plurality of fragmented social sites on the decaying urban scene: the total abandonment of inner cities by the federal government during the Reagan-Bush-Gingrich years; the national tolerance of a drug-and-gun culture; the massive cutbacks in the area of health, education, and welfare; and the cooptation and normalization of the culture of violence by the mass media and the toy industry.[11] This chapter, in asserting the dominance of a self-governing culture of school violence, has placed the spotlight on two zones that have become concealed at the level of pedagogical praxis. The first is the teacher's responsibility for encouraging students' moral development and the teacher's supervisory role *in loco parentis,* which has now been replaced with devices, guards, and technological systems seeking only to curb major incidents. The earlier emphasis on manners, politeness, and character development has gotten lost. The second zone, the direct correlate of the first, is the construction of a student body whose surface has become the active agency for real violence, destructive as well as self-destructive. What I have attempted to interrogate here is the "commonsensical" nature of some board-of-education and union credos that have become complicit in these processes.

When I suggested to an African American counselor, one highly respected by students and faculty alike, that it might be possible to bring teachers and counselors together so counselors could communicate some of these deepest-held student feelings about the need for structure and the breakdown of ordinary discipline, her thoughtful reply was: "It would be war. The teachers would feel you were infringing on their rights. They would go to the union." But teachers' unions and boards of education operate within a political and intellectual framework that, in the bustle of everyday business, is not often acknowledged. The next chapter will speak to the collusion of pedagogical theory in this process of creating and fostering a culture of school violence.

PEDAGOGICAL THEORY AND THE MIND-BODY DUALITY

My primary intent is to deconstruct the educational theory and institutional practice of modern humanism.
  —William V. Spanos, *The End of Education: Toward Posthumanism*

Humanism in East New York?
  —Teachers union official

A NOSTALGIA FOR HUMANISM

The preceding chapters have left us with two images that, taken together, capture the school system's response to the culture of violence, which, like all cultures, operates largely at the unconscious level. The first image is that of the teacher's deflected gaze, now turned fearfully away from eye contact with the student, thereby placing distance between the educator, perceived as pure intellectual, and the body of the student, perceived as the incarnation of a vexing youth culture with which confrontation would be unwise. This averted gaze stands for the avoidance of encounters over student comportment, the neglect of reminders about manners, the lack of even friendly and relaxed student-teacher exchanges—in sum, for the total rejection of the *in loco parentis* role.

If New York is emblematic of the rest of the country, then, the role of the teacher in the inner-city high school of the late twentieth century has been reduced to the realm of the intellect, and teachers are being charged purely with the custody of the mind of the student and with the cultivation of academic skills, as defined by state-dictated curricular requirements. Dealing with schoolwide discipline at the moment an offense occurs, communicating firmly but in a consistent way what is or is not acceptable etiquette, correcting students on the spot, enforcing school rules jointly with other teachers, teaching and modeling social skills, challenging adolescent beliefs and attitudes, allowing students the space to "open up"—in short, a humanistic interaction with the "whole" student—all these have become taboo areas for the lower-tier teacher. As a result, there is little insistence on personal responsibility, and students conclude that the teachers just do not care.

When I asked one of the top officials in the teachers union about what has happened to the role teachers once played in supervising students, about the humanistic enterprise of character development, and about "caring enough to correct," his immediate response was: "I think that's gone. . . . I mean you go through some neighborhoods in the Bronx and you see the curbside shrines of kids who were killed and this type of thing. . . . I think that ball game is over already. . . . I think that's just nostalgia. Humanism in East New York?"

The second image that has emerged is that of the metal detector, manifesting a response to violence that might better be described as an absence of discourse, since, despite the headlines after each tragic incident, silence and avoidance, rather than open acknowledgment, surround the topic. As noted above, official board of education statements attempt to minimize the amount of serious conflict and to locate the causes outside the school building, blaming lack of federal gun-control laws, the dangerous streets, intruders, or a "small handful" of troublemakers.[1]

The teachers union contends that the board is deceitfully underreporting violence and begs for more technology and guards as protection for its members. The board has now conceded that violence is underreported and has accepted as a remedy for this the diminishing of the principal's role and the enhancement of the chief security guard's role in the school (see Travis, Lynch, and Schall 1993 and Dillon 1993a). Adolescents' fears, their basic needs for self-preservation, and the dictates of the street culture to act tough are expressed through the semiotics of the concealed weapon. In the end, the most politically significant discourse is uttered through the decision to spend millions on weapons scanners and additional police and school safety officers, who are entrusted with the surveillance of the outer fringes. This technological escalation only elicits further responses of marginalization, nostalgia, and violence.

A SILENCE IN THEORETICAL DISCOURSE

I have already referred to the refusal at the level of educational praxis to recognize the new dualism that has evolved; legitimating this refusal is a corresponding silence at the level of educational theory. This strand of theory may be justly dubbed dualistic, because it dichotomizes the student, dismissing the importance of the teacher's connection to the body or bodily behavior of the student while emphasizing the teacher's relationship to the mind. With the blessing of these theoreticians, teachers are provided with a rationale that permits them to withdraw from all contact with the physical component of the adolescent person, thereby absolving themselves not only from the nasty work of disciplinary surveillance but also from the whole matter of forming human relationships.

I am not blaming teachers for their predicament; in schools of thousands of students, it is truly impossible for teachers, who must interact with over 150 students daily, to form the kinds of personal relationships students need during this formative period. Rather, I am taking aim at the unwillingness of theoreticians to see such interactions as desirable, even in smaller settings. Instead, friendly contacts are described as subtle cooption into the hegemonic system. Ironically, these doctrines, while distancing the teacher from the body and from what used to be called character development, simultaneously romanticize the body by refusing to attribute real lethal aggression to it. Unlike the gnostic dualism of old, this form of dualism envisions the body of the student, and in particular the inner-city student, as inherently good, as incapable of serious mischief, as almost already glorified, and certainly not in need of correction. This misrepresentation of the body is illustrated most clearly in the critical pedagogy of Henry Giroux, who has written extensively about the importance of revitalizing John Dewey's vision of public schools "as places where the skills of democracy can be practiced, debated and analyzed" (1988, 114).

Giroux's goal is to reformulate citizenship education in the public schools as a way of transforming, rather than defending, the inequities of the existing social order (1988, 10). He wishes to redefine teachers as "transformative intellectuals" who would work toward social justice by helping students acquire critical knowledge of the existing societal structures in order to transform them into more humane, emancipated institutions. In Giroux's utopian but sober and well-reasoned view, public schools would prepare students for active participation in a democracy by gaining some control over the sociopolitical forces that control their destinies.

But for Giroux, as for many "critical ethnographers," all school violence ends up being interpreted as "symbolic violence," which the hegemonic system perpetuates by "devaluing the cultural capital" that students possess (1988, 123). Symbolic violence is, in Giroux's use of the term, really synonymous with the idea of structural violence, which the Norwegian sociologist Johan Galtung expounded as the menace present in institutions even where no literal violence (understood in the more usual sense of the word) occurs. Thus, both terms are the equivalent of social injustice.[2] The legitimacy of this concept is not in question; the problem is that its exclusive use clouds our recognition of the presence of violence in the more usual, narrow sense. Absent among critical pedagogies is any hint of violence effected through student agency.

Giroux favors getting rid of "old-fashioned pedagogy" with its overemphasis on test scores and rote learning, arguably a worthwhile aim and one that he is hardly alone in promoting. But in distancing himself from right-wing notions, he also downplays teaching of such "old-fashioned virtues" as hard work, self-discipline, and perseverance. In this same vein, he finds character training that emphasizes punctuality and obedience to authority "profoundly detrimental." "Respect for family," "character development," "codes of civility," and "discipline" are not terms he is comfortable with, and he, like most critical pedagogues (e.g., McLaren 1986; Fine 1992), constantly identifies any use of them with right-wing discourse.[3] "School discipline" appears to have only one possible embodiment: the extremist measures exercised by Joe Clark, the bullhorn-carrying principal whose "get tough" measures endeared him to Ronald Reagan and William Bennett

Giroux's central concern is nothing less than a complete reinvigoration of American democracy through a re-creation of teacher education and classroom pedagogy. He would turn teachers into "transformative intellectuals" who would link schooling with the highest ideals of democracy and who would motivate students to become critical, politically active citizens. To accomplish this, students must be made aware of the oppression and injustice inherent in the present uneven distribution of power in society. Giroux attempts to move educational theory in the direction of a more radical and emancipatory form of critique by breaking down individualism, by creating a community rooted in social justice, and by establishing a pedagogy of hope. Students, having become aware that schools are not neutral political territory, would also become empowered to reconstruct the social order.

GLORIFIED BODIES

Commendable as are Giroux's objectives for teacher education, they remain permeated with the new dualism, which is based on a peculiarly restricted concept of the body as it manifests itself in the actualities of everyday schooling. Overcoming the mind-body duality, for Giroux, consists in a recognition of diversity and a celebration of human sexuality. The teacher is to be a caring person, but caring does not include admonitions, confrontations, or corrections; it seems to be a kind of caring that would applaud and revel in the student's sensuality.

Just as some gnostics envisioned all sin as emanating from an originary evil principle, so, for Giroux, all vice is to be referred back to a primeval source, the dominant society's oppression of its exploited victims. Giroux does not allow himself to contemplate the ways in which a cyclical relay of violence might function—replicating and escalating itself as it shuttles back and forth between "bourgeois" source and "plebeian" terminus, between the architectonics of the social system and the body of the inner-city student. In these frenzied urban schools, the violence of the one becomes the sign of the violence of the other to the point where no rigorously theoretical account of violence can be given. The "meaning" of violence becomes infinitely deferred, in the Derridean sense, the marginality of the subordinate term encompassing the marginality of the superior one. But the responsibility for coping with and ending the violence is not thereby lessened for those in control of the political and pedagogical machinery.

One searches in vain in the pages of Giroux or his frequent coauthor, Stanley Aronowitz (see Aronowitz and Giroux 1985), for any mention of the antagonistic semiotics of aggression with which the space of contemporary urban school life is flooded: hidden weapons in pockets, gunshots in cafeterias, murders in corridors, rapes in stairwells, arson in classrooms, techno-security in lobbies, violent episodes in students' dreams, mourning and sobbing of parents and classmates in local funeral parlors. It is remarkable, given their ambitious attempt to examine critically the root causes of the problems in contemporary American schooling, that Aronowitz and Giroux avoid this crucial topic of violence, which for them is, at best, something that happens to students, something inflicted on students, not something students perform.

For these authors, the body of the student, especially the body of the marginalized student, is seemingly inoculated against the ability to commit truly harmful or malicious acts. Actual violent misdeeds such as theft, betrayal, sexual assault, and physical attacks on peers and teachers are excluded from the scope of their concerns. They, like other social reproduction theorists, are so intent on discovering "forms of resistance" to the dominant culture that they fail to take their own reproductionist idea to its limits. Ultimately, this becomes a failure of ethnography, since they fail to report what is happening "on the ground"—namely, that the body of the inner-city student is not only a bearer of the counterculture, not only an active reproducer of her or his future lower-class career, but also a doer of violent deeds, caught up in a mutually destructive dialectic with the least humanistic face of the school system and of the other sites (e.g., prisons) outside the school.

It is my contention that, by pulling up short before arriving at the most devastating conclusion and extreme end-point of their theory, Aronowitz and Giroux and other radical theorists misrepresent the inner-city student essentially as a unitary subject, one heroically doing battle against an unjust system, one the students themselves would have a hard time recognizing. The inner-city student is portrayed as the originator of nonviolent action, actively rebelling against the dominant society, but never as an active agent of violence, a transmitter as well as a receiver of the culture of violence. Whether from insufficient exposure to inner-city schools, or through a calculated refusal to recognize the student as an agent of aggression, they ignore the occurrence of actual, concrete violence. The culture of violence destroys both the unified nature of what was formerly—albeit somewhat nostalgically—thought of as the "whole student" and the unity of the organized institution. Focused on classrooms, which they apparently still believe is the center of the research arena, and lacking an ethnographic base like the corridors of a lower-tier school, these theorists fail to attend to a fourfold postmodern fragmentation: of the student, of the teacher, of the monolithic institution of the school, and of the ethnographer-observer.

HUMAN AGENCY, UP TO A POINT

As Gary L. Anderson (1989, 256) has observed, Paul Willis's now-classical expression of countercultural resistance, *Learning to Labor* (1977), became the standard for critical ethnographies written during the 1980s, because it transcended standard reproduction theory. The cardinal point of Willis's educational ethnography was "the unintended consequences of the lads' oppositional culture formed at the school: how they systematically disqualify themselves from middle class jobs as the ironic effect of class conflict in the schools; how, without coercion, youths funnel themselves onto the shop floor" (Marcus 1986, 182).

In Willis's account, the inappropriate behavior of the "lads" he studied was not only a form of resistance; it became a device for their own later deprivation. For this, Willis is usually given credit for a singular intellectual achievement: he surpassed a simplistic and old-fashioned Marxist structural determinism, because his lads are endowed with human agency. They are not mere pawns of powerful economic forces; they construct their own (counter)culture, which has the paradoxical effect of consigning them to working-class jobs forever.

But Willis's theoretical attainment also has its limitations. Note that the whole metanarrative of modernity is present here: a coherent group of subjects (the lads); a structured institution against which to rebel (a fairly well-managed British school); a neutral ethnographic observer, Willis (who is not interested in changing his subjects' behavior). The fundamental ethos of the school is represented as "a nagging vestigial but insulting attempt to reassert the old authority," an attempt that "disqualifies the authority of the school in the eyes of 'the lads.'" Even the "successful" teachers who try to adapt to the new realities are seen as just doing enough to "contain the counterculture without provoking incidents on the one hand or collapse on the other" (1977, 81). I dwell on Willis's school because, despite the presence of the rowdy lads, it was still, at least at the time of his ethnography, a traditional school, not a "school" as I have been defining it above—an intimidating space beyond the control of teachers, "secured" by guards, and reinforced by armed police who routinely handcuff students.

Like Giroux, Willis is concerned to endow his research subjects with human agency, but his concern does not go so far as to endow them with the capability for true violence. Their truancy, fighting, and disruptive behavior are good for laughs, can be branded as inappropriate or countercultural, and irritate the devil out of some teachers. But, once again, there is no blood on the floor, no real aggression, no dead bodies, no police presence, no security-technology response.

The contrast between these analyses and our students' lives is startling. The following log comes from a Caucasian woman who stayed in touch with one of our African American students during the summer he spent in jail:

> I had quite a surprise today—[Lee] came back to school today! He came down to see me during his lunch period. This was his first day back in school. We had a really good talk. He said that he got the newspapers & postcards that I sent to him. We talked about school for awhile & then finally talked about the summer. It seems he had some horrifying experiences watching people hurt other people. He said that some of the big guys had knives & when he reported them to the [jail] guards that they didn't even check up on them. He seems truly frightened & says that he doesn't want to go back. He really is on the verge of wanting something different. We talked about high school and coming to classes and the effect it could have on your life. I really want to concentrate on pulling him towards other things to get him away from his neighborhood & the type of crowd he hangs with. I asked him what he missed this summer. He said his friends. I said what about his family. He said that they came to visit alot so he didn't miss them so much. I asked him if he missed home itself, its comfort, smell, & the feel of his own bed, admitting that that is probably what I would miss the most. He smiled and said that he did miss those things. He commented that he also missed celebrating his birthday which turns out to have been a few days before mine about two weeks ago. So I asked him if there was something he would like to do & he said after some thought that he would really like to go to the zoo. I thought this was an odd request after just getting out of jail but he was serious. I said "let's go." He said "When?" So we are—Ted [another tutor] is going with us & possibly a few more students next Saturday. I need to connect with him now because if he takes the next step he might make it.

A straightforward reproductionist reading of this excerpt would no doubt highlight the social injustice of putting yet one more African American youth behind bars. The writer does not indicate why Lee found himself in jail, nor need we delay on that issue here. My own reading of the text would emphasize the fact that the writer-ethnographer exceeds critical ethnography: she is actively engaged with Lee, not merely analyzing his meaning. This anecdote also allows us to see the school from the perspectives of the state and of the street. The guards' calculated disregard of weapons in the school is the perfect analog of the behavior of prison guards too fearful to check prisoners for weapons; the interactions between the state and the street in both spaces insinuates a language of violence mutually intelligible to adults and adolescents alike.

Contra the reproductionists, student subjectivity is not so easily characterized as mere bearer of the counterculture. It is part sensitive child (wanting to be taken to the zoo), part street-smart lawbreaker (with all the insights of a summer in jail), and part willing student (responding to a caring tutor). Students switch among all these personas while they inhabit the highly contested and (to them) frightening space of a fragmented educational establishment no longer interested in making the "nagging vestigial" attempts to reassert authority. As the union official I cited earlier implied, even thinking of the teacher as a disciplinary figure is now an exercise in nostalgia. Perhaps the crucial difference between today's inner-city school and the one in which Willis worked is this: his ethnography disclosed a traditional school facing the countercultural lads, whereas the students with whom we work are not presented with an established structure against which to rebel. Instead of a unified countercultural rebel force, we have a totally decentered student subjectivity pulled and pulling simultaneously in several different directions; instead of a school we have a "school," a fragmented institution, its former humanistic core reduced to seeking protection at the outer perimeters from the most egregious crimes. Entering students seek in vain for some kind of framework on which to construct their identities but instead find that violence itself has become "an institution possessing its own symbolic and performative autonomy" (Feldman 1991, 21). Borrowing Feldman's perspective, we need to grasp this discourse of violence, unfettered by causal explanatory burdens such as class or ethnic formations, and see violence as a historical process that shifts social sites and subjectivities and as therefore causative of ethnicity and class.

Reproduction theorists such as Willis and Giroux interpret street culture in school corridors as bright, celebratory, Rabelaisian festival, but it also reproduces itself on the body of the inner-city student as dark, Stygian destructiveness. In expositions of Giroux's type, nobody really gets hurt, and nobody really causes hurt. Students do not stab one another. Death and mourning are not within the horizon of their merely boisterous, merrymaking "subjects." But the premises of social reproduction theory lead to a logical conclusion its authors fail to appreciate: street culture in the school, rooted in the injustices of hegemony, possesses its own (de)formative power that is capable of transforming the student into an instrument of its own making, an instrument of violence. The body of the urban student is not "given" a priori as either tough, benign, or victimized; it is a constructed site that, faced with a dominant culture that has chosen to absent itself from supervising youth initiation rituals, often finds itself committing real crimes to certify its toughness. Students' subjectivities cannot be predicted in advance. Within the context of a "school," none of the existing ideologies— neither the machismo of the street, nor ethnic values, nor traditional pedagogy, nor humanism, nor capitalism, nor a deconstructed and reconstructed humanism—has totally occupied the doctrinal space. At any given moment, compliance, outright aggression, docility, antagonism, anger, and celebration may all be anticipated.

Portraying students as perpetrators of mere pranks, of more or less harmless acts of resistance to upset old-fogey principals, represents a distortion of the ethnographic base on which theory should be built. It also shields a naive Rousseauian philosophy of the noble savagery of human nature, which understands adolescents, and most especially marginalized adolescents, as basically good kids. It undertheorizes violence. Positing the student as an active agent of violence, on the other hand, is not an endorsement of the existing social order. Rather, instead of excusing adolescent actors as victims of an unjust system, it represents them as so far victimized that they have become, at times, perpetrators.

In their zeal to do battle with ultraconservatives, critical pedagogues undermine whatever might still be recoverable from the Western humanistic tradition after it has been deposed from its imperialistic throne. Giroux, for example, takes one conservative author to task because "he views schools as places that should transmit values instead of critically appropriating, contesting, and engaging them" (1988, 43). Right-wing refusal to recognize the existence and equality of students' indigenous languages and cultures is matched by the refusal of radical discourse to recognize either the dark side of student conduct or the worthiness of teachers' values.

Giroux and the social reproduction theorists do not contemplate the possibility of a more balanced pedagogy. Such a pedagogy might be pulled tautly toward a recognition that students bring their own cultural assumptions and forms of etiquette to the educational encounter and toward an endorsement of self-confident communication of teachers' own values and standards of behavior, ones they expect students will meet. At the same time, teachers can help students critique the attributes of society at large and their indigenous cultural forms. This is not difficult to do, as the following excerpt illustrates.

> [Caucasian female tutor's log]: Paul [ninth-grade student] came down and brought me this tape to listen to. It is by a group called NWA (Niggers with Attitude). Paul and I were talking about music and I had just read this article about this group NWA getting censored by the FBI. I was curious and wanted to hear the music and find out why. . . . He lent me the tape to discuss in our group. I was very surprised to find that no one in the group could define censorship. So we talked about what it was and what it meant and whether it was right or wrong. The kids had some very interesting views on it and it grew into a very interesting discussion on human rights. Then I played the song in question called Fuck the Police. All of a sudden they changed their minds. They thought that this was too violent and should be censored. I thought that it was an interesting switch and we are going to discuss it further next week.

Given the proper forum, students may strongly critique the culture of violence as embedded in rap music or other cultural trends; in the above vignette they seem to be even ahead of their tutor in this respect. Their reaction represents a direct challenge to Giroux's optimistic picture of "street-corner culture" as a benign and innocent phenomenon with no admixture of violence, crime, or fear. For Giroux, when teachers focus on problems of order and control, they are defining the student as the cultural "other." He would have us interpret cordial relations between teacher and student as a device of control (1988, 126) rather than as a prerequisite for the discovery of knowledge or as a genuine striving for the *communitas* of which Turner speaks (1969, 94).

BEYOND CRITICAL PEDAGOGY

However valid its critique of the neoconservative ideology of the 1980s, the radical discourse of authors such as Aronowitz and Giroux (1985) proves inadequate when brushed against the multiplicity of contradictory rituals—some playful, some deadly serious—inherent in everyday life in the inner-city high schools of our era. Today's schools force us to go beyond critical pedagogy and reproduction theory, even that of the "culture of resistance," without denying the advances these have made in the debate with conservatives. For, in truth, these students are being stretched in more than just two directions, compliance *with* or resistance *to* a biased system. Contradictory ideologies pull these high school students, who are still forming identities, in many different directions. One fifteen-year-old girl, discovering she is pregnant, tells a female tutor that her mother will throw her out of the house if she keeps the baby, that her pastor warns her that abortion is a serious sin, and that her drug-dealing boyfriend wants her to "make a baby boy" for him. What, she asks, should she do? The tutor, like a counselor-in-training or a psychiatric resident, needs to learn how to refrain from proposing her own solution and allow her tutee to make her own decision. But the presence of the tutor and the influence of her values are undeniable. Ideally, she listens to the multiplicity of voices within the individual (and within herself and, insofar as she is being supervised by me, within me) and helps the student reinforce voices that have been stifled through neglect or violence. Without this support, the adolescent finds herself alone in trying to sort out the multiple signals she is receiving, only some of which the community may legitimize.

Another of our tutors had the following conversation with a fifteen-year-old boy who had just learned that one of the girls in our program had had her face badly slashed by a group of girls:

> N: What happen? You get in a fight? [The tutors tell him what happened and N shakes his head disdainfully.] I'da kill dem.
> Tutor: N, she was outnumbered. Anyway, violence is no answer to violence.
> N: I give my girl one a dem coat. She so sweet.
> Tutor: Well, if she's so sweet you better tell her not to wear it in Brooklyn.
> N: I give her a piece [a gun] too.
> Tutor: What if the cops find a gun on her? You could get her in trouble.
> N: She know what to do. I teach her. You gotta carry dem in a brown paper bag in your pocket. I got search by the cop tree times—dey fin' a gun on me an' arres' me. I tell 'em it in the bag 'cause I find it in the playgroun' an' I'm taking it to the police.
> Tutor: And they believed you?

N: Sure, 'cause I walk in the direction o' the police station. If they believe me they gonna believe my girl.

TUTOR: If you have a gun, someone's more likely to use a gun on you. Guns make people less safe.

N: Not my girl. I show her how to use it. She know how to shoot.

Students sometimes tell us that their mothers, though reluctant to see them carrying weapons, recognize their need for protection and survival. The value systems of responsible adults, parents, or school authorities become transformed by inexorable street logic, which has already become embedded in the gestures, consciousness, and emotions of the student. I have known judicious principals who have deemed it best to allow students to keep their weapons, on given occasions, for their own protection. But even hardened school authorities are often shocked when, at a disciplinary hearing,[4] a mother, instead of chastising her child for fighting, blurts out that she or he should have attacked the other student even more viciously. All such events need to be reinterpreted not at the level of individualistic psychology, as aberrations of spiteful parents or irresponsible school officials, but as realistic sociological appraisals of the student's need to survive within the culture of violence and her need to "adapt" to it. Although we never condone violence as an answer and we strongly attempt to dissuade students from fighting and retaliation, we find ourselves at times questioning whether we should dissuade a young girl from carrying a razor for protection on a dangerous subway line or in a remote and unprotected school stairwell, even though all the regulations forbid it. We find it difficult to argue with a girl who assures us the only way she will get respect on her block is by threatening people. Yet the possibility of switching to a discourse of respect still exists. And confrontations by adults over rules are welcomed by students: "[Tutor's log] The other three boys are the real challenge. H will not keep the Walkman off. I told him I would rather not take it away from him since he was old enough to be treated with more respect, but after many reminders, I finally decided to hold onto his headphones for the duration of the session. He seemed almost relieved by this."

We find ourselves facing a new question, one we never thought we would be asking: should we accommodate this culture of violence or should we resolutely repudiate it in every case? What are the ethics of permitting participation in the culture of violence, even when the motive is the benign

143

one of arming the student with survival skills? The clearest example of this dilemma occurs whenever we are faced with the issue of reporting child abuse. Should we scrupulously adhere to the state laws and report the abusive home situation the student, in painful desperation, has manifested to us, or should we explore other alternatives such as psychotherapy? The very reporting will, perhaps, only result in an angry parent's retaliation on the student or a placement in an equally abusive group home.

DECENTERED STUDENTS, DECENTERED "SCHOOLS"

The culture of violence transforms the dynamics of a school beyond the point at which quick fixes and prescriptions, found in manuals of school management and applicable to traditional schools, are workable: maxims about formal and informal organizational structures, leadership styles, teacher autonomy, and the like. Legal boundaries, insurance requirements, and union regulations become considerations in almost every decision. The new teacher who volunteers to stay after school and work over and beyond the call of duty is reprimanded by the union chapter chairperson. The one who consistently neglects duties may get a letter of reprimand, but everyone knows that a cumbersome due-rights process may drag the issue on for years. Hence the reluctance to enforce behavioral standards on teachers and the quiet acquiescence to the constant infraction of small rules, forms of polite conduct, and norms of etiquette. Underneath everything is a tacit recognition by all that a whole domain of delicate issues will never be addressed. The teacher wearing the dirty sportshirt with a pack of cigarettes protruding from his breast pocket will not be reprimanded, just as a student with a reputation for toughness will not be confronted by guards. Guards mention quite often—with a mixture of pride and resentment—that they are the only group in the school required to follow a dress code.

Students are quick to perceive the connections between authorities' disregard of minor school rules and small breaches of manners and their inability to prevent major transgressions such as the carrying of weapons. This deliberate overlooking of students' small (mis)behaviors sets the stage for students to breach the rules of etiquette; these breaches can escalate to hostile performances and, ultimately, to violence. The gaze of authority, such a pervasive bugaboo to Foucault, is more noticeable by its absence than by its presence. Thus, inner-city students are left to their own devices, to their own network of fearful, deflected gazes,, and this creates not the regime of discipline and docile bodies, so feared by Foucault, but a zone of sporadic and random violence:

> JD: What causes most of the fighting? You have seen so many principal's suspensions.
> PRINCIPAL: Stupidity causes it; [this] is the only way to say it. Girls, when they get into a fight, I'll hear more often than not, "I walked down the hall and she rolled her eyes at me. Or she said something about me." It's one on one, then it becomes 5 on 7. Then you have the out-in-the-open fights over guys that's constantly goin' on. The guys will fight over girls. The guys will get in a fight if you're up in the cafeteria. Kids are very protective of their clothing and, you're up in the cafeteria where it's very crowded and whatever, and if I'm leaving my bench and I step on your sneaker, and I don't say "Excuse me" quick enough, or even if I do, . . . I put a mark on your sneaker . . . these two kids are going to go at it. If they bump each other on the stairwell those kids are gonna go at it, they may not even know each other. And then there are other things, things that happen in the neighborhood. You have a party on Saturday night where somebody spoke to another girl and instead of doing it on the outside they'll wait until they get into the [school] building, cause they have more friends around them. And then there are also ethnic things. You'll have kids going after other kids just starting something because a kid's Haitian.

The code of the streets becomes the rule of school hallways once legitimate authority ceases to exert its vigilance and surveillance. Students not only need to look tough in order not to be attacked; they need to anticipate the hard gaze of the other and confront it with their own callous glare. At times, they need to take preemptive first strikes. E, one sixteen-year-old girl, discussing the violence on the streets, pondered the enigma of the phenomenon of the gaze: "[You could be killed] just for a look. One of my brother's friends had got shot in his back just 'cause he had looked at this guy."

In his study of facial engagements, Erving Goffman (1963) discusses the special role that eye-to-eye contacts play in the communicative life of a community: they ritually establish an openness to verbal statements, but, in societies where public safety is not firmly established, they can be a prelude to assault. Certainly, urban streets cannot be said to be places where public

safety is firmly established. When our Brooklyn students travel to unfamiliar areas such as Manhattan, they often return and report that "They look
at you funny." This reaction is usually given a racist interpretation; here I
am emphasizing more the out-of-control nature of urban public space. Ideally, the relaxed, friendly gestures and the smiling eyes in a school environment would provide an antidote to the hostile repertoire of gaits, postures,
and demeanors that we have all subconsciously internalized as part of normal behavior on urban streets. But displays of hostile glances are common
in the daily life of the unsupervised, and therefore unprotected, urban
street-like space of a lower-tier school:

> D, for example, was entering the tutoring room when he was dis-
> tracted by another boy who was in the stairwell trying to get
> through a door which was kept bolted by security guards. The boy
> kept calling to D through the window, asking him to unbolt the
> door to allow him entrance. D, fearful of contravening the hall
> dean, did not let the boy in but did maintain eye contact with the
> boy for a few seconds. When the boy finally got through he sought
> out D and said, "I will get you. I see where you walk home."

The code of the streets takes over immediately with the withdrawal of a
sound and moderate disciplinary authority that would ideally involve the
coordinated effort of the school community. The street culture becomes far
more consequential in fostering conflict than interracial or interethnic disputes. In a school of forty-one nationalities, the pivotal factor is not whether
the Panamanian students are conflicting with the Haitians this year or with
the Jamaicans or with some other group. "You gotta hurt them and hurt
them first," one student told me. In the face of this prevailing ethos, ethnic
affiliations become secondary to violence, which is permitted free rein as an
independent structural formation. Three boys, all Caribbean immigrants
and up to this point friends, became ensnared in its grip:

> [Tutor's log]: Today is a depressing day. R [Grenada] and C [St.
> Vincent] who have been best friends fought each other. It appears
> as though U [St. Lucia] is becoming very friendly with C and this
> made R very jealous. . . . A nickel debt incurred by U triggered the
> blowup. R's hostility toward U was reprimanded by C ("You're not
> a real friend") and out came the fist, foul words and fury. The fol-
> lowing day R brought in a razor to cut C's jacket which was then

ripped. A day later, in a recurrence of the incident, C was scraped on the lip with the razor.

GRAND NARRATIVES

Thus, the neo-Marxist, social reproduction, and "culture of resistance" narratives are no longer adequate to account for the appearance of the "school" anymore than the conservative theories are. By focusing on causal explanatory devices, these theories minimize or ignore the culture of violence that has overwhelmed the schools. The culture of violence is now more appropriately conceived as a spatiotemporal intersection of street violence and policing technology.

But this culture appears in numerous places and eras: schools are just one site among many in the deteriorating urban locales, the 1990s just one point in a continuum stretching back beyond the 1960s, 1950s, and 1940s into the very origins of modernity. The phenomenon of aggressive behavior did not begin in the 1970s or 1980s with the large buildup of uniformed security officers. We cannot locate its origin in the postwar era (no matter what films such as *Blackboard Jungle* may make us think). Microfilms of the *New York Times* contain numerous instances of shocking behavior and crimes perpetrated by high school students of the 1920s and 1930s. Nor can we place all blame on the relaxation of teacher surveillance, due largely to union pressures since the 1960s.

But this line of inquiry misses Foucault's essential point that Bentham's panoptic ideology of discipline, even when it was more effectively exercised than it is nowadays, was applied at precisely the pressure points at which modernity was always breaking down: schools, hospitals, prisons, and other institutions designed to "serve" the poor. This is also the lesson of the Benjaminian dialectical image: the arcadelike ceiling that promised the "stars" to a generation of Brooklyn students was a rude progressivist illusion that, combined with the deceitful spectacle of commodities, was another form of control needed to cushion the blow that the harsh reality of the factory world would deliver. The modernist school's constraints and domination of the body was the pedagogical equivalent of the discipline demanded of the factory labor force.

In his excellent study of the origins of Central High School in Philadelphia, David Labaree recounts how, prior to 1859, "students received demerits for disciplinary infractions, which were then deducted from a student's grade point average at the end of the term" (1988, 17). No doubt, for nineteenth-century New York City schools and American schools generally, moral education and character training were major goals of public schooling. Labaree records that Central High School students were evaluated 1600 times every term for either scholarship or *conduct!* He continues: "Like Bentham's Panopticon, [John] Hart's high school was a mechanism for training the unblinking eye of moral surveillance on hapless subjects in order to induce self-regulation. The leaders of the early Central High School were happy to impose public norms on the private interests of their students" (1988, 19).

This brief excursion into history is intended to demonstrate that the need for controls has always existed. The important question that needs to be asked is, What caused the controls to break down? If a persuasive history of this breakdown were to be written, I believe that, after listing all of the usual economic factors of an unrestrained and unjust capitalist culture, it would also highlight the important components of the American "culture of indulgence," which William Damon (1995, 21) has articulated: the misguided childrearing practices that shield children at home and at school from hard work, firm rules, and consistent disciplinary practices.

A first step, then, in pulling away from the current impasse is to place teachers in a pedagogical context in which they will be able to engage and to challenge students' daily performances as well as their sometimes uncritical interpretations of contemporary events, the mass media, general culture, youth culture, and their own indigenous lifestyles. Not everything that is indigenous is authentic. Although the culture of violence is not to be identified with the so-called subaltern cultures, neither are these to be conceptualized as being immune from it, given the propensity of the street culture to overlap all cultural formations, social classes, artistic genres, and ideologies.

The position I have carved out is at odds with the right-wing stance on education, which envisions the student, especially the inner-city student, as (at best) a *tabula rasa* on whose surface the teacher is to inscribe values. It also contests, at the other extreme, the Deweyan position, which conceptualizes the ideal teacher as one who should be reluctant to assert her own values, even when purged of the onus of a Western, patriarchal hegemony: "Thus Dewey left the teacher in a deeply ambiguous position—an instructor who could participate but never pronounce, offer suggestions and share in decision-making but never determine, think what might be best for students but never utter it" (Diggins 1994, 313).

A VULNERABLE ETIQUETTE

If one agrees with the basic proposition that the meeting of teacher and pupil is about something more than the mere communication of information and skills and that "something more" consists of assisting students to construct both their individual identities as well as a common sociocultural tradition (a just *communitas*), then it is important to recognize that two competing processes are interwoven within the text of today's urban educational institutions: the phenomenon of violence and the narrative of traditional education, however one may choose to characterize that tradition. It is absolutely vital for schools to confront the culture of violence.

This does not mean that adults should assert "traditional values" over youthful "wild behavior." To conceptualize teacher-student dialogue in this way would be to misunderstand the nature of dialogue, to think of it as an interchange between two autonomous and unitary individuals. In the "ideal" model of dialogue,[5] a sociocultural tradition does not precede the dialogic encounter but is built through the very dialogic process (Maranhão 1990, 5). To reach this new level of intercultural understanding, the teacher may have to take positions on values with which the student may disagree. Teachers and principals may profitably tell students (not in so many words), "My values are better than yours!" Youth who insist, for example, that homosexuals, lesbians, the Jewish people, and various ethnic groups have no right to exist or that rape and "wildings" are acceptable behaviors— acceptable because supposedly rooted in some cultural or ethnic form— need to be confronted directly but in such a way that does not humiliate. All of this is unexceptional—one might even ask why it is necessary to state such obvious truths.

The sticking point comes not so much in challenging ideas but in interrupting students in mid-performance precisely because their behaviors are unacceptable. Suppose you are on the subway. Four boys are putting their graffiti tags in full sight on the windows of the car door. They are also harassing passengers, horsing around, wrestling, and making everyone uncomfortable and tense, but people are ignoring them, with downcast eyes. They are a nuisance and even a danger to themselves and others. What do you do, assuming that no transit police are readily available? Most people choose to do nothing. But a few generations ago, adults would have reprimanded these youth. That does not happen anymore. If teachers and educators also look the other way in the schools, they allow the code of violence to replicate itself unabatedly in the one place where it can still be challenged and arrested.

Let us consider, without commentary, several ethnographic snippets that relate to this theme of direct challenge to student misbehavior before drawing some parallels or contrasts with contemporary pedagogical hermeneutics.

A) D [another tutor] and I have been working with a kid named Y. I kicked him out of my eighth period group. I refuse to let one kid ruin a learning experience for the rest of them, so I told him, "Look, Y. This is a voluntary program, but it works both ways. I don't have to take a student that I don't want to, so if you don't want to work, I'd like you to leave right now." He said he would leave, but hovered in the threshold of the door. I insisted he leave or I'd have the guard escort him to class. He essentially dared me to do so and I went to get the guard. This scared him into leaving, but not without threatening me first. I would not like to be his teacher.

B) One student came into our crowded tutoring room and fired up a cigarette. Everyone was aghast but one of the men tutors, Juan, soon went up to him and told him that this was not permitted. The boy complied right away.

C) [One white female tutor writing about an African American student with whom she had been working for over two years at Alpha School, including giving him a 7 A.M. wake-up call in the mornings]: I just could not understand though, how his family could ignore his absences from school. I guess I really can though. L is not "cutting" in the typical sense—his brother left the house and is hanging out with the guys. L stays home . . . and I really do believe he's taking care of the family. His is the father role. He takes his grandmother to the hospital or doctor's office. He will go take care of his aunt who has an anxiety attack. He'll take his grandmother to see her son, L's uncle, in the hospital. I'm sure he's doing all these things for them so they don't see the school as the priority. What is L going to do with himself? What do they want for him? Well I know one thing, the GED program is going to be tough to get into. After school on Wednesday I went to see Ms. A to see if they had graded his test. They had. He was reading on a 7th grade reading level. What to do? I had a sinking feeling. She said, "He's got two strikes against him! One, his reading level is below what we accept! Two, his attendance record is horrible!" I had a feeling this was not going to be pretty. "But there are options. I could refer him to a GED program that will focus on bringing his reading level up to par. Or, I could admit him into our program on probation and if he's got one unexcused absence he's out of the program!" I have a particular sense of urgency in L's case. I have been working with him for two years and he's one of my "special" kids. I've invested a lot of emotion in him. Maybe he senses that and does not want to let me down and that is part of [the reason for] his no shows, I just don't know. But there really is no one else plugging for him in the school so I am very fearful of next year. There is no connection for him. I feel that if I don't make the connection now he'll be another statistic next year. I really had hoped to make this connection with Ms. A. I just don't know how it will go. I just dread that he will drop out.

D) E is slouching in the corner of the tutoring room. He adopted that corner and would sit nowhere else. He has a sallow complexion and a sour expression on his face but when he smiles he looks like a different boy. I sensed that he wanted to work, but that protective shell which so many of the boys adopt prevents others from seeing his eagerness. He is dour and taciturn around males, with the exception of M [a male tutor]. They have struck up a delightful rapport, mainly consisting of bantering about football teams and advice to the lovelorn. Initially he would get angry at me if he couldn't understand a math concept. Now he understands that asking questions is not a sign of ignorance.

E) [Female tutor's log excerpt about a Chinese girl at Gamma School]: Oh Boy. I think this is the strongest case of a clinging crush I've ever had from one of my students.

F) I ran into G [a Vietnamese student] on Tuesday leaning against the wall in the hallway outside the cafeteria amidst masses of screamy-meamy students waiting their chance to enter for lunch (barred by security guards asking for their program cards which say they have lunch this period). He looked sullen and isolated. I greeted him and asked what was up. . . . He beamed a smile and said in his own way "Maybe I come with you?" Seizing the opportunity to rekindle our friendship I encouraged this. We then went [to the tutoring room]. Over the week, G then maintained regular attendance. It was a different G I saw, and got to know much better. He did not seem to want to study, which is unusual for him as well as for other Vietnamese students I see. He just wanted to talk. He shared a lot with me about his life in Vietnam and the incredible struggles he went through to get here as well as the heart aches and trials and tribulations he and his family went through in Vietnam. . . . He was open and honest. I saw a real vulnerability there that "reeked" of pain.

G) [JD fieldnotes]: We took our students on a trip to Albany with the purpose of lobbying the State legislature to continue funding of the program. One Caribbean student, asked by a Senator in his office—which was crowded with professors, graduate students, and other people who had come up to lobby for various programs—what he liked about our program and why it should continue, replied that passing into the tutoring room from the school corridors was "like going into a church, mon." He added: "these guys [pointing to the tutors] are my shrinks."

I do not wish to preempt all possible readings of these excerpts by presenting my own "definitive" interpretation; each log could be read as an analysis or critique of the program, the schools, the ethnography. For my present purpose—the emergence of a new theoretical discourse on discipline—I would suggest that the key question is whether the "caring" exhibited by the tutors in logs C, D, E, and F and summarized by the comments in G ("like going into a church, mon"; "these guys are my shrinks") is enough to offset all the negative forces pulling students in an opposite direction, one diametrically opposed to graduation and a productive career—presupposing, of course, that some reasonable possibility of a satisfying career exists in the real world. In light of logs C–G, logs A and B take on new meaning.

Log A seems to reveal a side of our program that is the exact opposite of what I have been advocating: here we, frustrated, end up contemplating calling the security guards. Did the tutor make the wrong decision? Could he have handled this in a less confrontational manner? Should he have taken Y. on earlier? Might Y. have responded differently had he been talked to privately, away from his peer group? At the very least, this little episode reveals that a "small group" context does not itself eliminate such confrontations. These questions are the stuff of our Monday seminars. But the central consideration to be stressed here is that not all discipline arises from the teaching interaction itself. This notion is, of course, the polar opposite from that of Dewey, who hated authority and pretended that if order had to be imposed externally, outside the student's intrinsic love of the subject matter, the teacher had failed. But it is not always true that turning students on to the sheer joy of learning will guarantee they will conform to acceptable codes of behavior. Dewey knew only schools, not "schools."

In log A one boy seems intent on disrupting the learning of the others, and in log B another boy seems to have no concern about the rights or sensibilities of the others. Both logs illustrate the need for the tutors, as a group, to have a coherent plan concerning what is or is not acceptable behavior—and a corporate will to enforce that plan. But the most fundamental point to be made is that logs A and B depict only stages in the process of genuine caring, techniques to get to the stages represented by logs C–G. In another case, some of the tutors helped a student find a job, housing (to get away from an abusive father), and admission to college, because they cared enough to work as a team and to stay with him until all these things happened. Perhaps, then, failure should be defined not as a trait inherent in the students but as the consequence of an adult society not trying hard enough, not caring enough to provide the proper settings, and not caring enough to confront. Logs A and B (confrontation, challenge) need to be placed in the perspective of logs C–G. Another way of saying this is that discipline becomes only one important appendage of "caring."

Caring and confronting often produce a changed perspective on the part of the student. Code-switching from tough, rude,or counterproductive behaviors (ranging from disruptive hallwalking to attacking others) to polite, productive etiquette should not be thought of as precisely homologous to the linguistic process of code-switching from, say, "standard English" to a nonstandard form or a foreign language. I believe it is unfortunate that many scholars of language (oral historians, sociolinguists) are too ready to blur a distinction that should be drawn between various ethnically based speaking and performing styles and abusive, threatening, or aggressive discourse. Walter Ong (1990, 44) has rightly commented on the way oral cultures tend to strike literate people as extraordinarily agonistic: "Growing up in a still dominantly oral culture, certain young black males in the United States, the Caribbean, and elsewhere, engage in what is known variously as the 'dozens' or 'joning' or 'sounding' or by other names, in which one opponent tries to outdo the other in vilifying the other's mother. The dozens is not a real fight but an art form, as are the other stylized verbal tongue lashings in other cultures."

But, without contesting the validity of observations of this sort, it remains a legitimate question to ask where style leaves off and the culture of violence begins. When does a sound concern for the student's linguistic and cultural sensibilities end up mystifying the issue of violence? When does oral art exceed its form and become derogatory of "mother"? Do not verbal tongue lashings ever shade into "real fights"—either intraculturally or especially when cultures interact? Log D provides a convenient illustration of what I am trying to get at here. Perry Gilmore (1985) describes this kind of slouching body language as "stylized sulking," a nonverbal behavior characteristic of a "black communicative repertoire," similar to interactional competence in a nonstandard vernacular (e.g., black English). In his view, such styles are misinterpreted by teachers as indicative of a "bad attitude." The implication is that the dominant culture (represented by black as well as white teachers) associates this style with lower social groupings and thereby forces students to give it up. But other interpretations are equally plausible: does anyone care enough to challenge such behaviors? Might a teacher not point out that such postures may be acceptable in one social setting but not in another? Is such a posture as wholly innocent as Gilmore portrays it, or does it manifest a will to disrupt—which needs to be brought to the attention of the adolescent? Are these interpretations, which conflate certain performances (dozens, sulking) with ethnic styles, tributes to the ethnic group in question when the violence is blurred over?

IDYLLIC ETHNOGRAPHY

The determination to show the inner-city student in a noble light worthy of Rousseau induces many writers to eliminate all references to student-initiated violence from their ethnographies. In Michelle Fine's study of a New York City public school (1991), for example, Latino, black, and urban youth generally are portrayed as keen analysts of discrimination, but, in her version of inner-city life, student-initiated violence is nonexistent. Despite her several disclaimers to the contrary, white teachers are usually depicted as insensitive dolts while black female teachers do "extraordinary amounts of emotional work" for little recognition, and the white principal is completely out of touch. References to violence are eliminated from her text, and aggressive behaviors are certainly never located at the body of the student, the point of enactment at which subjectivities are constructed. Dropouts, pushouts, and potential dropouts are characterized as feisty victims whose "voices" the system has attempted to silence but who are less depressed and less conformist than those who stay in school. In the process of leaving, their bodies are "exported" out of the school, or the students make rational and mature choices to leave and thereby serve as critics of the system. Incredibly, although rejecting almost everything else in the self-portrait of this lower-tier comprehensive New York City high school of the mid–1980s, Fine accepts its own statements regarding the absence of violence, a version that fits neatly with her central thesis. "It had low rates of student violence," we are told (1991, 2). There is no room in her representations of students for self-deception, deceit, or enactment of violent action. Student assertions are automatically to be believed simply because they are student assertions. Students never lie to themselves or to others, never work authority figures against one another to get their own way.

By contrast, here is one tutor's daily log: "A.D., the boy I spoke to you about who keeps getting deeper & deeper in trouble has been a cause of concern for me & I've been trying to think of ways to help him. First I caught him lying to me about his lunch period—when he claimed he had no program [card] to prove my allegations incorrect I went to the program office & got a copy of his program. When I confronted him the following day with the evidence he admitted that 'I got him on that one.'"

WITHIN FINE'S narrow framework of innocent student subjectivity, the only violence evident in the text is the symbolic violence of a school system that is to be relentlessly blamed for everything. Teachers are never to criticize students' performances. All explanatory power is located in institutional oppression. If students are accorded any agency at all, it is certainly not an agency reproductive of the violence of street culture. In attributing all causality to the heartlessness of organizational structures, Fine monopolizes all analysis, since in disagreeing with her one seems to be defending the system. She circumvents the site at which power is enacted: the politicized body of the student. Students speak with a single innocent "voice," one capable of capture only by the sympathetic ethnographer, and there is no room for code-switching back and forth between a discourse of violence and a plethora of other competing discourses.

These ethnographies paint an idyllic picture of inner-city students but do no favors for them. At most, these texts tacitly assess student behavior as "not really bad," as mischievous, as prankishly contrived to demonstrate resistance toward various aspects of a class-structured society. In fact, many student performances are supersaturated with violence and deserve serious attention, such as was provided by one female tutor in Beta School:

> T came by during his usual time, fourth period. We spent the entire time talking about how he could avoid getting into a fight with a bunch of people who were out to get him during lunch, and about related issues. Here's the story, as told by T: There's this guy R, who is apparently disliked by a lot of people, so finally yesterday, someone beat him up. Everyone around was glad he got beaten up, and everyone was saying how they wished they'd been the ones to do it, and [in T's words] "I had some diss for him, so I said that I wish I'd beaten him up. This girl who was standing next to me heard me say it, and she told R, and she told him a bunch of other things I didn't say, and so now he's out to get me." Apparently R knows he can't fight and beat T, so he is getting a bunch of his friends to do it for him—he told T so. Apparently R is pretty bad news—"He hangs out with the worst kind of people. You don't want to have anything to do with them." So we talked about what to do—the upshot of that was that he'd stay in our room during lunch today, and see if the situation would diffuse. . . . But we spent some time talking about how these things go, how some people seem to like to fight, about how out of proportion fighting and hurting people seems to be to what is being fought about.

Students do need help in learning how to relate to peers, parents, and teachers. But by insisting on explaining student behavior through the narrative of "resistance," the critical pedagogues minimize the scope of violent behavior and even celebrate their informants' "getting one over" on authority figures. Students are "feisty" or "sassy" but never violent. Since the theoretical perspective is locked into the narrow explanatory device of resistance to oppression and historical deprivation, the psychological aspects of violence (e.g., in child abuse, in alcoholism, in individual family pathologies) cannot be examined. The result is that a two-dimensional adolescent subjectivity is depicted, one that either reveals or camouflages the resistant self, one untroubled by the need to code-switch amongst a multiplicity of behaviors, some of which are deeply rooted in the terrifying culture of the streets. In this genre, kids are never self-rejecting or self-alienating; they always reject authority figures. Finally, these authors conflate linguistic and cultural determinants (e.g., use of Creole languages) with behaviors that are de facto socially unacceptable in any cultural context. The possibility of encouraging a student to develop linguistic and cultural competence in *both* the dominant society and in the home culture does not appear to be a viable option for these authors.

MAPPING A NEW MYTHOLOGY OF VIOLENCE

In summary, it may be said that this muting of a discourse on violence is conspicuous throughout the mainstream liberal and critical literature. On the right, violence is predicated of the subaltern culture, misinterpreted and magnified by various forms of "cultural deficit theory." On the left, as we have seen, if the topic is not deleted altogether, it is rationalized through foundational theories ranging from reproduction to symbolic violence to Rabelaisian celebration of aggression. Tenacious violence seems to beg for profound explanatory origin myths, and the theoreticians discussed in this chapter arise to fulfill that need. For them, violence is ultimately explained as pure resistance to poverty and unjust socioeconomic conditions.

Allen Feldman (1991, 19), writing about Northern Ireland, rejects the notion that violence is just a pathological symptom of some deep-rooted cause, however that may be defined (religious intolerance, discrimination, lack of housing, unemployment, fiercely held ideologies). He disagrees with authors who "locate political violence as a surface expression of 'deeper' socio-economic and/or ideological contexts. In this perspective the issue of descriptive adequacy is rarely brought to bear on the acts of violence themselves, but only on the putative origin of the irruption. Violence is denuded of an intrinsic semantic or causal character."

FOR FELDMAN, it is in the act of violence that agency is disclosed. He finds that other commentators on violence in Northern Ireland treat it as a "derivative symptom." By so doing, they are blinded to the ways in which violence can be a causative factor in mutating ideologies and in changing the ways in which violence is interpreted and conceptualized. Similarly, school violence is not adequately explained by assumptions about underlying causes (inner-city poverty, racist teachers, hegemonic ideologies of school systems, and the other causal explanations of social reproduction theory).

The task that remains is to begin to discover a new mythology for explaining school violence, one more fitted to contemporary realities and therefore more serviceable in guiding us in another direction. Before approaching that task, however, we must first look at one current—and very popular— attempt to cope with violence, one I shall be claiming is merely palliative.

VIOLENCE: THE LATEST CURRICULAR SPECIALTY

Violence does not simply occur "in" a space, whether public or private; it is implicated in the very production and maintenance of the distinction between spaces.

—Mark Wigley, *Heidegger's House: The Violence of the Domestic*

E is pregnant. . . . We headed to Planned Parenthood. . . . On the train ride back, we were both silent, and . . . we stopped by a coffee shop to talk: "Everybody thinks they know what I should do. My mother says I should keep it but that if I do, she'll throw me out; S [the boy] wants me to get rid of it, but he won't help me pay for it." "What do you want to do?" "I don't want it, but it all seems so painful." . . . An interesting piece of graffiti was left on the table by E. . . . She had written "Mother" and below that "beautiful"; next to it she had written "father" and below that "asshole."

—Female tutor's log excerpt

How to Get an Antiviolence Grant

What I have been referring to as a discourse of avoidance regarding school violence is not the only discourse. One strand of discourse currently featured in the educational literature—and widely reported in the press and on TV—has been attempting to address the topic directly. In 1993 the *New York Times* reported on this trend under a headline that read, "Schools Try to Tame Violent Pupils, One Punch and One Taunt at a Time." The article relates how this novel approach concentrates on teaching children peaceful alternatives to conflict within a classroom setting. Federal agencies are now making millions of dollars available for "conflict resolution" classes, for creating "safe haven" rooms in schools, and for "peer mediation" programs. Getting a federal grant has become simple: just start your own conflict-resolution program. "Conflict resolution" has become the buzz word of the 1990s: gym teachers and ESL teachers are suddenly being converted into conflict-resolution teachers, and community-based agencies are coming into schools, each one marketing its own unique curriculum and methodology for teaching nonviolence to children and youth.

To reduce the sharp increases in violence, many psychologists and public health specialists have recommended teaching children and youth ways to handle their emotions more positively. The foremost proponent of this approach is Deborah Prothrow-Stith. She, together with her coauthor, Michaele Weissman, writes that her program is based on the assumption that "truthful information about the risks of fighting could and would change students' attitudes about fighting and, over time, their behavior" (1991, 161). Using the successful national campaign against smoking as her model, she builds her program on the idea that "individuals who understand the health risks confronting them are more likely to make healthy decisions." Applied to the issue of violence, Prothrow-Stith is convinced that teachers and other professionals can work with adolescents "to help them develop the cognitive capacity and moral reasoning power to turn away from the dangers on the streets" (p. 18). Once students understand clearly that violence is harmful to their health, so the argument runs, they will surely abandon it the way many smokers gave up smoking.

Citing Kohlberg's stages of moral reasoning, Prothrow-Stith contends that if young people reach the stage in which they "have the cognitive ability to understand the world they live in," and in which "they can see beyond themselves and understand their own actions in a moral and legal context," they are more likely to act in accordance with the moral logic they have learned (1991, 62). But to know the good is not necessarily to do it.

However necessary it is to develop students' moral cognition through teaching, this can be no substitute for the central mechanism of delivering ethical standards to adolescents: the encounter between mature adult and maturing adolescent in an existential situation, where values conflict or are challenged, where the outer borders of conduct are tested and defined.

The schools in which we operate all have violence-prevention courses, peer-mediation programs, and conflict-resolution programs. Following a particularly virulent period of violent episodes, a principal will increase the number of these courses. Our own program could just as easily be labeled a violence-prevention program, since, as many of the log excerpts in this book testify, we spend a great deal of our time attempting to convince students that some of their behavior is self-destructive. But neither our program nor the violence-prevention programs are the solutions to the problem of systemic school violence.

Statistics can be trotted out to "prove" that these violence-prevention classes and other cognitive approaches have culminated in a decrease in fighting and physical violence. The specialized teachers who conduct these sessions often describe them as stimulating and exciting. A tenth-grade teacher enthusiastically related to me the successes this approach was producing in her students. In the same breath, she also related how many students, reconciled briefly and superficially during a conflict-resolution session, go outside after school and finish their fights. That same week, the principal had asked me, in desperate tones, to do a study of why a sudden eruption of violence had occurred. The partisans of conflict-resolution courses and peer-mediation programs partake of the same ambivalent discourse of violence referred to earlier: on the one hand, they report how, thanks to these courses, the school has become an "oasis of safety"; on the other hand, they refer to the latest stabbing incident or the latest fight that was discussed in the conflict-resolution course. Unlike the social reproductionists, the conflict resolutionists locate violence primarily in the students, in their homes, in the community, on the streets—anywhere but in the structure of the school itself. In their search for origins, violence is in the "other," not the self.

VIOLENCE AS A CURRICULAR SPECIALTY

This newest response to violence is not only inadequate and flawed, it also distracts from a fuller understanding of the etiology of the anarchic behavior. By making violence prevention the latest specialty—a course offering added to the curriculum (and one that crowds other basic required courses out of the schedule)—this movement attempts to circumscribe the phenomenon and to "cure" it without adequately diagnosing it. In these "schools," the majority of teachers (those not involved in teaching conflict-resolution courses) become confirmed in their view that dealing with violence and aggressive students is a subspecialty that they had better not get involved with because they are neither trained in this area nor given that specific responsibility. Conflict-resolution teachers who have gone through a few weeks of basic training in this esoteric specialty have now been added to the list of those who have whittled away at the teacher's role, which used to encompass more responsibilities.

But the most basic flaw in promoting violence-prevention and conflict-resolution curricula within schools is even more subtle: it consists of substituting the hypothetical for the real, the past and future for the present, discourse for performance. As James Q. Wilson (1993, 249) suggests, adolescents learn behaviors more through an osmotic process of daily interaction than through theoretical talk about ethics. But violence-prevention and conflict-resolution courses help educators avoid existential confrontation and engagement. Violence prevention deals with past behavior, conflict resolution with future behavior, and both are convenient ways of escaping behavior in the present. It is one thing for a teacher within a classroom setting to discuss "cases" (real or imaginary, drawn from students' lives or from the newspapers) after the fact; it is a totally different thing for a teacher to define the limits of conduct with a student who is behaving transgressively, at the very moment the student is assaulting another student, defacing property, engaging in unacceptable behavior or unacceptable speech (e.g., telling a teacher to "fuck off"). It is one thing for a principal to add violence-prevention courses to the curriculum; it is a totally different thing for a principal to challenge *all* the teachers—and the entire school community—to adopt and enforce a uniform code of conduct—in brief, to resuscitate the now almost forgotten *in loco parentis* role.

Deborah Prothrow-Stith's approach has the advantage of recognizing that the social setting in which a young person grows up plays a major role in the phenomenon of imitative violence. No one can argue with her efforts to help individual students in their struggle with angry feelings or to teach them new ways of behaving and relating. Our tutors discuss these same issues with their students, although their conversations usually grow out of an academic context. In contrast with the social reproduction theorists, Prothrow-Stith squarely faces the reality that students do display seriously aggressive behaviors that culminate in harm to themselves or others. And she believes in the capacity of young adolescents to change their behavior.

How Antiviolence Normalizes Violence

How can one have any misgivings, then, about something so apparently beneficial as conflict-resolution classes? My reservations stem not from my reluctance to confront the sensitive but necessary topic of violence education but from a concern that creating these classes as the chief pedagogical response will further normalize the already normalized violence. The subtextual message is, "We expect this school to be violent, so let's talk about it." Rather than operating from the assumption that violence is unthinkable and unacceptable, violence-prevention courses give the entering students—especially those from overseas—the impression that violence is an institutionalized part of American life and that they might as well learn to cope with it. Violence-prevention courses also create the impression that schools are doing something—other than using metal detectors—about the problem, even though they do not address the fundamental causes. A violence-prevention curriculum, then, is one more method that has evolved for distracting attention from the real issues.

It is in real-life experiences, not just in classroom discussions about morality, that adolescents and young adults learn to accept that different actors in the social world have differing perceptions about where limits are to be drawn. It is in existential confrontations that mature adults assert their own values through their insistence on high standards for academic work or their determination that students show respect for the environment, property, one another, the teacher, and themselves. It is this inability to cope with teacher-student disciplinary encounters that blocks these writers from theorizing the phenomenon of violence. Once again, we are faced with a neognostic duality, an assumption that intellectualized dialogues of the classroom are sufficient to embody morality and the acceptance of societal norms.

I have argued that students are often agents of violence. Conflict-resolution courses tend, however, to place the whole burden of the introduction of violence on students; likewise, they place the burden of its eradication on student-student dialogue. Like explanations that focus on one race, ethnic group, or sexual group as the source of violence (e.g., males are more aggressive than females), conflict-resolution courses posit the phenomenon of violence *in* a group or an individual, not as jointly constructed through the interaction of agent and institution, individual and society. The corridors of an inner-city school provide convincing evidence, on the contrary, that school violence is jointly constructed through the explosive chemistry of aggressive students and unmanageable "schools."

Conflict-resolution approaches, in summary, differ from social reproduction theory in that they recognize the existence of violence in the student. However, they too have to be judged as part of the discourse of avoidance, because they want to deal with asocial conduct either before the act

or after, not *in actu,* at the moment of transgression. Older students, said
to be peer mediators "trained in conflict mediation" by conflict-resolution
teachers, ask younger bellicose students if they can agree not to bother one
another, not to call one another's mother obscene names, not to insult one
another. If they "feel comfortable" with such an agreement, they shake
hands, congratulations are extended all around—and the fight resumes the
next time they look at one another. Faculty continue to ignore student conduct in public space, and classrooms are turned into privatized mini-courts
in which the onus of the culture of violence is shifted onto the two students
who are encouraged to "work out" their anger, mutual hostility, and differences—and to create their own ethical expectations, since the adults have
opted out of this task. But conflict-resolution enthusiasts are convinced of
the efficacy of their newfound religion. Peers, they tell us, will listen to their
peers. And any adult dialogue with youth about behavioral expectations is
branded ineffective "preaching." They are, it seems, in possession of the
truth; why, then, one wonders, does the school still need eighteen security
guards to patrol the halls?

THE STUDENT AS ORACLE

Conflict-resolution approaches to school discipline have the subtle effect
of further withdrawing educators from puberty-ritual encounters with
youth; but they are not the only ones that do so. Some brands of feminist
research seem to believe in this withdrawal as a matter of principle. Carol
Gilligan's reconceptualization of girls' adolescent development and Michelle Fine's analysis of female sexuality in the context of inner-city schools
are two of the clearest examples of recent attempts to diminish and, indeed,
to disparage the active role of adults in the *rites de passage* of adolescents
into adulthood. Here adults are to be passive listeners.

For Carol Gilligan and her colleagues (e.g., Janie Victoria Ward), students, especially young women, are conceptualized as full-time victims of
violence, never as part-time perpetrators (1988, 175). Partitioning adolescents into those "who commit violence" and those who "must live in the
midst of it" sets up two separate species of youth, the good students and
the few bad apples. Gilligan's approach is to interrogate the good students,
the passive victims of violence at home and on the street, about their moral
theories of violence, a questioning that inevitably leads Gilligan and her
coresearchers to discover concerns about "justice" (mainly in boys) and

"care" (mainly in girls) (1988, 172). Girls and women are not represented as perpetrators of violence; they are mothers who have lost sons, wives who have lost husbands, little girls who have lost fathers.

These authors' interests lie in investigating students' moral values through research. The values of the researcher, as social scientist, are presented as neutral; researchers never suspect, debate, or doubt students' values; in the final analysis, the values of the researcher do not really matter. As for teachers, Gilligan's basic stance is that they are not supposed to teach answers "but to raise questions which initiate the search for knowledge" and, in the spirit of discovery, "to listen for what is surprising." Neither teachers nor researchers, then, have any moral values worthy of communicating to students; they are there to listen. Gilligan's ideal adult is a passive questioner and a good listener; Gilligan's moral constructs are elicited through her version of dialogue in which the adult listens and the pupil does all the talking.

The idea that truth emerges out of the dialogic relationship certainly has its place, but students also need to be made aware of what moral constructs mean to others outside this dialogic relationship. In the spirit of "whole language," adolescents indeed have a deep need to be listened to and to be understood (whether for their ethical views, artistic opinions, or arithmetic insights), but they also need to be taught moral values, watercolor techniques, and the quadratic formula, items that may never emerge from dialogue even if the partners sit around and talk all day. The youth with whom we work respond to adults who are not just passive listeners but who also define the limits between acceptable and unacceptable behavior in an existential situation and help them think through the consequences of their actions: "Nate D. also has improved his grades some. He may only fail two courses this term in comparison to all but two last term. He has been so respectful since I had that talk with him. He needed someone to draw the line. S [an African tutor] has a great rapport with him and I think he really needed a man to talk to."

One might conclude that, just as reading should not be taught in a decontextualized way, so too behavioral standards and etiquette need to be taught in context, which frequently occurs at the moment of the infraction of a rule. The girls with whom we work are neither pure victims nor pure perpetrators; the culture of violence requires them to perform the same machismo script that one normally associates with males:

Today was a really rough day. It started off with one of our students (a ninth grader), M. S. [a girl], getting stabbed in the head by another girl in the hall. It doesn't seem that she was seriously injured but nonetheless the incident was tragic. It set the mood for the whole day. N [a boy] saw the whole thing and was really affected by it. I felt this was something that would be good to discuss in group today so that we could get our feelings out. It turned out to be a good way to deal with it. N, O, P, Q, R [boys], and S [a girl] and I had a really amazing discussion about the stabbing. Then we talked about weapons and violence, which led to talking about protection. It's amazing to me that the alternatives to not being involved with the gangs and possies that these students belong to is to them to be a target. Their fear of being attacked leads them to attack first. They feel that it is a safer alternative than staying away from these gangs. N would never have struck me as the violent type, he always seems so together and considerate, and when we began to talk about the end results of this kind of warfare and doing things that one might regret later he said that he already had a regret. He rolled up his sleeve to show me a huge scar on his arm and the two fingers on his left hand that would never move again from being slashed with a knife in one of these gang wars. My heart really hurts. I didn't know what to say and I was rather glad that the bell rang and relieved me from having to say anymore than that I was sorry that that had happened to him. It must be the hardest position to be in for these kids, and they have no other experience to help them make better decisions.

Gilligan and her fellow researchers categorize the concerns of adolescents into two groups defined by gender—"justice" (derived from the mostly violent boys) and "care" (derived from the mostly nonviolent girls). These categories are then used to rethink the developmental theories of Kohlberg and Erikson, which Gilligan believes are male oriented. She then finds that there are "clear sex differences with respect to violent action" (1988, xxxvii). Since wisdom—moral wisdom—is generated through careful listening to teenagers, a whole new agenda develops for the field of education: it needs to develop the "art of the voice" (1988, 156)—that is, it needs to heed the voice of the adolescent. Gilligan's ideal teacher, presumably, is one who listens at the feet of the teenager, whose voice, especially that of the female teenager, now transformed into Delphic oracle, is able to topple classic developmental schemata.

I am not questioning whether Gilligan's constructs fit the realities of the young men and women she has studied; they simply do not correspond to the realities of New York's lower-tier schools. The social inequalities have transformed girls not just into victims of violence (with the inwardly directed ailments Gilligan describes, e.g., anorexia) but also into perpetrators of violence toward others, a behavior commonly associated only with boys. The best "caring" an adult can offer is often a well-defined set of firm limits:

[Beta School, female tutor's log]: I have been working with K from the beginning. She comes during her lunch period with three other girls and we work on different subjects together. At first, she came into the room, sat down with C, one of the other girls, and they just listened to their Walkmen. When asked if they wanted to do work, they grumbled "no" and continued to eat their lunch and ignore me. Therefore, I began focusing my attention on M and R who wanted help with their homework. I didn't know what to do with K and C at first because it seemed a waste for them to attend (although it was their lunch period) without doing any work. Finally, on a day when M and R were absent I was able to get through to them. I asked them why they came if they were just going to sit there. "The people who come here want to learn—there is no room for you two to just sit around pretending to do something constructive." K said nothing and C mumbled, "I want to practice reading." Surprisingly, this little talk made a difference. Thus began my work with C on reading (she is a very poor reader) and K, who acted like she didn't care about anything until I focused my attention directly on her. She still remained very wrapped up in her own world, writing stories to herself that she is not fond of sharing with others. K did not show up for tutoring on Tuesday or Wednesday. I was a little surprised because although she wasn't always prepared to work, she had been consistently attending up to this point. I checked with the attendance office and found that she was absent both days. When she returned on Thursday, I could tell something was wrong. She had a grimace on her face and her shoulders and head were bent. At first when I asked her what was wrong, she said "nothing." I said that I was surprised because she had been absent for the past two days. I think that the fact that I showed interest in her whereabouts made her more willing to talk to me. She told me that she had to go to court because two years ago she had been involved in a fight where she slashed another girl with a razor. I have to admit, even though I feel pretty shockproof most of the time, I was surprised that this girl that I had been spending all this time with had done such a thing. Of course, I didn't respond in that manner to her—instead, I asked her to explain what had happened. She was very upset because the girl is now accusing K of having shot her—it seems the girl had a gunshot wound from a different fight (according to K) yet is blaming it on the fight with K. I had to hold my feelings in as I listened to her tell the story. I realized that she had no idea how to solve the conflict peacefully. There are no skills or prior experiences in her repertoire that would instruct her on how to put an end to an ongoing conflict with another person without someone getting hurt either emotionally or physically. Unfortunately, K is not alone—it saddens me to realize that the intense feelings many of these kids have on a daily basis often blow up in their faces. These feelings must somehow be channeled into more productive matters—they can get mad, but then, let's help them to use this energy to do something positive for themselves, their schools, their neighborhoods. Another idea that I think about is whether I am pushing my values on a person who lives in an area that may not accept this type of resolution. For instance, if I teach her to assert herself productively (meaning getting her point across without ignoring the other person's feelings) who is to say the other girl would not in turn slash K? Obviously, for K to negotiate herself in the "real world," she should have these social skills in her repertoire. But how do we reach all these aggressive kids so that they respect each other's non-aggressive behavior?

We are operating here in uncharted waters. The truisms of psychoanalytic narrative, conflict-resolution theory, and standard educational verities yield to a totally new cultural horizon, a world in which all the rules have changed because whatever adult protection a "modernist" society used to provide to youth is now completely lacking. The tutors and I find ourselves actually contemplating whether or not it would be more productive to arm our students with social skills better adapted to the culture of violence! We have passed from Gilligan's paradigm of traditional Western psychology to a world in which only violence makes sense. These girls are abandoned to their own peer-originated devices, and it is very difficult to see how "care" is coming through as a dominant theme. Gilligan's characterization of boys as more violent than girls and her claim that there exist clear sex differences with respect to violent action are singularly unhelpful for those interested in trying to understand and deal with adolescent aggressive behavior of either gender. Feminist discourse that tries to downplay, overlook, or otherwise excuse the actual violence perpetrated by girls adds nothing to our understanding of the co-constructed nature of the phenomenon. We need to become more enlightened on how girls' subjectivities become suffused with the street culture, how they adopt, to their own detriment, a self-defeating machismo ideology that concludes in violence for themselves and others, as well as how they resist this same exploitation (see Bourgois 1989, 11).

TOO LITTLE OR TOO MUCH CONFRONTATION?

Michelle Fine, like Gilligan, wants teachers to listen, not contribute to the dialogue. There can be no doubt that the silencing of a discourse of desire, about which Fine writes, exists in the context of public schools, and in New York City high schools in particular. But educators need to do much more than create a context in which female voices can get a hearing; they also need to raise their own voices and, at times, challenge female and male adolescents' sometimes immature assumptions. This discourse again portrays students as victims, is intent on disclosing "silences" nurtured by the school system, and fails to pay attention to the jointly constructed nature of the culture of violence. But our own interactions with urban youth indicate that they want and need more, not less, confrontation.

Fine's depiction of the school system—in particular, the New York City public school system—as intolerant of students' opinions is off the mark. Her representations of New York City high school teachers—especially white ones—as overbearing, controlling, intolerant, and silencing can no doubt be substantiated by her "ethnographic examples," but if an ethnographer with no desire to prove a thesis spends any time at all in these schools, he or she will find a spectrum of behaviors ranging from the compassionate to the outrageous—far more irresponsible than even Fine's depictions.[1] Horror stories about insensitive guidance counselors, racist teachers, and offensive white principals could easily be multiplied on a scale far beyond Fine's descriptions: [tutor's log] "Another student, Brenda, was talking about one of the teachers she had that commented that he didn't like black kids and then hurriedly added that he was just kidding. It is pretty amazing that these teachers get away with this kind of stuff. I hope we get a chance to talk about this soon." We have known teachers who—in the presence of female tutors—have made unbelievably crude sexual remarks to a whole class; when we tried to complain, we ran into union objections. How is it possible to create a systemic environment that can permit these sorts of interactions to happen? The overriding feature of New York City lower-tier high schools today is not that teachers and counselors have excessive influence or are too involved in students' lives; rather, teachers are situated in a structure that allows them too little of such involvement. Granted, closer involvement with moral instruction might entail the potential for abuse, but it is not the case that teachers are too active; rather, teachers have withdrawn—or have been forced to withdraw.

Teenage girls speak openly to our female tutors about their sexual predicaments, fantasies, and hopes, and they often do so precisely because the tutors are the only ones who will listen. This happens not because we are more sensitive human beings than the teachers but because the structure of these mega-schools militates against intimate student-teacher contacts. These girls often begin their conversations by stating categorically that neither their mothers nor their teachers nor the guidance counselors know anything about this situation and that they (the girls) prefer to keep it that way. If the situation warrants it (e.g., the girl is pregnant, the girl thinks she is pregnant), tutors often persuade the girl to seek out a compassionate guidance counselor, who in turn makes the referral to a health clinic, hospital, or family planning agency. Usually, the tutor will accompany the girl on her visit to the school guidance counselor and to the clinic or hospital. These sessions are not "celebrations" of teenage sexuality but sober and complex conversations—such as the one alluded to in the epigraph—about alternatives, about responsibility, about available community resources, about using precautions next time, about regrets, and about hopes for the future.

Fine is highly suspicious of what she calls "a discourse of female sexual victimization" in public schools, which, she claims, "represents females as the actual and potential victims of male desire" (1992, 34). Fine does not see girls so much as victims of male desire but as victims of the dominant society—mediated through the school system—which persuades girls that they are objects of male desire; hence her deemphasis on dialoging with girls about the potential dangers of adolescent sexual activity. Such declarations mask Fine's own discourse of victimization through which she consistently portrays minorities and women as victims of an oppressive system.

Indeed they are victims, but Fine does not allow them any true agency of collaboration in their own self-destructive behaviors. Fine's representations are at a far remove from what is actually happening in the New York City public schools. It is true that smaller schools would provide many more opportunities for students to engage in profitable discussions about sexuality, and no one would want to defend the shortcomings of the current sex education curricula, but the teachers and counselors we work with are not just naively and prudishly telling kids to "say no," nor are they "recommending marriage," nor are they particularly biased toward heterosexuality. Witness the following excerpt from a white female tutor's log in which open discussions on family planning and sexual orientations are part of a day's work for a student in Beta School, and not just in her interaction with the tutor: "S [a sixteen-year-old African American student] called me yesterday, but I got home too late to return her call, so I did this afternoon. I confirmed that we are going to make the phone call together this Wednesday to set up an appointment at Planned Parenthood. Aside from that, we talked about an article she's writing for the school newspaper about male strippers—she's going to Chippendale's to interview some of them!—and about the elections, and about going to college."

Exhortations to encourage adolescents to explore a "discourse of desire" are not particularly helpful for adults helping students to think through the consequences of decisions related to sexuality. On the contrary, part of sex education can (and, I believe, should) arise from adult-adolescent dialogues in the context of real-life situations. Consider the following log in which a group of women tutors help a high school girl question her own assumptions: "D.N. [a seventeen-year-old girl] came down this morning. She was talking about how the Phys. Ed. [male] teacher always wants to talk to her. She said he gives her tickets for concerts. She doesn't like him but still flirts with him. We cautioned her on this because her actions might be misinterpreted & he might think that she's interested. She seemed rather surprised that this could happen since she never agreed to go out with him but the more we discussed this the more it made sense to her."

Sexuality and Literacy, Humor and Courage

The "discourse of desire" that Fine claims to be missing from New York City public high schools is, in reality, alive and well:

[Female tutor's log]: I told the kids they could write about anything that was on their minds. J [a girl] wrote a mash letter to G, although she later changed the name of the addressee to N [another boy] as G was threatening her with bodily harm. J wrote that she loved his color and his big juicy lips and luscious butt. She said she wanted to kiss him and that she loved his [blank line] as well. It wasn't hard to fill in the blank. She wrote in almost perfect standard English and she spelled "luscious" correctly. . . . She didn't break my one cardinal rule which is "thou shalt not diss" [= disrespect] so I really don't have a problem with the paper.

If the above excursion, which might be dubbed literacy through sexuality, causes some bafflement, what are the consequences for praxis and educational reform of the following log excerpts? I cite without commentary:

The kids pass a prostitute on the street who flashes her private parts. D [a boy]: "That's New York for you." M [a girl]: "That's it. I'm gonna go bust up her ass."

G and D [two Caribbean boys] announced [to L, their white female tutor] that white women were prettier than black women. I asked them how they would feel if a black woman told them that white men were nicer than black men. "L, that's true! White men nicer!"

T [a fifteen-year-old boy] on the street says he wanted to find a store that sold "cheap gold." Was it for a present? "Sort of," he said. It was for himself, but he planned on trading rings with a girl. "Do you think C would like these? I buy for her." Turns out T has a big crush on C. S [another girl, to T]: "If you buy a present for a girl even before you go out, she thinks you're buying her." S got mad at T: "Nice girls don't want that." "Some girl only like you if you got money and a car," said T. "Some girls only like you if you're a nice guy," we [the female tutor and S] replied. We convinced him not to buy the earrings and suggested that he invite her to go Xmas shopping or go out to lunch or, better yet, get to know her first.

[Female tutor's log]: After the party, she pulled me aside and said, "We have to talk." She has a prescription for the pill, but now she's feeling apprehensive about taking it. The side effects are frightening to her, particularly the prospect of gaining weight. [Result: the girl comes over to the tutor's apartment the following weekend to talk.]

Often, graduate students are asked very personal questions about their sexual lives; they are frequently perplexed as to how to deal with the adolescents' direct questions: are you gay? are you straight? did you ever have an abortion? and many, many more. It is important to know how to handle such situations, to appreciate that, in asking such questions about the "other," the youth are really manifesting concerns about themselves: they are trying to discover their own sexual identities. Compassionate listening is an absolute requisite, to be sure, but students also need someone who will challenge their assumptions about sexuality and their stereotypes about gays and lesbians; they need someone who will develop a warm and caring relationship yet know how to draw a firm line, when appropriate. Tutors or teachers should not, for example, allow students to manipulate them into disclosing information about their own sexual history; this serves only to distract from discussing the students' own problems. Students need to be told that they should check with a doctor or a nurse; sometimes they have to be taken to a clinic almost by hand. In short, even in sexual matters, they need someone *in loco parentis,* especially if the parent is not fulfilling that role.

CARING ENOUGH TO CORRECT

At a social gathering, a fifteen-year-old black American student did an impersonation, with great affection, of one of the West Indian female tutors who is respected by everyone in the program and who was not present at the time. This young man, known as one of the "young guns," a group that has had its share of serious run-ins with the police, tells the tutors and the other students that the tutor was the first person in his life who ever cared enough to tell him that he "must" do something. Such direct guidance, apparently, was not something he encountered with his teachers or perhaps even at home. Yet it was something he desired, expected, and felt to be an expression of genuine affection.

It is not easy for a female tutor (or for anyone, for that matter) to confront a tall, good-looking, street-smart, wise-cracking young man and tell him what he must do. How should we read such an incident? Is this young man completely without morals, a *tabula rasa* on which the tutor is inscribing a code of ethics, as the right-wing might have it? Or is his very desire for structure, and her supplying it, a reproduction of the dominant social order, as the critical pedagogues would have it? I do not find either explanation satisfactory. How, then, are we to interpret this inculcation of "good" behavior and this learning of a new moral language?

In his review of James Q. Wilson's *The Moral Sense* (1993), Alan Ryan questions Wilson's view that learning morality is similar to learning a language and asks, rather cynically: "But what next? Ought we to abduct the offspring of incompetent single mothers and teach them standard morals along with English? If so, how? What would be the equivalent of a remedial English class for morally slow learners?" (1993, 55). Our work with inner-city youth affords a perspective on adolescent morality that has nothing in common with the one Ryan seems to be suggesting here. In sarcastically suggesting that a concept of remedial morality for "ghetto youth" might be compatible with Wilson's moral philosophy, Ryan misses the point that the concept of remedial English is as defective a concept as the notion of reme-dial morality is. "Ghetto youth" do not arrive at the schoolhouse door as moral illiterates, a point well understood by Wilson, who simply—and, I believe, correctly—envisions schools as entities designed to foster and de-velop students' native moral sense.

The notion of "street" needs to be elaborated, lest it become reified and conflated with "culture of violence," as has happened in both popular and scholarly discourse. The whole field of popular culture attests to the rich-ness and aesthetic complexity of street culture, of which parades, theater, and performance in the Caribbean, in Latin America, in early modern Eu-rope, and in the United States are only the most spectacular part (Mukerji and Schudson 1986; Davis 1986). Thus, without falling into the trap of branding any form of popular culture (mass culture, "folk" culture, youth culture, etc.) a form of social decay—an elitist perspective (see Brantlinger 1983)—we need to explain how, like the dominant culture, and perhaps because of it, the street culture has become vulnerable to penetration by a code of violence. The school in turn becomes infected by and infects these social locations outside school.

But we must also believe that adolescents are capable of code-switching to another moral register if the community of adult educators will only lead the way. Although it is not always easy to distinguish mere norms of polite-ness from standards of morality, we may still begin with the hypothesis that inner-city adolescents (like adolescents or adults anywhere) have a legiti-mate code of manners and morality that they carry with them from family and social group to school. This code is not deficient, but it may be quite different from the norms of politeness and moral conduct that obtain for the dominant society. The functions of educators, then, become complex and manifold: to respect the social norms the student brings from the home setting; to disrupt, where appropriate, those social norms with others that obtain in the dominant society and that the student will have to learn in order to succeed; and to expound moral standards of justice, equity, and respect for the most destitute.

In other words, the teacher must become a critic of both worlds—the dominant and the subaltern—and help the student to become the same. No two public school teachers will agree on which are the norms of the dominant society or on the universal standards. Clearly, before schools can obtain a consensus on the uniformly acceptable rules of school conduct (and before American society can obtain a consensus on a common morality), subaltern values will have to be respected and the "dominant morality" will have to be demythologized and purged of the excesses that have accrued in the course of Western history. But if educational leaders do not work toward this goal of some yet-to-be-defined and uniformly accepted code of behavior, then they will continue to abandon the playing field to the culture of violence.

CHAPTER SEVEN

"YOUTH'S YOUTHFULNESS": AN ALTERNATE VIEW

I begin this chapter with an extended series of log excerpts written by a white European female tutor about her relationship with a Beta School girl from the Dominican Republic, V, who was initially attracted to our program when she saw the photographs of students we had pasted on the outside of the tutoring-room door:

> February 15: She seemed like she wanted to talk to me, but at the same time I felt like she might decide to walk away at any moment. She's having a hard time with one of her teachers who is kicking her out of his class because she's been absent too often. The reason she's been absent is that she's been having to go to the hospital, but the teacher won't honor the doctor's note. . . . Eventually she came inside the room, then she sat down. I got her to fill out one of our forms, even though she hadn't said that she wanted help with her school work, but I still had the distinct feeling that she might just get up and leave, and sometimes having the student fill out that form can sort of put the person at ease, and it gives you a context for asking about the family. . . . Well, in the next hour or so I certainly found out about her family. "I don't like my father. He abuses me. He used to beat me. Sometimes he beat me with a whip. See, when I was a little girl, I used to think that my father was the most loving man. Until one day we were at a shopping center, and he was talking to a woman, and I was hungry, so I went up to him and asked him for a dollar so I could get something to eat, and he looked at me and said, "Who are you? You're not my daughter." Her father has other women, and V would tell her mother, but her mother wouldn't believe her. One day she proved it to her mother—she took her to see her father with someone else. Then everyone was upset and her brother told her it was all her fault. Her mother works, her father doesn't. They all live together, including her brother and two sisters, both of whom have had abortions and/or kids. Then: "The reason I have to go to the hospital is I'm preg-

nant." She's going to have an abortion. Next week, at N Hospital—
she trekked all over town, to four different hospitals, by herself,
to be accepted somewhere to have the abortion done, and to get
Medicaid. She's thirteen weeks pregnant. Her ex-boyfriend at first
"didn't believe me that I was pregnant. Til I proved it to him. And
then he said he'd get a job. But he just hangs out on the street.
When I realized that he wasn't going to help me, that's when I knew
I'd have to take care of myself. I had to do it by myself." "Do you
want me to go with you?"—"Are you sure?"—"Yes, I'm sure." You
should have seen her face. She didn't smile. But that look—I'll
never forget it. I almost started crying—she didn't. She took out the
forms from the hospital to show me when and where. She has to go
in twice, once on Wednesday and then on Thursday to have the
abortion. I'll go with her both days. John and Peter, you know what
I did later—I came to see you, and talked to B [a nurse in an STD
clinic, who had lectured in our seminar, to whom Peter and I referred the tutor—JD] about the actual procedure. She gave me a
step-by-step rundown of the procedure, explained why she'll have
to go in twice instead of once, told me what to expect afterwards.
This gets to me every time I hear it. . . . Oh, I gave V my phone
number, too, and told her to call me any time, if something happens,
or if she gets worried all of a sudden. . . . "It doesn't matter what
time it is—you can call me at three in the morning if something
bad happens and you need someone to talk to."

February 16: The more I thought about it last night, the more it
became clear to me that I'd have to go in today to talk to V some
more, and also to talk to Mr. W., who is her guidance counselor. [In
our conversations with the tutor, who by this time had decided to
rent a car so that V would not have to go to and from this ordeal
on a subway, my assistant and I had recommended that the tutor
talk with Mr. W.—whom we knew to be a compassionate person—
and that she try to get V to talk with him before going to the hospital.—JD] There were just too many unresolved questions about
what was going to happen. What will happen after the abortion?
It's not the kind of thing you can hide so easily, given the way you
are likely to feel physically and emotionally, so maybe she should
tell her mother. And if she doesn't, how appropriate is it for me to
play a role in this? I was pretty sure that she'd told Mr. W., but in
case she hadn't, would it be appropriate for me to tell him? I decided
to talk to Dr. L. [an assistant to the principal on loan from the

central board of education] first. Also, all the questions about logistics: How would she get there, should I drive, but what about insurance and liability if something happens? What if there are complications afterwards—is there a clinic near her house that she can go to? She's getting the abortion done at N Hospital in Manhattan, and she lives way out in East New York [one of the most troubled areas in New York City—JD]. So I talked to Dr. L. first. Then we found Mr. W., who, as it turned out, did know. As a matter of fact, he'd gone through the whole decision process about whether to keep the baby with her. We talked for a long time—also about my feelings. Am I going to be ok doing this? Yes. Yes, I'm emotionally involved, and yes, it won't be easy. But there is no way I would have considered not doing it, and in any case, anything that I may feel is nothing compared to what V has to go through! That was pretty much my thinking/feeling about it. Mr. W. thought that telling her mother was not likely to be good. In his words: "She'll probably beat her up and kick her out of the house." With respect to D, the father of the baby, they both agreed that he's bad news. "He's about as low as you can get. He's being destroyed by the drugs. He doesn't have long to live." After this I met V and took her up to our [tutoring] room. We talked for a good hour and a half. She was under the impression that she'd have the abortion, and then she'd go home and feel fine and go to school the next day. I told her that it's not likely to be like that. That it will probably hurt some, and that it will probably leave her feeling very shaky and very vulnerable. Again, we talked about a lot of other things, too—her family, her feelings about D and his not being there for her now while she's going through this. Also, at some point, she said that she really would like to have the baby. At the hospital, they had done a sonogram and shown it to her on the monitor. "And here's the head. . . ." Seriously! That's what she said. But before I really responded to that she said she didn't have a choice—having the baby was just not an option. So I'll see her Tues., and then the ordeal starts on Wed. But, as V said: "I can't wait for it to be over."

February 20: V mentioned on Friday that she wished she could keep her baby, and I was not sure what to do if she brought it up again. Do I go through the whole decision process with her? In an impartial way? I asked Mr. W. He said to let it lie—certainly not to bring it up if she didn't (remember that he already went through it with her once). But if she brought it up, he said to discuss it with her, and by all means impartially. *She* is the one who has to make this decision, it has to be hers, not mine, because she will have to live with it. What he said made sense to me. As it turned out, though, V didn't bring it up again. Third period V stopped by, and I spent the time talking to her. We talked about her cousin C [a girl] who is moving back in with V's family. V seems to be a good friend to C although C apparently uses drugs and has stolen things from V in the past. C is also pregnant. Her boyfriend, who is on drugs, kicked her out—that's why she is moving back in with V's family. V said she would stay with D if he got his own place, just for that, for having a place to live. My first impulse was to say NO! You should never have a relationship with someone because you want something material from that person! But I didn't say it, because something in my head said, "Wait, who am I to tell her not to do that?" Living with D, with all that may involve, may be a heck of a lot more pleasant than living at home! Can I really tell her that this is something she should not do? She is probably a much better judge of that than I am.

February 21: Went to Beta School in the morning. I felt calm, but I realized once E [the team leader] came in and third period started that I wasn't. What if V didn't come fourth period? I was nervous. . . . The bell finally rang. V came before the bell for fourth period even rang. She's looking very serious. She just saw D, and "we settled some things." "I'm not going steady with him no more. He'll see. He says he has to go to class, he has to take a test. I asked him: 'How many tests have I missed to be with you?' An' he didn't say nothin'. He stood silent. 'Are you goin' through this? Do you have to go to the hospital? Are you feelin' any pain?,' I asked him. And he didn't say nothin'. He just stood silent." We left the building and went down the block to F Avenue for a slice of pizza—D had given her money to get something to eat. V ordered a slice, then went across the street to get a soda, since "it's too expensive here." We caught the train at the F Avenue station, just up the block. We talked about the procedure, how it was going to feel. And about a lot of other things. D—"We've been together for over a year. It's gonna be two years. I've never gone with a guy this long. I really care about him a lot." "Yes, I can see that you care about him." "That's why this is so hard." I told her that whatever happened she shouldn't be afraid to ask questions. If you're worried about something, if there's anything you want to ask the nurse or the doctor,

or, if you get scared—ask. Say how you feel, if you're scared, or if
it hurts. Or, if there's anything you want me to ask, you can ask me.
"I know," looking at me and smiling. She knows how to get to the
hospital. Waiting for the elevator: "I always get nervous walking
into this place." She didn't seem so nervous. She got signed in, got
her Medicaid cleared (she just got the card in the mail yesterday—
just in time). Then the waiting room. They had all sorts of brochures. She pointed out one on "safe sex," said it was real good. "I
read it, and there was some stuff in there I didn't know. And I told
some of my friends about it." I took one of the brochures and
opened it, looked through it. "Did you understand everything in
here?" She was worried about diseases. Can you get diseases from
smoking? From smoking herb? From doing drugs? No—those
things might make you less healthy, so you might get a disease more
easily, you might be more susceptible to it. But you can't get a disease from doing drugs. But you can gets AIDS if you shoot up and
share a needle with someone who has it. She wanted to get checked
to make sure she doesn't have anything. "V, do you have any reason
to be worried? Does it itch—does your vagina itch, or does it smell
funny?"—"Yes."—"For how long?"—"Two or three months." (!!)
So I told her that this is a long time, and that she definitely needs
to get it checked. I explained that there are a lot of different diseases
that you can get. Some are really serious like herpes and gonorrhea,
and then there's others that are really harmless and really easy to
get rid of—you just put in some cream every day for a week, and
that's a pain, but the infection is gone. So it may be something totally harmless. Later we were talking to a nurse and found out that
her blood test showed her to be negative for gonorrhea, syphilis,
herpes, and all that. V still didn't mention the itching, so I told the
nurse. She asked V how long she'd had it, and if it was on the inside
or the outside, and why she didn't say anything before. Why didn't
you tell the doctor? V just gave her a blank look, like "don't you
know?" But this was later. Meanwhile, we're in the waiting room.
The amount of wrong—totally wrong, just unbelievable—"information" being exchanged among the patients was incredible. If two
things happen at the same time, one is assumed to be the cause of
the other. Abortions cause cysts. Drinking causes diseases. I tried
to untangle some of this—especially that which pertained to what
V was going to go through—to one of the other patients. "No,
abortions don't cause cysts in your uterus. They just found them
now because they did the sonogram for the abortion. Cysts are

common."—"They are?" (relief)—"They're like lumps some people get in their breasts, or on your arm or wherever."—"Oh, yeah, I've got one here on my arm, see?"—"Well, they're just like that. They're usually harmless—you just have to watch them, and maybe have them taken out if they grow and get in the way." The ease with which she accepted what I said as fact surprised me.—V returned from the procedure—"the laminaria"—shaken up. She walked into the waiting room with that look on her face, of pain, of having been through something horrible. She's been crying. Not a smile anywhere in her, at this moment. "It hurt, man!" We just sat for quite a while, then walked up and down the hall a bit, just to make sure that the way she was feeling was more or less stable. She had some bleeding, and the nurse got her a pad and reassured her that this is normal. Then we left the hospital and walked some more—it was a beautiful day out. She was hungry so we again had pizza—I took her out. While we were walking she said to me, "Tell me something about you! You know a lot more about me and I don't know anything about you." So she asked me if I'd had a lot of boyfriends in high school (no), and if I'd ever had a serious relationship (yes). I just answered her honestly and straightforwardly. I felt that this certainly wasn't a time to worry about whether this was appropriate in a "teacher-student" relationship. She had opened up to me and let me see things about her so much in the last few days that I felt that if she wanted to know something about me I would certainly tell her. It somehow seems to tie in with having respect for her as a person. I'm just writing—I hadn't thought about this before. We took the subway back. I got off at [a subway station], she continued on home. (I picked up the rental car and drove home.) This was a long day . . . (6:30 by the time I got home). I'll see V at 6 A.M. tomorrow at her house.

February 22: Woke up early, took one more look at the map, and drove over to V's house. It was before six in the morning, still dark out. V lives in the area that's just on the border between East New York and Brownsville. There were few people on the street. Two men were doing what looked to me like a drug deal. Some unloading of five or six trucks was going on on one block. V's block is all storefronts which of course are shuttered up at this hour. No doorways and no parked cars. Good: I can see everything that goes on on this block while I wait. She lives in an apartment over a store. This seems to be the only residence on the block, all the other buildings are just one story high and stores. I'm ten minutes early. So I park in the middle of the block. The neighborhood is unbelievable—I won't bother describing it. But being here at six in the morning, as a woman, alone, in a brand new white car, I was definitely nervous. I will be able to see anyone who enters this block, but what will I do if someone does come walking down the street? Someone did, in fact, a few minutes later. I started the car and drove around the block. V came out exactly at six. Her mother had given her a hard time about leaving so early, even though V had told her she had a zero period class to go to, and had brought her bookbag. The first thing she said to me was: "I'm really glad that you are going with me!" I replied, feeling very serious: "Well, you're welcome!" She liked my driving: "You're real smooth." We drove down Fulton and over the Brooklyn Bridge. V: "Wow, this is exciting!" I had to explain to her what a blinker is. We drove up the FDR Drive, and she was telling me how her father and his friends, and her friends, are always driving drunk, and are always racing each other. We got a parking spot right in front of the hospital, at a meter. And we were just on time, with about ten minutes to spare. On the fourth floor we checked in and waited. Most of the people there we'd seen yesterday already. Y came in with her entourage again, bouncing on the balls of her feet, smiling, energetic. Then she sat down and held her stomach. V was just sitting. She was definitely feeling pain. Y's entourage consisted of her mom, her mother's boyfriend, and her friend R. They had a tape player with them—Y held it on her lap. The TV was blaring. V was quiet. She and Y compared notes about how they felt—yes, it hurt when they put in the laminaria yesterday. After a while they called all the patients in to get changed into these robes. They came back out. V kept trying to pull the robe closed so that it would cover her knees and her legs completely. She said that she felt embarrassed to have to sit here in a nightgown and a robe, with men being in the room and all. After a while they went to lie down in the room behind the nurses' station, and I went to sit there with them, at V's request, until the nurses told all the visitors to leave. Then I stood outside the room and looked through the window. Y was throwing up. When they were taken to the back, to the operating rooms, I went back to the waiting room. Every once in a while I went for a walk outside. I tried to read but between being tired and being worried about V I wasn't too successful. I paced the hall until the nurses told me to stay in the waiting room. At twelve thirty, the head nurse called me over and told me that V was ok, and that I'd be able to see her in about two hours. I was so relieved, I felt like screaming "Yeahhh! She made it! She's ok!" So much for distancing yourself emotionally. I turned around to face everyone in the waiting room, and just had this huge smile on my face. . . . I finally got to see V about three hours later, just through the window at the nurses' station. She was lying on a bed and eating something. She saw me, waved at me, and did not smile. At about four thirty, I saw her in person. God, that look on her face. She just sat down on the first chair by the door. I went over and sat next to her. And this was it. It was over, except that it wasn't. "When I get home, I'm going to tell my mother, I don't care what happens." They had given her three kinds of pills. One of them had to be taken, "three times daily for four days." I had to explain to her what that meant. This was to get her uterus to contract to its normal size. The other two were Tylenol and birth control pills. She went to the bathroom. Y came from there and told me V was crying. I went in there. Again, I sat down next to her. "Nothing good ever happens to me," she was saying. She threw her arms around me and she was crying and crying. I just held her . . . "Oh, V." But it's not like her to cry for long. After a few minutes she stopped. And she said: "Except that something good did happen: You're here with me." We were the last ones to leave. The nurses were closing down everything—another day's work done. Driving home took about an hour and a half, through Manhattan traffic in the rain and the dark and in rush hour. I think renting a car was the right thing to do. V again referred to my driving: "When I have a car, I won't let anyone race in it. I just want people to drive like you and me." I thought the "like you and me" was interesting. And we talked about her telling her mom. . . . I dropped her off, then I returned the car. The worst was over, and it was so nice to be walking, to be rid of the car, to just be walking down the street. . . . All of what I saw in those two days—right now I could not put any of it into words. It was just this huge chunk of life. Am I still the same person I was two days ago?—Writing this ten days later, there's still a lot I haven't put down on paper. I could have written so much more: just everything I saw, all that was said, and all that just was, that's there, and that I was there to see. It took me about a week to find my balance at all again. It's not just the abortion. It's the fact that I got a look at what it might be like to live like that, without education about all the things we take for granted, from basic facts to how things work. And I got a look at what that means for the way you live your life, the way you have to relate to people.

February 23: Gave V a call. She's feeling exactly like yesterday. She told her mom, who reacted in a totally unexpected way: she was upset that V had not told her before, and said, "You need a hug from your mother!" So that was good. I'm glad!

GOING THE EXTRA MILE

What would be a proper exegesis of this text? What should be my own reading qua ethnographer and program director? In a given week, multiple examples of abusive relationships, unplanned teenage pregnancies, suicidal thoughts, or other crises manifest themselves in our program. I am hardly a neutral observer, any more than the tutor or V are. How, then, is one to situate the body of the tutor in the text so that she does not become merely an "objectivist lens"? Each of my graduate assistants would produce a different reading. And what lessons does such a text have for anyone interested in lessening school violence?

I will organize my own comments around the central characters involved: myself, V and her family, school personnel, and the tutor. Also, there are at least three levels of textuality here: the written document of the tutor's log; the verbal text (i.e., the dialogues the written text purports to transcribe and interpret); and the social text, the actual situations V herself has been experiencing (e.g., encounters with her father at the shopping mall, visits to the hospital, etc.) that the verbal texts of V's stories recount.

MYSELF

Although I advised the tutor every step of the way, I was a relatively minor actor in this drama. My assistant and I played a supporting role by referring the tutor to the nurse who ran the STD clinic, by giving permission for her to rent the car, and by being available for consultation. As a former Jesuit priest, I had my own feelings of ambivalence as I guided the tutor through this process, thereby becoming a collaborator in the deed, although this was by no means the first time I have had to face such a dilemma. The ethics of abortion is not the issue here, since V had made her decision before the actions described took place. My interest is in drawing out the relevance of this thickly descriptive ethnographic text to the complexity of schools saturated with violence, to the corresponding demands that violence places on the teacher-student relationship, and to the need to remythologize that relationship.

V AND HER FAMILY

Even an antiabortion activist might be struck by the pathetic sight of V, thirteen weeks pregnant, trekking all over town looking for a hospital and trying to get covered by Medicaid. If the tutor had not appeared in her life, V would have had to continue this dreary process alone. It seems that all it took to lure her into our program was a smile from the tutor. I am also struck by how a simple act like filling out the routine "intake" forms together can become a bonding and tension-breaking experience. How would Foucault read this bureaucratic moment? Is it the exercise of power, the forced extraction of the desired knowledge about V and her family? The pervasive spread of panopticism? Are we coopting her into our own brand of humanism?

I am also struck, as anyone would be, by the severity and cruelty of the father's abuse.[1] I also note that V tested the tutor's reactions to the tales about the home abuse before she decided to reveal the pregnancy and her plans for an abortion. As for the forlorn boyfriend, his casual response is perhaps predictable, but it does not lessen the abandonment V feels ("I knew I'd have to take care of myself"), nor does it lessen her attachment to him. I also note the regrettable absence of any resource in the school to work with the boy, whose pathetic gift of money for a slice of pizza perhaps symbolizes his own total helplessness. Most basically, V's decision needs to be interpreted in the context of a home life saturated with drugs, violence, instability, and a father who gets his kicks out of racing a car while intoxicated. Accounts like these make it easy to understand why inner-city educators roll their eyes when piously lectured by "effective schools" advocates on the importance of promoting parental involvement in the youth's education. Although the written text does not disclose the teenager's moral reasoning leading to her decision to abort, we can guess at some of its components, given the completely unstable home life. It does, however, raise the valid question of how much more a school could do in working with abusive and alcoholic families—and thereby have a greater impact on the total community—if the setting were smaller and the staff less pressured.

SCHOOL PERSONNEL

One may wish to blame the school system's inadequate sex education program for the girl's deplorable ignorance about "safe sex," although one is also free to wonder, despite all the absolutely valid statistics about the efficacy of sex education, how much good it would have done in this case. When V's crisis finally was brought to the attention of the guidance counselor and the principal's assistant (both, as it happens, white males), they responded most competently and sensitively. If one wonders that they do not "go the extra mile" to the extent the tutor did, one must also remember that they are charged with working with hundreds of students daily, she, only with a few. I cannot even get too angry at the dim-witted teacher who kicked V out of class: had he known about the pregnancy, he might have acted differently, and V chose not to tell him. And if Mr. W. misjudged what V's mother's reaction would be, and if he was less than empathetic with the boyfriend, he at least walked V through the decision-making process in a most compassionate way.

TUTOR

I note the tutor's extraordinary efforts to give V the support and love she needed. The tutor's presence at V's side as she underwent this painful experience, which she otherwise would have had to endure alone, was clearly crucial for V's emotional health, but what are the ramifications of such nonacademic interaction for educational practice and critical theory? How does it help us define and clarify the responsibilities of schools?

This tutor (who was hired because of her ability to tutor mathematics) stretches herself well beyond what anyone might expect of her: she shares her phone number, invites V to call her at any time, decides to rent a car for V's comfort and privacy, bravely ventures into a tough neighborhood alone, and conducts an impromptu sex education class in the hospital waiting room. She plays, in effect, the role of an activist medical anthropologist, interpreting and mediating between the concepts of the Western medical system and the explanations for disease and sexuality held by V and the others in the waiting room.

Within our seminar, I would applaud the tutor's decision to make herself vulnerable and to share some of her own personal life with V at a time when V felt so vulnerable. I would, however, note that such self-revelation is normally not desirable, since such questions take attention away from a serious examination of the student's own sexual issues. I would also agree with the tutor's judgment not to question V's plans to continue her relationship with D and to move in with him, at least at this time, when V's world is crumbling around her. But at some future date, when the timing is right, it would be most appropriate for the tutor to help V to think through the consequences of her desire to move in with D. I would challenge the tutor's statement that V "is probably a much better judge of that than I am," since, almost certainly, V would be moving from one abusive situation to another. But, as any counselor knows, V needs to come to that conclusion herself and not just accept the opinion of the tutor. At the same time, the tutor's initial reaction to protect V from future harm, her impulse to help V think through the consequences of living with this boy, also needs to be respected as a more mature resolution to V's living dilemma. Such an impulse, which the tutor restrained, arises not because she comes from another ethnic group or income level but because she has the maturity of someone who has negotiated the snares of life in late-twentieth-century Western society a little longer and with more resources at her disposal.

The Totalizing Vision of Antihumanism

My reading would be totally at odds with some postmodern theories that would see in the contrast between maturity and immaturity just one more oppressive and hierarchical binary opposition, like white and black, male and female, or rich and poor. William Spanos (1993, 198), for example, views such affirmations of maturity as another way to reproduce "the dominant sociopolitical order":

> Postmodern theory—neo-Marxist, deconstruction, genealogy, new historicism, critical theory—has not adequately thought the relationship between the student revolt in the late 1960s and the simultaneous precipitation of what has been called the generation gap: the emergence for the first time in Western history of a youth culture, a symptomatic consciousness on the part of the young of their "oppression" by an institution of learning (and its pedagogical apparatuses) representing a sociopolitical order perennially validated, empowered, and reproduced by the privileged status it gives to adulthood in the name of the prolific metaphysically derived opposition between maturity and immaturity.

In other words, to set oneself up as "more mature" is, for Spanos, the equivalent of placing oneself in a "supervisory" position, and supervision is as abhorrent to him as it was to Foucault. "Supervision" automatically equates to "oppression."

Let us consider whether, in this "humanistic" encounter between tutor and tutee, we are observing oppression. What is taking place in the relationship between the tutor and V is hardly the "domestication of the revolutionary energy of the young" or the metamorphosis of a Hispanic girl into a white male role, a transformation so feared by Spanos (1993, 200).

I argue that Spanos's epistemology should be challenged on two essential points. First, in reconceptualizing ideal education along the lines of the pedagogy of Paulo Freire, Spanos conflates the dialogic aspect of teaching with the totality of the teacher-student relationship. Teacher and student, we are told, should enter into a "reciprocal deconstructive learning process, one in which the oppositional teacher becomes a student and the interested student a teacher" (1993, 202), the teacher now experiencing what it feels like to be subjected to the disciplinary gaze. Such an educational philosophy has delusions of omnipotence: it wishes to extend its valid insights to encompass all aspects of teaching and learning, to become a totalizing vision. To accept the concept that not all knowledge is immediately generated through the dialogic relationship does not, however, equal an "oppressor ideology" or the "absolutizing of ignorance."[2] It simply represents a recognition that the student needs to be aware of what things or concepts mean for other people outside the context of the immediate dialogic relationship ("I had to explain to her what a blinker is"). In other words, while knowledge constructed through dialogue is to be valued as essential to the pedagogic process, it is also true that not all knowledge is or should be so conceptualized. Constructivism is splendid, but it has limits.

The second point to be made is that this absolutizing of dialogue derives from Spanos's inversion of the hierarchy of maturity and immaturity. Henceforth youth, romanticized and portrayed only as marginalized and oppressed, is now invested with maturity, which has been stripped from the "grey-haired" and humanist professoriate (1993, 205). He conceptualizes "youth's youthfulness" in such a pure, unadulterated way; there is nothing negative in youth culture, which is referred to always in an uncritical and unproblematic light. Absent is any analysis of popular culture, only enthusiastic references to rock music and the "arts of the people" (207).

Such naivete is almost charming. When inner-city youth watch music videos with us, they often critique the more violent aspects of rock, rap, and slam-dancing. Even more shocking for a critical theory that devalues

191

"banking" education,[3] these students also listen respectfully to our critiques of postmodern art forms[4] and sometimes accept them. Moreover, allowing immaturity to somehow take precedence over maturity[5] is, at the very least, a misapplication of Derridean deconstruction, which never intended a total inversion of the received order of priorities (cf. Norris 1987, 35).[6] Should the tutor have sought emotional help from V or allowed V to drive the car to the hospital, since apprenticeship, for him, implies oppression and a lack of respect for youth's youthfulness?

Reflection on the log excerpt, however, raises a more central consideration, one to which all of the above remarks are merely preliminary: why does the tutor so stretch herself to meet V's emotional and physical needs? In inquiring into the tutor's motivation, I am not so much interested in her personal motives as in a possible ideological orientation. If one can safely assume that such "caring" and extension of the self beyond the call of duty emanates from a humanistic tradition, or from some demythologized form of humanism (be it secular humanism, liberation theology, or traditional Judeo-Christian humanism), then several philosophical issues emerge. If this be humanism, then I would contend, contrary to those who style themselves oppositional intellectuals (Spanos) or transformative intellectuals (Giroux), that the struggle should be to inject more humanism, not less, into the traditional school and that the school systems are currently failing students not by "over-disciplining" their bodies but by ignoring them— that is, putting teachers and counselors into such impossible managerial positions that they are forced to ignore them. The inner-city school that V attended had its hands so tied by incredibly large numbers and by ancient structures that it was able to give her the attention she needed only once the crisis erupted. Early intervention might, had it been able to get to her earlier, have prevented the pregnancy altogether. Whatever the reason, V's body was ignored by the system. But the goal of the tutor (or of our program) in focusing on emotional support should not be mistaken; there is no question here of just "doing social work" and ignoring the cognitive. The tutor's (and our) ultimate goal was to help V acquire the social and cognitive skills needed to be promoted, to graduate, and to have a productive career. But focusing on the academic is useless while V is absorbed with sexual and social issues—these must be dealt with first or at least simultaneously. Once these concerns are met, the struggle with the academic content of the curriculum (including the struggle to destroy the oppressive elements in it) becomes immensely easier.

THE ANTHROPOLOGY OF THE STUDENT BODY

But critical pedagogy is not comfortable with the body. It prefers to restrict its discourse to the cognitive and the mentalistic: the introduction of hitherto marginalized Third World texts and the interrogation and destruction of the Western tradition. What is at stake here, by contrast, is the whole nonacademic and "messy" side of student life, the side that university professors never have to worry about because student personnel services are expected to take on the responsibility. All these events take place far from classrooms, academic offices, and professors' apartments. The student basketball game that dazzles the crowd turns into a lethal nightmare when guns appear or when the crowd overflows and crushes people to death and the lowly guards and student union personnel are said to have been negligent. These "youth culture" phenomena reveal themselves as Walter Benjamin's "dialectical images" (Buck-Morss 1990, 58–77) because of their potential, in the context of the fracturing society of late-twentieth-century America, to flip quickly from celebration to decay and to subvert original meanings and intentions. The joys of teenage sexuality mutate into the gloom of unwanted pregnancy, abortion, or AIDS. The glamour of MTV and consumerism—wholesome at one level—participate in the culture of violence at another. A friend feels betrayed or frightened, gets a gun, and kills a classmate. Essentially, these are parental issues, and the educational establishment must decide how far it should go in assuming responsibility: when to draw the line between etiquette and rudeness, how to cope with the consequences of earlier abuse, what is the prudent thing to do, given the legal and liability insurance aspects of any issue. This nonacademic side of student life can range from worrying about spectator behavior at a basketball game to checking for weapons use to fending off personal and sometimes violent attacks against one's person—all areas about which postmodern theory and critical pedagogy have nothing to say. Their silence extends from after-school bull sessions to wild, carnivalesque corridor riots, from innocent student parties to Dionysian revels, from compassionate conversations to ugly scenes of girls' gangs pulling one another's hair.

A large segment of current academic writing frequently implies that the traditional system is "exercising power" over the bodies of students and is guilty of using excessive discipline. In fact, an ethnography of the nonclassroom space reveals exactly the opposite: in inner-city schools, power over the body is being relegated to a low priority through the superficial treatment it receives at the hands of the guards.[7] All of these commentators essentially want to define the teacher-student relationship within the privatized framework of classroom space; nonclassroom space remains unthought. Furthermore, in their view it is not just the school that is seen as reproducing the dominant society by privileging discipline and "maturity"; even parents are seen as unconsciously doing the same by "setting examples" by their behavior (Althusser 1971, 156–57, cited in Spanos 1993, 197)! Again, none of this "theory" reflects the reality of daily life in inner-city schools: it is not derived from an ethnographic base but from debates with other theoretical positions. Lower-tier teachers, as indicated above, have almost completely withdrawn from even the pretense of being role models. This is due in part, perhaps, to such theory, but it is due mostly to systemic developments and the predominance of fear. The anthropology of the student *body,* therefore, as well as its extensions into space (in the form of emotion, sexuality, food, clothing, weapons, exercise, and school-building architecture) and time (in the form of sloppily-computerized class programming procedures, cutbacks on teachers' prep time, antiquated bell schedules, frequent holidays, the almost total lack of after-school activities and sports, students' highly unorthodox home schedules, after-midnight TV watching, truancy, attendance and lateness problems) remains undertheorized precisely because the nonacademic surveillance of students is conceptualized, by unions and theory builders alike, as an undesirable holdover from a paternalistic Eurocentric era.

Students, precisely because they are inner-city students, are envisioned as not requiring supervision, as living in a prelapsarian, innocent state of nature, incapable of inflicting violence, only of suffering it. The body itself is romanticized and "celebrated" to the point where the schools are admonished to deny the meaning of the social dramas they see unfolding before their eyes everyday: the cold hard fact, for example, that most teen pregnancies end up being unmitigated disasters for the girls themselves, even where the schools provide parenting programs: "[Tutor's log] As we talked, she [a seventeen-year-old tenth grader] began jotting down her first thoughts—the responsibility, the fact that she can't afford to raise [her one-year-old baby girl] alone, the missing father, her determination for her child to receive a good education in order to 'make something of herself.'"

To which intellectual resources may a teacher turn in learning to cope with such exigencies? According to Michelle Fine (1991, 79), "a genuine discourse of desire would invite adolescents to explore what feels good and bad, desirable and undesirable." According to Spanos (1993, 199), we should revolutionize liberal education, which now colonizes and pacifies youth's youthfulness. According to Aronowitz and Giroux (1985, 42), the real problem teachers are now facing is that they are overburdened with "numerous noncurricular tasks such as bus duty, cafeteria duty, and playground duty that needlessly constrain their time and teaching abilities." Is one to conclude, then, in this new pedagogy of nonsurveillance, that the teacher is to eschew all attempts to interact and to challenge, to avoid informal nonclassroom contacts, to refrain from questioning these young women's need to be nurturers before they themselves are fully nourished, to have someone depend on them before they themselves are fully independent? Is the teacher to exult in celebrations of youth's youthfulness and submerge all mature judgment about the realistic potential of these girls—and boys—as future parents? Or is the teacher perhaps just to avoid playgrounds, cafeterias, and school buses altogether to avoid being confronted with the messy, the violent, the bodily, and certainly the nonacademic side of student life?

These bankrupt solutions lead me back to my final reflection on the log that opened this chapter. Allow V's statement ("I just want people to drive like you and me") to stand for a powerful adolescent hope that there is some way out of the culture of violence. It represents V's determination to fashion some portion, at least, of her own identity on the model of the tutor's behavior. The tutor's performance is in competition with a number of other dramas vying for V's allegiance. But exposure to the tutor does more than just set her up as a role model. It affords V the opportunity to code-switch to behaviors that emulate those of the tutor by building on her own already-present native repertoires of morality. It transcends all of the academic discussions fixated on ethnic and racial identity (V could not care less that the tutor is a European woman). Most important, it presents V with a behavioral modality that enables her to resist being sucked into the vortex of the street culture, which has infiltrated her home, family, peers, and school. Something good did indeed happen here: the tutor was there for V when V needed her. The point is not that V is "expected to feel grateful to the liberal society" (Spanos 1993, 199) because she is a minority student. The point is rather that the teaching relationship occasionally blossoms into commitment, friendship, love, and caring. If the tutor's behavior be "humanism," then make the most of it. If two white males at Beta School helping V at this critical stage flies in the face of feminist doctrine, then welcome to the postmodern world of inner-city schooling.

REMYTHOLOGIZING INNER-CITY SCHOOLING

Post-Modernism . . . rejects epistemological assumptions, refutes methodological conventions, resists knowledge claims, obscures all versions of truth, and
dismisses policy recommendations.
                —Pauline Marie Rosenau, *Postmodernism and the Social Sciences*

I concluded that it is not a question of getting beyond myth . . . but rather of
inventing new and more salutary myths, myths to counter the destructive
myths of violence, domination, patriarchy, and hierarchy.
                —John D. Caputo, *Demythologizing Heidegger*

The preceding chapters have advanced the thesis that a culture of violence has become pandemic throughout New York's lower-tier high school
system. Some readers may also see in this depiction of New York a reflection of their own communities and of the general response to school violence across America. In making such declarations, I realize I have come
close to the kind of banal alarmism that has appeared in pedagogical journals since the late nineteenth century (with titles like "Is Our Educational
System Dangerously Adrift?"). Although my ethnographic vantage point is
from within the walls of the schools, the central message of this book is not
that the schools—the inner-city schools in particular—are isolated and self-
contained islands of violence. These "schools," as tumultuous as they are,
must be understood as part of a larger tumultuous society. Both parts of
this proposition need to be affirmed: if one blames societal ills as the single
causative factor, then school reform becomes trivial and unimportant; if
one puts all the blame on the schools, then they become the scapegoat for
a much larger societal pathology.[1]

The fact that the commodity of violence is so highly perceptible, so
shocking, when observed in the school setting should not cause us to conclude that schools have a monopoly on it. Since violence is the antithesis of
everything schools are supposed to stand for, the truly frightening thing is

the rapidity with which all of us who sojourn in these "schools" become adjusted to this anticulture. The fright I am alluding to here is not the vicarious, distant, chill a literary critic or an ordinary reader feels when reading a work of literature. It is the sudden consciousness that one has been surrendering to the normalization of violence all along and that now that adjustment is not sufficient to cover the latest shock. Violence has suddenly closed the distance and has moved close to me (the ethnographer or the program director) in a very personal way.

As I write on a sunny Friday afternoon, my concentration is pulled away from this text. I want to make two phone calls. The first is to a trusted street-savvy friend to ask him if the advice I have given to one of my women graduate students—whose tutee just divulged highly self-incriminatory information—will put her in great jeopardy. By receiving this criminal information, the tutor could become the target of street violence herself. At the same time, if she and I take no action at all on the information we both have, we could be collaborating in the passivity that generates social injustice in America and against which I have been inveighing here. What are my legal obligations in this unfamiliar land where going to the authorities may considerably worsen our situation? As tutor and as ethnographer, we are both caught up in a *crise de conscience* thrust upon us by the culture of violence. We are both potential recipients and victims, and we are both possible transmitters and perpetrators of the disease. Angry and frightened, we find ourselves in exactly the same position as the "schools" and students I have been trying to interpret.

The second phone call I want to make this weekend is to a mathematician friend to ask her the best way to explain to a ninth grader why $-10 \times -10 = +100$. Thus we come full circle to the "school" as an admixture of the normal and the violent. Normal schooling or culture of violence? The key question, then, which has no single answer, becomes, How can our society and our school systems begin to address and reverse this process of normalization? If the above critique of the myths by which theory and praxis live has any validity, how are we to remythologize urban pedagogy, and how are we to reshape and renew the circumstances of schooling for this most disenfranchised segment of the youth population?

The trends reported in the previous chapters have not been abating—on the contrary, they are on the increase. Since I began writing this book, the New York school system has purchased airport-type walk-through (or "archway") metal detectors for fifty schools and has created a new set of high schools exclusively designed for "very disruptive and violent students" (Dillon 1994). The news about the new metal detectors appeared, as it usually does, after another tragic shooting of one more student in a lower-tier high school. The news about the creation of "disciplinary schools" was a direct response to a new "get tough" federal education law that requires schools to suspend for at least a year those students who carry guns (Newman 1995a). Transferring the gun-carrying student from the school of origin to a corrections academy presumably satisfies both the advocacy community (which is constantly criticizing the board's suspension of students and has been successful in eliminating the concept of expulsion altogether) and the Washington hardliners who want to appear to be doing something about the nationwide proliferation of guns in schools. In their eyes, it is the gun-carrying student who needs to be marginalized and expelled from society, not the guns themselves. But insiders within the system all recognize that the plans for these new schools sound suspiciously like the notorious "600 Schools," which were set up and then disbanded by the courts during the 1970s, because they were judged to be dumping grounds for troublemakers. In terms of the analysis I have been advancing, it is critical that we understand what is happening. If the whole system is geared toward generating these huge lower-tier "schools" of last resort, which, as we have seen, nurture the culture of school violence, and if one subscribes to the philosophy that the real problem in these "schools" is a small handful of really bad troublemakers, then it follows that one is perforce required to create a sort of subbasement to the whole pyramid, a set of lower-than-lower-tier "schools" to which the "really bad" students may be transferred, a space where the distinction between school-qua-dungeon and school-qua-panopticon becomes very blurred indeed.[2] Since these youngsters are not quite eligible for the criminal justice system, the board's only alternative would be to expel them altogether and let them roam the streets all day, clearly an unthinkable political option.

As I finish writing this manuscript in the fall of 1995, the issue of school safety has emerged from the wings and has taken center stage in New York City politics. Tragically, both sides of the current debate—whether to place guards under the direct supervision of the police department—are in

agreement on basic assumptions that are diametrically opposed to the propositions I have been advancing here.[3] A report will soon be issued as a result
of public hearings, but all indications are that it will simply repeat similar
documents of the past twenty years. The previous report, written in 1993,
supposedly to "rethink school safety" (see Travis, Lynch, and Schall 1993),
may serve as an illustration of the mentality that drives policy on school
violence issues and will continue to do so in the future.[4] Seen in this light,
the current controversy—which pits the mayor, who wants in effect to aug-
ment the police presence in the schools, against the board, whose members
are content with making cosmetic adjustments to the present system—becomes relatively unimportant, since both parties are moving school discipline in the direction of law enforcement, the antithesis of what I have been
advocating here. Depressingly, no one in the city seems upset that inner-city
truants, pursuant to the mayor's orders, are now being dragged from street
corners in Brooklyn (I have never seen this in Manhattan) each morning
and deposited in the lobbies of schools, handcuffed!

Using the Travis report, then, as representative of the direction in which
school officials are taking the system on safety policy, I will summarize—
and dissent from—each of its main components before formulating my own
mythology for dealing with the issues of schooling and violence. Along the
way, my own version of the minimal requirements for promising reform will
become clarified. In crafting a set of hopeful proposals, of course, I am
perversely violating one of postmodernism's central edicts—referred to in
the above epigraph—that the realities of today's shredded society make it
futile even to contemplate making public-policy recommendations. But in
trying to find more systemic ways to cope with the violence and to revalue
discipline and moral instruction, I have no illusions about returning to the
ethos of some past, largely imaginary, utopian school community. In the
present climate, any solutions have to be local, ad hoc ones, constructed
through a consensus-building process that takes into account, as far
as is possible, the full complexity of the roots of violence. If my approach
seems negative, beginning with admonitions about what not to do, it is
with the hope that, through this *via negativa,* some light will be shed on
the path to follow. I begin by singling out one item that is largely, but not
completely, outside the control of educators; unless this item is taken
seriously, all of the rest will unequivocally fail. After that, all of the

considerations fall within the scope of what people usually think of as pedagogy.

ELIMINATE GUNS FROM AMERICAN SOCIETY

Why single out guns from the multitude of social pathologies that beset contemporary American culture? Surely, media violence, drugs, alcoholism, domestic violence, and the present Republican-led economic abandonment of inner cities rank high in their consolidated impact on the construction of aggressive behavior and violence in schools. And, one could object, every newspaper reader is aware that boxcutters, not guns, are the current weapons of choice for students trying to smuggle weapons through metal detectors. It is precisely because the National Rifle Association would no doubt use this kind of argument that it is so pernicious. The lethal nature of the gun is, in fact, the hidden signifier creating the climate of fear that causes the school to install more metal detectors and the students to carry other weapons. Mere "bullying behavior," which we have had with us as an identifiable school trait since at least the mid-nineteenth century and which European schools still see as their chief discipline problem, has escalated immeasurably since the advent and proliferation of handguns in the inner city. Working with students who are known to have committed murders, or who sprayed bullets all over the front steps of a school, or who have been involved in illegally transporting Berettas and 9 mm Glocks from northern Virginia to Brooklyn—all situations we have had to deal with in the last few years—immediately begets an incomparable idiom of fear within the school culture in ways that other forms of violence do not. Guns equate to violence on an exponential basis; our society has no more need of them than we do of cigarettes. Not only is there no need for guns, but, as Garry Wills has recently shown, the "right to bear arms" has been totally misinterpreted by the gun lobby and its lawyers and law professors (Wills 1995). As indicated earlier, school boards and unions should not use the lack of gun control as an excuse for failing to do everything they can within the school structure to eliminate violence. But, in reality, they are fighting a losing battle as long as the Senate and the House remain puppets of the gun lobby. Schools, parent associations, and sensible Americans everywhere need to organize to counteract the NRA and to work for the total elimination of guns from American society.

Stop Relying on Technology and Law Enforcement as the Prime Tools for Achieving School Discipline

The cardinal premise of the Travis report is that schools should begin to learn how to manage themselves by imitating the methods of the more sophisticated police departments around the country. The current reliance on metal detectors and guards is taken for granted and is never questioned, even implicitly. The teaching profession has become entirely excluded from the serious business of keeping order in schools, presumably a brawny job to be handled by professional police and guards trained in police tactics. School discipline, it seems, is too important an issue to be left to mere teachers. The "safety staff" (i.e., guards) is there, with its technological gadgetry, to ensure order so teachers can get on with the purely cognitive business of teaching. Throughout, the report suggests that if principals were not so benighted they would turn to law enforcement agencies with their sophisticated knowledge of police procedures in order to produce safer schools: "The Panel examined the current approach to school safety within the Board of Education using the lessons learned in the fundamental re-examination now underway in the policing profession" (5).

The "policing profession" is thus being held up as *the* exemplary model for educators in their attempts to achieve order in schools. According to the panel, the "rethinking" of school safety should parallel the "rethinking" currently taking place in more enlightened segments of the police world: "We recommend that in many respects, large and small, the Division [of School Safety of the Board of Education] should look for guidance to the practices of other law enforcement and public safety organizations, and then tailor those practices and policies to the unique environment of the school" (xvi).

The panel manifests no awareness that there might be some unforeseen consequences or by-products of this general philosophy or that it is, in reality, not a "renewal" at all but a mere continuation of the present philosophy. The guards in each school are encouraged to learn from "their colleagues in other policing circles" who—so it is claimed—are gradually reducing their reliance on traditional police methods in favor of more collaborative processes.[5] The ethnography of the corridors has demonstrated for us just how successful this approach has been.

Don't Rely on Committees and Planning Processes

The centerpiece of the panel's recommendations consists of an elaborate and inclusive planning process that would have to sound perfectly reasonable to an outsider not familiar with the system and its hierarchized strata:

> The Panel endorses the idea of a school safety plan, coordinated by the principal and drawing upon a variety of resources within the school. This approach . . . is also consistent with the Chancellor's philosophy of school-based management and shared decision-making. But to bring this concept of the safety plan to life, the planning effort must extend beyond the walls of the school to bring additional resources to bear. The Panel envisions a planning process which occurs around a large table, large enough to include students, teachers, parents, guidance counselors, probation officers, police personnel, local business leaders, youth service providers, and clergy. At the head of the table sits the principal who, both under the regulations and in the life of the school, assumes a coordinating role. (38)

Once the foundations of technology and a basic police presence have been established, the trappings of democracy can be paraded out, replete with a puppet figure: the principal. But the purpose of the report is to shift the relations of power away from the field of education (embodied in the figure of the principal) and toward the field of law enforcement (embodied in the techno-security officer). The principal—now dubbed a coordinator—will, conveniently, still be there to be blamed if things go wrong, as they surely will. The placid tone struck by such committee-drafted reports exhibits no recognition that frazzled high school principals actually have little power now, that they have been placed in impossible managerial situations, that they are already holding regular meetings with a broad-based array of community resources. But no one is asking why discipline-through-committee-meetings is not working.

All the principals I know consider the system's "school-based management, shared decision-making" initiative to be pure public relations "hype" that the media swallowed hook, line, and sinker.[6] The approach itself was based on the highly debatable assumption that principals hold an excess of power that should be devolved to the staff level. In fact, lower-tier principals find themselves with no direct power over custodians, guards, cafeteria workers, or even teachers (the latter are protected by a twenty-five-year history of union-board agreements). The "big lie" surrounding many supposedly liberalizing policies in education is that the principalship is a dictatorial, omnipotent office whose power needs to be shared. In fact, many incumbents find themselves in extremely weak managerial positions. This fragility also helps to explain why these principals are often required to overcompensate for this organizational flaw by compromising, cajoling, or even, at times, using highly domineering tactics.

The system, qua system, does not trust the position of principal:[7] the Travis report places the principal at the head of the table playing this "coordinating role"—another way of saying that she is not to play a managing role. The "large" table meetings visualized by the panel are, as noted, already taking place and are generally worthless mechanisms for achieving a safer school ambience. I participate in several such "safety" councils, which unfold as little more than "show and tell" sessions in which members of board-funded community-based organizations commend themselves on the efforts they are making to reduce violence; one or two parents recount the latest horror stories; the police, mostly silent, complain about how students, when confronted, defy them; and the local clergy reveal their intentions either to infiltrate the school or to close it down altogether. If there are any teachers present—and often there are none—they sit passively by, listening to the litany of criticisms. Occasionally, an upstanding teacher will express the fond hope that we all make it through to the end of the term without a major incident. The guards, too, are often present, also mostly silent, and aware that they report to a different authority. When the meeting breaks up, the beleaguered principal is left facing the harsh realities: how to find the culprit who set off a large firecracker outside during the safety meeting itself, what to do about the chief security guard who is on cocaine. Police and guards return to their posts, charged with "handling" the discipline problems such as putting out the toilet-paper fire in the one boys' bathroom that remains open.

I recognize that criticizing collaborative and participatory approaches is tantamount to opposing democracy. But, with due apologies to John Dewey and Paulo Freire, high schools, which are essentially spaces of interaction between adult teachers and adolescent learners, cannot be models of pure democracy. The main actors who need to sit down, take ownership of their school, and agree on the basic cognitive and behavioral standards and on the parameters of acceptable etiquette are the teachers and the principal.

These conversations need to happen early, before the school year begins, before guards, police, clergy, parents, students, politicians, academicians, and local agency heads are invited. The dirty secret of the New York City schools is that principals and teachers, teachers and guards, are not talking to one another, at least not in any cohesive way, about the details of school discipline. That the traditional teacher-principal dyadic relationship has fallen apart is part of the story of the previous pages. The very large table envisioned by the Travis panel capitulates to this basic weakness: in desperation, the plan grasps at straws, suggests talking to anyone and everyone about "security", but does not really expect the principal to sit with teachers and guards and agree jointly to formulate a uniform code of school etiquette and expectations that are realistically enforceable. Of course, the path I am recommending here is quite unrealistic—and cannot actually happen—in the setting of the mega-schools. That is why it must be combined with what follows.

STOP CONCEPTUALIZING VIOLENCE AS ADHERING IN THE "OTHER"

The authors of *Rethinking School Safety* do not seem to be able to imagine a school devoid of security guards and metal detectors. Their central thrust, on the contrary, is an insistence on the need to upgrade significantly the role of the guards, the supervision of the guards, and the whole Division of School Safety. Thus, policy meetings at a citywide level become long wrangles over what the supervisor-to-guard ratio actually is and what it should be (1:180 or 1:80 or 1:12?). In a typical euphemism, the authors write that the rapid growth of the Division of School Safety (from 200 guards in 1969 to over 3200 in 1994) "reflects the changing nature and escalating level of crime *in our City* over the past two decades" (xv, italics mine). Crime is conceptualized as a culture of violence originating outside school buildings and somehow creeping in. The function of the guards and technology is to arrest "the Other" at the front door, before it enters.

That violence is a trait inhering in us, in the board's history and structure, in the often discourteous scripts that teachers and school staff act out every day and not in some plague invading the school's immune system is not a consideration within the panel's purview. Violence is deemed to reside in the Other, not in the self or the self's practices. No reexamination of the role of the teacher or of teacher styles is called for here: teachers are barely mentioned in this report—they appear as silent actors in a talkies film, as bit players on the school safety scene. When referred to at all, they are conceptualized in ways that would never ruffle the feathers of union leaders. They are spoken of as potential victims of violence who should not fear for their own personal security, as harried instructors who, "standing alone in a classroom . . . should not come to the distressing conclusion that they are more disciplinarians than educators" (Travis, Lynch, and Schall 1993, 3).

Following this philosophy, the report parrots the teachers union attitudes I referred to earlier. Even when teachers are timidly given some disciplinary function or other, it is always with the disclaimer, "We are not suggesting that teachers become security guards." It is to the guards that one looks for maintaining the brunt of school discipline. "Discipline" thus becomes a bad word when applied to teachers, a good word when applied to the security guards. Teachers are mentioned as one voice among many at the roundtable meetings, never as an authoritative voice in the production of a safe school. The report never contemplates the teacher as a mature person having expectations for social or cognitive behavior, as a responsible adult conscious of the need to set an example of courtesy, as a team member accountable for helping to foster the identity of the institution, or as a moral instructor concerned with providing leadership and helping to construct a communal code of values.

The most basic ideas of courtesy—that students might learn to express gratitude by hearing teachers say "Thank you" to them and to one another, for example—are never alluded to. These small issues of courtesy are not seen as connected to safety or security, because the main focus is always on the issues of weapons interdiction, arson prevention, and the like. The small issues take time, care, and a concern for the individual character of each student; large issues focus on the larger group and the precautions needed to protect it. As the principal quoted in chapter 3 said, "they're watching the lights [on the ID card machines] and not the faces."

To be sure, some teachers are to be providers of the conflict-resolution courses. The point is not just that board policies fail to conceive of the teacher as an adult *in loco parentis;* they also refuse to see the self of the educator or the educational establishment as a potentially violent entity. Teachers are seen essentially as neutral agents in moral and behavioral matters, and that is the way students see them, too.

As a result of the contradictory signals society has been sending them, teachers are left in a state of confusion as to the role they are expected to play. I have heard a special education teacher, close to tears, pose her dilemma to union officials at a public meeting: was she supposed to physically intervene and break up fights, and thereby risk bodily injury, or not intervene, and be accused of shirking her duty? If she chose not to intervene, a small riot might ensue; if she did intervene, she might risk a lawsuit for putting her hands on the body of a student.[8] All the union officials could offer her were warnings about the dangers of physical intervention ("You will not get insurance coverage if you are injured!") and recommendations for more conflict-resolution training.

CREATE SMALLER SCHOOLS BUT NOT AT THE EXPENSE OF LARGER ONES

It has now become conventional wisdom that the creation of smaller high schools is the single most important element in the synthesis of the chemistry of reform. Up to ten years ago, only a small group of researchers were arguing that smaller schools would be safer and more productive learning centers than the larger ones and more cost effective in the long run. Today, this doctrine has been widely embraced in most proposals for restructuring schools—embraced in an all too unquestioned, uncritical way. In educational circles, "smaller schools" has become part of the litany of 1990s buzzwords: "Research shows that schools with strong principals; schools that are not too large; schools where discipline is fair, but firm; schools where teachers are imbued with high expectations for every child; schools where parents are drawn into the educational orbit, are schools where learning takes place" (Prothrow-Stith and Weissman 1991, 168). The Travis report accepts this smaller-is-better doctrine: "While not strictly falling within the Panel's purview, we noted two policy initiatives now underway within the Board of Education that hold long-term promise for providing safer schools. First, the Chancellor's stated policy of developing smaller schools, or breaking up large schools into "houses" within the school, could well result in safer institutions" (34).

The crucial consideration that no one at the central board seems willing to discuss is that the city's recent policy of developing smaller schools does not take into account the impact of small-school creation on the lower-tier schools. "Every time you create a Vision School, you further damage a lower-tier school," I have been told over and over again by the principals and assistant principals in the "schools" in which we work. The fundamental flaw in the effective-schools movement, now heavily funded with foundation money, is that it has defined its mission in terms of the individual school. What the movement fails to grasp is that the task of creating, reforming, or restructuring a single school—though obviously a highly demanding task—is a comparatively easy trick to master. The real challenge that faces large urban systems is not the creation of an individual small school, or even a plurality of such entities, but beginning to restructure the entire system. This can only happen by destroying the factory-sized "schools" of last resort at the bottom of the pyramid and, from their ashes, creating brand new smaller schools to absorb all of the original population. Most small-school creation in New York occurs only because the creators have extraordinary political clout, and when it does happen it drains the surrounding bigger schools of their best students. To be effective, small schools must be created throughout the system, not piecemeal, not school by school.

If the lower-tier principals look on board press releases about the creation of fifty small schools with a jaundiced eye, their response should not be judged cynically as resistance to change but as a realistic appraisal of the citywide situation. The creation of a small school usually begins with the careful organization of a single grade with a manageable number of students (about sixty). The following year, those students move into tenth grade, and a new group of sixty is admitted into ninth grade; in four years, a total school population of 240 is achieved. With careful student and teacher selection, it is easy to see why such schools are quickly declared models and why educators, parents, the general public, and researchers are so attracted to them. The inevitable effect of such a move has been to draw the more able students away from the lower-tier schools with populations ranging from 2000 to 5000 students and to ship the "least desirable" students to them.

Whatever may have been the case regarding the conduct of these factory schools with their European populations at the earlier part of this century, they have all become the schools of last resort today and therefore impossible institutions to manage. Thus, principals of these big schools, with good reason, look on all small, model, Vision, magnet, ed op, charter, and effective school ventures as just more skimming and political placating, especially since many of these efforts, announced with great fanfare, never get off the ground as planned or have no serious educational program at all.

In New York City today, there are fifty-nine very large high schools (out of a total of 197 high schools throughout the city, counting the new smaller ones) that are considered dangerous enough to have eighteen to twenty security guards and extra guards who screen students every day for weapons with metal detectors. These are the huge "schools" thought of as belonging to the lower tier. Reform must begin with the total destruction of these "schools"—not with single small-school experiments that will be proclaimed success stories worthy of dissemination elsewhere.

The key issue, then, is not whether to create smaller schools but how to create them. It is clear that smaller schools are the only way to address the major reform issues. The pivotal issue the board must face if it wishes to address the issue of violence is whether to continue to form small schools one at a time and independent of the rest of the system, totally ignoring the presence of the larger nearby schools, or to begin to destroy the lower-tier system by closing down the larger schools one by one and reopening them as multiple smaller units. This latter course of action may seem like radical surgery, but unless New York City's lower-tier mega-schools of 2000–5000 students are completely destroyed, the culture of violence will persist.

What kinds of resources would such a policy entail? To break all of these overcrowded institutions down into smaller schools of 200–600 students would mean an expenditure of funds larger than any present-day politician would deem remotely reasonable or even imaginable. At a time when educational resources are being slashed at every level, this proposal sounds like a far-fetched ideal, but unless the system moves in that direction, the present situation will not change. Why am I so convinced that smaller schools can work?

In the alternative schools of about 250 students each, students sense a profound change in the quality of the adult-student relationships. One principal whose alternative school was located in a blighted neighborhood, only a few blocks away from Alpha School, explained: "Each student has a first name here; teachers have a first name. Everybody knows everybody else; there is no anonymity." This principal's own seriousness of purpose and her professional demeanor combined with the small school size to produce a staff willing to offer individual tutoring for students. The student in such a school realizes, "Here, I have all I need to succeed. Here I am being treated as an individual."

Once a school has done all this, it has the right to exact demands of its students. Once it has gone the extra mile to provide the student with all he or she needs, it has the credibility to say to the student: "This is an academic setting dedicated to success; we ask you to pay for this. Now here is our price of admission." If two students begin fighting, they both know they will automatically be asked to leave. The school communicates to the individual student a crucial message: "It is not our job to worry about you; it is your job to worry about yourself." The school demands scholarship and attendance. Even students with histories of failure rise to the occasion. None of this would happen without the total small-school environment: a policy that does not specialize in taking the "best" or the "worst" students but is willing to accept all comers; a school that is operated by the staff under the leadership of an energetic principal; a staff that is caring; a staff that does not abhor structure and disciplinary enforcement. But the "creaming effect" of the recent wave of small-school creation is not there.

One alternative school in which we work with a school population of 180 had four students killed by gunfire during one summer alone. In the same school sixteen girls (out of a total of ninety-five) returned pregnant after the summer break. These schools often break the student population into small teacher-led "family groups" of ten or twelve students each in which personal issues as well as academic ones are discussed openly. At the same time, these schools, as opposed to the mega-schools, have at least a fighting chance to set clear standards and to communicate basic expectations to students. In short, they are excellent models for what the overpopulated lower-tier schools could become if they were shut down and then reopened on this "alternative" model. Conceptualized in the early 1970s as havens for dropouts from the "regular" schools, they have now become havens of safety and therefore more desirable than the schools for which they were originally designed as alternatives. Yet no one is looking at them as systemwide models for the deconstruction and reconstruction of the larger schools. In a reformed system, the security guards could be almost eliminated, except, as in the alternative schools, for a single guard stationed at the front door.

SET COMMUNAL PARAMETERS

Tutoring rooms, I recognize, are not the same as small schools. Nevertheless, we have learned, often the hard way, some lessons that might benefit any small learning environment. We hold weekly meetings in our tutoring rooms in which all of the tutors and mentors close the doors, throw the students out, and talk frankly among themselves, about how they feel the program is going, about what people find to be irritating with one another's styles, about how to maintain order. (Why didn't you say anything yesterday to that new boy who came in playing his Walkman and threatened Eve when she asked him to take it off? How come you were late today? I had to take over and tutor your students for you! What should we do about the girl who refuses to work with a male tutor? How should we handle Z, the girl who lives alone with her religious grandmother, who believes Z is possessed of the devil and who hits her in the stomach with a broomstick because she believes she is pregnant?) In order for teaching and learning to take place in a room of nine graduate student tutors, each of whom is working with one to five students at any given period, agreement has to be reached on what the ground rules will be: no "dissing" of tutors or peers; respect for the space and rights of others; no physical abuse or acting out; consideration for one another's "styles"; no weapons; consistent expectations about attendance, minor rules, and completing assignments. These rules are always a work in progress and need to be restated in one form or another week by week. Beyond the rules, however, is a philosophy of interaction with students. To be successful, tutors have to take a proactive stance and find ways to seek students out; they cannot sit in the tutoring room like office-bound psychiatrists and expect students to come to them. They cannot fear adolescents. They have to approach them, be present for them, be available to talk with them—about anything—in the corridors and cafeterias. They have to "hang" with them after school, go to their basketball games, go to their parties and dances, eat with them. They have to take them on trips to artistic and cultural sites—always in small, manageable groups. They have to set up small discussion groups on sensitive topics (parenting, violence) even at the risk of having this strategy backfire at times. Finally, they must confront them when their discourse or behavior is outrageous—but without taking one's own behavior too sanctimoniously.

Once adults have made themselves available and made themselves vulnerable to youth, mutual interests can suffuse the teacher-student relationship. Puberty rites can begin. The adolescent, now beginning to feel comfortable with the teacher, even in the presence of the adolescent peer group, begins authentic dialogue on issues of common interest. Along the way, she catches the twinkle in the teachers's eye and begins to realize that the teacher's structure ("discipline") is just another game—but perhaps a game it would benefit her to play. Discipline becomes demythologized for the student and he sees it for what it is: a scaffolding for friendship, a means for constructing communitas. What is more, the adult, by refusing to show fear, by interrupting the adolescent performance, opens up an indefinite continuum of vulnerability to her own selfhood. What if the adult is wrong in challenging or in interrupting what he believed to be an inappropriate youth performance? The adult might even find himself being corrected, being challenged by the youth, and, lo and behold, the youth might be right! This also happens, of course, on academic matters, but in morality, the adult's conduct is supposed to be always appropriate. The upshot is that the adult might even have the opportunity to admit to the youth that she was wrong—and not just on an academic issue. Communications get mended, and a learning experience has occurred. Discipline, then, not for discipline's sake, but for mutuality, for inclusiveness, for community.

There are other dangers, more intrinsic ones: the tutor or teacher who does not know how to handle these opportunities for closer, more personal relationships with youth, who gets "caught in the transference" of feelings, as psychiatrists are wont to say, who relies on the more intimate relationship as a way of obtaining her or his own personal gratification. Even one major scandal can engender such negative publicity that a program's—or a school's—reputation is destroyed forever. The dangers, therefore, are great, and supervision is needed. But the danger of not involving ourselves again in the rituals of youth initiation, of not creating a new panopticon of a different order, and of not remythologizing the educational theory that undergirds these daily practices is far greater; to abstain from the puberty rites is to remain in the present downward spiral of violence currently engulfing our schools. We do not have to perform the initiation rites perfectly, but we do have to start performing them again.

RECONCEPTUALIZE TEACHING AS A VOCATION,
NOT AS A PROFESSION

Even if we could wave a magic wand and transform all of the mega-schools into homier, more secure, "alternative" settings of a few hundred students each, the central issue of the redefinition of the concept of "teacher" still remains. I have been contesting throughout that the classical holistic concept of teacher is fast becoming lost to memory; if this is so, how would we unnostalgically redefine it for our imagined smaller schools of the future? How are we to reformulate the persona of the teacher after decades of accent on the cognitive and intellectual side of the role, a concomitant retreat from the body, and the almost complete abdication of engagement in the rituals of adolescent initiation, which always entail strong emotional and moral dimensions? How can we remythologize teaching for these smaller, more personalized settings in such a way that they would begin to look very much more like some of the small-scale tutoring-room vignettes described above rather than like some of the sadder, violence-infused, large-school narratives? How can we create learning venues where students can describe to a teacher how painful it is to live in an alcoholic home and not feel embarrassed about asking questions about the Pythagorean theorem?

I begin with the assumption—one based on our experiences in the alternative schools—that teachers, once in the smaller settings, and with the minimally decent working conditions they do not have in the larger schools, would be receptive to the notion that they are something more than mere conveyors of mathematical, scientific, or literary information. My remythologized teacher, therefore—let's say a math teacher—is a creature/creator who, in her or his everyday work within the confines of a small-school setting: (1) is attuned to all of the rethinking going on in the field of mathematics education, including linkages to language arts, literacy acquisition, and the like;[9] (2) discloses—through mathematics itself—the inequities of the current social and political order;[10] at the same time (3) makes demands on students for schoolwide—as opposed to mere classroom-wide—behavior; and in so doing (4) helps to create a learning environment that will give all students an opportunity for dialogue about the realities of their youthful lives and about their plans for the future. If these roles are played out in a context in which fellow teachers, from the first day, are acting in concert, and in which all teachers are provided with the time for study as well as with resources for consultation on sensitive issues, the result is a total school communitas of mutual respect, support, and learning.

Many teachers are trying to play this role at the present time. The problem is that, given all the negative working conditions, they cannot be expected to play it well enough. In these huge settings, the name of the game becomes not a sincere desire to do everything you can to motivate students to come to school but to do just enough to convince the superintendent that you have taken all the reasonable actions anyone could be expected to take to make that happen. "Going through the motions," rather than "going the extra mile" becomes the order of the day. A reconceptualized teacher role will demand a kind of support from supervisors that teachers are not now getting. Encouragement, concern, caring, and love will have to replace the attitudes many teachers now face: suspicion, lack of support, lackadaisical efforts, and sometimes harsh criticism.

These prescriptions are not given as a kind of school-management manual. There are actually many of these, some quite excellent, on the market (e.g., Jones 1987; Mendler 1992); but, like much of the "school reform" literature, they are written for schools, not for "schools," which need to be led away from the culture of violence and reinvigorated. The path is full of underbrush, and the final shapes of these reinvigorated schools are still uncertain, but their contours may be imagined by contrasting large and small settings, small tutoring room and mega-school:

> [Female tutor]: L came down [to the tutoring room]. When L used to come down he'd always leave his cap on—which tended to give the impression of the non-entity—the being that faded into the woodwork—now when he comes down he regularly takes his hat off—he seems more alive. I've definitely fed positive reinforcement when in the past he'd taken the hat off. But he's a face now; there's a personality now in his body language. We chatted for some time—and he initiated the idea of wanting to do work: "And what shall we work on today?" He said he was doing well in his computer math class but that he was having difficulty in his regular math class. By the time we finished chatting it was time to go and we set math as the priority on tomorrow's agenda.

> [Fieldnotes; faculty meeting at a large school]: Everyone agrees that the first floor bathroom is a wreck. So many things are happening

in there (setting fire to toilet paper, smoking, doing drugs, threatening other students who enter, hanging out during classes, breaking mirrors) that we have a fire hazard. Some advocate closing the bathroom. As of now, one guard has been assigned full-time outside the bathroom. The guards and deans complain that they can't be in every part of the building at the same time. Others say we need more security guards. But central headquarters will not let us use the two or three guards who are sitting down at the front door after the morning scanning sessions. The principal: "We are crying for help . . . exits 4 and 10 are now de-magnetized—that means kids come in and let friends in and who knows what. We need more of the volunteer patrols with the buttons." Someone suggests that we should adopt the practice of doing what one vocational school does—locking the bathroom doors after the break between classes. You can only go to the bathroom during the breaks between class. "Now we keep asking kids in the corridors during classes: Do you have a pass? it's hectic." Then, from out of nowhere: "We need to address the poor scholarship in grades 9 and 10; three-quarters of the kids in the building are failing. They are terrifying us with their firecrackers, fire extinguishers thrown out the windows, false alarms, etc." The guards can't figure out why these kids are destroying their own bathrooms. One was actually questioning why the kids need bathrooms. Horror stories about the student who defecated in the sink and about who had to clean it up. Who will monitor the bathroom when the guard goes to lunch? etc. etc.

[Site visit to small, alternative school]: An hour later I visit the small alternative school just down the block from Alpha School. While I am standing talking to the principal in the corridor, a group of five boys noisily exits from the boys' bathroom, laughing and joking. Their behavior could not be described as disruptive but nevertheless if it were a few decibels higher, it might disrupt a nearby class. L, the woman principal, looks directly at all five culprits, raises an eyebrow and says, "Are we going to have to institute a system of one-at-a-time in the men's room?" They all look down sheepishly. She does not let them off the hook; she expects an answer. Finally, each one mumbles "No," or "I'm sorry." They troop off, smiling at one another and at her. I don't at all feel that L's performance was for my benefit.

[Male tutor's log, large school]: During 5th period, as I went looking for a student, I overheard a confrontation between two security guards and a couple of students. The students (boys) were taunting the guards, yelling abuses at them, "dumb mother fuckers." The guards were basically helpless and kept telling them to get to class. The students wouldn't go. They kept yelling, "C'mon, mother fuckers" and finally the students left (more of their own free will). The guards, I think, felt a little helpless and I felt this for them as well.

[Male tutor's log, same school]: I crossed the street to shortcut to the [school] entrance. Just then I spotted A. Now I have been working with A almost all year. Somehow he took a shining to me at the beginning of the year and we have hit it off ever since. He is one of the program's biggest nuisances and successes at the same time. Often he comes merely to use me as a pass to class or to get out of class altogether. I generally give him what he is after which is mostly attention and secondly a pass to class. And since I have trusted him, he has returned my trust. The other week I brought him [to the university] for the Saturday class. I gave him some money for lunch and a token home. The following week he wanted to share his lunch with me and buy me a donut at the bake sale. So I know he has somewhere a deep sense of reciprocity and fairness. To most everyone else in the school that knows A he has neither. To most he is a troublemaker and a pain. So anyway, I see A on the corner, but not before he saw me. He had already started toward me with a smile on his face when I acknowledged him.

"What's up, A? How are you doing?"

At this his look changed and his cool face took over his overexposed happiness. I'm sure he couldn't be "uncool" in front of this group. He was watching the rappers [on a streetcorner outside the school] also . . . this was where the action was and that is always where you can find A.

"Yo David man . . . I'm not comin' to school today."

"You're not? Why not?"

"Yo man. . . . I'm just not comin'. I don't want to."

"But man, what are you gonna do? Hang out here all day? You gotta come down and talk to me. Otherwise I'll be bored. You want me to be bored all day?"

"No, man. . . . I donno. I just don't want to come."

He looked over his shoulder in the direction of the rappers who were still consumed in the hypnotic sounds which filled the neighborhood. We were talking over it. A was moving around alot. As I acknowledged his decision and began toward the entrance, he called:

"Maybe I'll come in and see you later."

At this I nodded and continued across the street and into the school. I could still hear the loud pounding outside. Even in my 3rd period class on the fourth floor I could hear the bass and feel the music.

Transform the Role of the School Safety Officer

I recognize, of course, that in any realistic scenario for the future, the school safety officers will not disappear. I have dared to imagine a series of smaller, more intimate, schools that would have, perhaps, only one guard at the front door to screen visitors. But I am also pragmatic enough to understand that my utopian hopes for large-scale creation of such schools will not happen soon, given the federal, state, and local budget policies of the 1990s. Nor is it realistic to imagine that the security forces will not continue to expand, in New York and throughout the country. But that does not mean that we have to persevere in our single-minded thinking about the nature of their role, as mini-police. If American secondary teachers wish to continue to emphasize the cognitive aspect of their roles, they could, at least, work out more imaginative ways to address what William Damon has so aptly called the changed "moral atmosphere of the school" (1995, 198). In a word, the permissiveness that has pervaded American home life and school life has now gotten out of hand, and we have called in the police and security guards to restore order. If the guards are indeed relating to students in unorthodox ways that were never foreseen in the first place—forming emotional attachments with them—perhaps this phenomenon needs to be recognized and discussed openly instead of simply forbidding "fraternization" with students, as is now the case.

As the teacher quoted in chapter 3 said, the guards are "like camp counselors" for the students. They are, however, camp counselors without any preparation for the job. Perhaps the guards' career-development needs should be reexamined, and not just by faculties of law enforcement and criminology. The disciplines of psychology, psychiatry, social work, education, sociology, and anthropology need to be tapped. Perhaps the guards' training—a mere two-week period after high school—should not be placed uniquely, as is currently the case, in the hands of the police, lawyers, and law enforcement personnel. Perhaps the guards' training should be completely rethought, giving them the opportunity to attend college and graduate schools. Perhaps the disciplinary systems of other countries should be examined through international education studies. France and Belgium, for example, have a "surveillant" system whereby university students act as disciplinary aids to teachers and perform other duties as well. Instead of continuing on our present course of identifying guards more and more as auxiliaries to police (giving them peace officer status, placing them under the supervision of the police department, allowing more and more police into the schools), why, even if we retain the guards in large numbers, can we not nudge the whole system in another direction? Why cannot their role be rethought as "corridor mentors"? At a very minimum, why cannot a school's teachers and guards begin to meet with one another to ensure that they are together in their approach to students?

CREATE A NEW PANOPTICON

How does what I have been advocating differ from a return to the sheer classical panopticism that Foucault so feared and perceived to be at the origins of bourgeois modernity? If I am correct in assessing the inner-city lower-tier secondary school as the embodiment of an ideology of antipanopticism, a lack of caring enough to enforce the "microphysics of power" and the minutiae of etiquette, is it even thinkable that what is needed is a return to the disciplinary days of old in order to cure the violence? Clearly not. As I have indicated throughout, the game has now become far more complex. What can it mean to teach virtue inside a culture of violence when the outcomes stand a good chance of becoming totally counterproductive? Why take the weapon away from the student when she or he may need it to get home safely? How, then, are we to remythologize the future of inner-city schooling on a small-scale basis?

The essence of the old panopticism was meticulous surveillance, a concentration on the details of "gentlemanly" etiquette, together with all the myths of patriarchy and domination that implies. In Foucault's reading of it, its purpose was the exercise of a power aimed at domination and coercion. But in the present climate the irony lies in the fact that, although there is much surface panopticism, at the level of lived experience there is a complete lack of concentration on detail, on the niceties of etiquette, values, manners, discipline, and morality. The mentality behind the technology of metal detectors is profoundly opposed to minute surveillance. "Just turn on the archway metal detectors and keep the weapons from coming through the front door," it seems to be saying. This ideology of distrust has flooded the daily life of these "schools" with violence and is antithetical to the original humanistic enterprise of character building and community formation.

But there are also legitimate exercises of power, ways of using power for emancipatory ends, for creating a unified communitas with a harmony of rules based on a respect for diversity. One of the many ways we deprive youth in inner-city schools is to deny them the same kind of caring, attentive, and consistent enforcement of expectations and of rules that was associated with elite schooling simply because those disciplinary forms of caring were originally tied to a patriarchal, hegemonic ideology. What I have been suggesting here is that it should be possible, by looking into ourselves and by getting in touch with the common humanity that unites us with our students, to create a new, more humane, caring panopticon—to distinguish this insistence on high behavioral standards and on the rights of the Other, which students strongly expect of us, from any nexus to domination, economic injustice, and oppression. The demythologized egalitarian image of discipline that thus emerges is not that of the dyadic "role model" of the young aristocratic boy learning how to emulate the older male aristocrat, being introduced to the devious ways of patriarchy, but that of a community of ethnically and sexually diverse young—or older—adults making themselves available to an equally heterogeneous group of youth, with the aim of equipping them with the intellectual, social, and ethical competencies they will need in order to cope with and to transform the societal structures in which they will have to live.

NOTICE

ALL PERSONS ENTERING THIS BUILDING
ARE REQUIRED TO SUBMIT TO A METAL
DETECTOR SCAN AND A PERSONAL SEARCH
IF NECESSARY, TO ENSURE THAT WEAPONS
ARE NOT BROUGHT INTO THIS BUILDING.
BAGS AND PARCELS ALSO MAY BE SEARCHED
BY MEANS OF METAL DETECTING DEVICES,
BY HAND OR OTHERWISE.

ON SOME OCCASIONS, ALL PERSONS
ENTERING THE BUILDING WILL BE SCANNED.
ON OTHER OCCASIONS, ONLY A PORTION
OF PERSONS ENTERING THE BUILDING
WILL BE SCANNED ON A RANDOM BASIS.

REFUSAL TO COOPERATE WITH
THE SEARCH WILL RESULT IN THE
DENIAL OF ENTRY
OR DISCIPLINARY ACTION.

A JESUITICAL FANTASY

The Jesuits were justly renowned for efficiency, the maintenance of high scholastic standards . . . and improved discipline.
  —Aldo Scaglione, *The Liberal Arts and the Jesuit College System*

A TRIVIAL INCIDENT

Hurrying down to our tutoring room in the basement of one of New
York City's neighborhood high schools, I was in the process of opening the
stairwell door, just down the hall from the principal's office, when suddenly
three female students burst through the door from the opposite direction,
pushing me aside, while they ploughed on, seemingly unaware that any code
of etiquette had been broken. My anger surged. After all, hadn't my adult
male body, clad in suit and tie, gotten to the doorway first? "Doesn't any-
body teach manners in these schools anymore?" was my first thought. Then
came a moment of remorse: why should such a trifling event, singled out
from all the other incidents—transgressive and nontransgressive—happening in the bustle of a crowded high school corridor be worthy of even a
passing mention? Didn't this sort of thing happen every day back at the
university? What role was racism or patriarchy playing here? Here I was,
after all, a white male of European extraction wandering around a school
with a student population that was 75 percent Hispanic and 25 percent
black.

I mention this one incident from my ten years of experiences in New
York City high schools not only because my momentary irritation marked
a clear cultural boundary or simply in order to depict a facet of my own
troubled subjectivity as a researcher but also because, beyond my personal
annoyance, this stairwell platform became for me a kind of stage, representative of many other student performances that educational ethnographers
such as Willis (1977) might interpret as "oppositional culture" at work,
resistance to a regime of power. Or Foucault (1973) might have seen my

angry reaction as a clear manifestation of the "power" that generates and infiltrates all social relations. At the very least, here was I, the ethnographer, inattentive to the way in which I was projecting my own cultural practices onto the "other" (Rabinow 1986). Perhaps the whole project of "proper manners" (with all the bourgeois overtones that phrase carries) needed to be called into question. What pedagogical lessons were to be drawn from this clash of styles? Much more basically, what position was one to take regarding the larger issue of how moral values, rules of politeness, and appropriate behavior are to be consciously communicated in schools?[1] What position was even feasible in an inner-city school at the present time? In short, what room was there in urban education today for a "disciplinary regime" intent on reclaiming some re-demythologized forms of what used to be called "manners" or even "character development"?

THE DISCIPLINARY "GAZE"

The fantasy would not leave me—a fantasy or memory of what the response to such a breach of etiquette in a public space might have been in my own high school days. Of course, the presence of girls at a Jesuit prep school would have been unthinkable in the 1940s. In any case, the likelihood of such an occurrence would have been greatly reduced by the ubiquity of the principal, Father John "Black Jack" Lenny, whose presence, it seemed, was in every corridor simultaneously. I think of him now as a kind of incarnation of Jeremy Bentham's tall and imposing panoptic tower, a Foucauldian bad dream. His black leather—and polished—shoes were always planted solidly in the corridor as if rooted there. The school hallways were, for him, not mere passages to somewhere else, sites of transition from classroom to classroom; they were a place of sojourn, a public space to be enjoyed.

In a word, he gave you the impression that he owned the place, which, in a sense, he did. Touching the top of his shoes was the hem of his black wool cassock, the next item you saw if you dared allow your eyes to survey his frame from bottom to top. Most students just kept their eyes riveted to the ground as they hugged the side of the corridor on their way back from Thursday morning confessions in the Gesu Church, because his steady glare filled the whole corridor. Few engaged in a staring match with him, and those who did had to be prepared for the inevitable invitation to come over for a chat, which might or might not be a friendly one. As in the original panopticon, you never knew whether you were being inspected because

Father Lenny's scrutiny was theoretically perpetual and yours was turned inward. You were always off balance in his corridor; he never was.

Just below the waist, his thumbs were securely tucked into his tight cincture; further up, his jaw protruded, challenging all comers. His body projected a series of mixed messages, which students could not fail to pick up as they passed in review: "I belong here; I'm not sure why we ever let you into this place and I'm less sure that I will ever let you graduate but, on the whole, there is something about you I like." His eyes were capable of smiling, but usually they just stared directly at yours, singling you out from the 850 other "preppers," letting you know that he knew exactly what crimes you were contemplating and that you had better not try them. If his booming voice did summon you over for a few minutes, all of your classmates wanted to know what had transpired as soon as you returned to your homeroom.

But my fantasy did not end there; it mixed these memories from my adolescence with my early adulthood when I, somehow attracted by Fr. Lenny and his ilk, became a Jesuit myself. In all, I had spent twenty-eight years of my life in schools and colleges of the Society of Jesus, as novice and as student, as teacher and priest, as faculty member (department of theology) and administrator (dean of students) in a Jesuit university. I made the most consequential decision of my life in 1967 when I decided to leave the Jesuits and the active Roman Catholic priesthood in order to marry.

It is important to understand the chemistry that used to operate within Jesuit high schools at least up to the 1950s or 1960s, and perhaps even later. In those days, we used to joke, not without a basis in reality, that although Jesuit schools advertised themselves as "*conducted* by the Jesuit fathers," they were, in fact, *run* by the Jesuit scholastics, young men not yet ordained who had already been in the order for about seven to eight years and who were required to get three years of teaching experience prior to going on for the study of theology, ordination to the priesthood, and future work as a Jesuit. There were also a few lay*men* teachers in these prep schools (never any women!), but the group of youthful scholastics set the tone and dominated the school. As an alumnus of that era portrayed it:

> It wasn't just the scholastics' intellects that won us over: Because they had just emerged from years of being shut away in a seminary (most of them entered the Society at 18, after graduating from a Jesuit high school themselves), they were bursting with gregarious-

ness, raring to coach teams and direct plays and make themselves available to students after school. The best of them functioned more like older brothers than professors—role models that few of us could resist trying to emulate. (Drabelle 1993, 21)

What would have happened if the little public high school doorway scene I described had taken place in a Jesuit high school in the 1940s or 1950s? Despite all the camaraderie just described, such a transgression of manners would not have been overlooked. The offensive students would have been called back to the doorway immediately. Then the Jesuit would have fixed his eyes on them for an eternity in stony silence. If he did not already know them, he would have gotten each of their names (it is unthinkable that they would have refused to identify themselves). He would have made sure that they knew that he knew who they were. Anonymity was impossible. Then, proceeding in the most unhurried way, he would have made them feel as uncomfortable as possible. He would have had them retrace their steps, rehearsing the whole doorway scene perhaps two or three times, making sure that they understood the rule of courteous conduct for walking through a door. He would have matched their performance with a little performance of his own. Finally, he would have allowed them to go on their way, making sure to give them a honey-sweet smile as an antidote to their sullen faces. Meeting them by chance a few days later, he might make an oblique reference to the incident so that this infraction now became converted into a bond between them, the stuff of stories at future class reunions.

An Attention to Detail

In *Discipline and Punish* (1979, 140), Michel Foucault singled out the Jesuit colleges of seventeenth-century France as involved in the process that raised discipline to an art form, fostered the emergence of a "micro-physics of power," and contributed to the supervision of "the smallest fragments of life" in the modern age.[2] Education of the intellect in these schools was understood to be inseparable from the acquisition of piety and good manners, and acquiring good manners implied discipline.[3] It is instructive to note that when the early Jesuit colleges of Europe were at the height of their reputation for scholarship—the Collège de Clermont in seventeenth-century Paris,[4] for example (Lacouture 1991, 241)—it was not scholarship per se that was their number one priority. The Jesuits' own formation was inspired by the maxims of Ignatius Loyola, their founder, who was constantly concerned that their love of the religious life and dedication to the acquisition of solid virtues would cool when they began to become fascinated with secular studies—the humanities, mathematics, and science.

From a purely "disciplinary" perspective, Jesuit schools of the twentieth century were a mere shadow of those of the seventeenth,[5] but even at this late date small things were not overlooked. Nothing was too minor to merit concentrated attention. Every item was grist for the mill and convertible into a learning experience. Jesuit teachers learned how to execute these small techniques of control not from "methods courses" but informally, from their Jesuit brethren, the way one might master magic tricks. What was the young teacher supposed to do if he walked into an unruly and untidy class in which bedlam was breaking loose? If the mere appearance of the Jesuit's black robe was not enough to quiet things down (and usually it was), then he should focus on a very small item, say a crumpled piece of paper on the floor, and, in a very low and measured voice (stage whispers worked wonders), ask a student sitting nearby if he would please pick it up and place it in a nearby waste basket. He might even pick up a few scraps himself. By this time, the entire class had usually gotten the intended message: if this teacher has troubled himself so much over such a trifle, surely he will not tolerate any major nonsense, so the only alternative is to settle down with the algebra text.

This obsession with detail filled every niche and alcove of a Jesuit school. It was accepted dogma that every student was expected to study three hours per night; teachers consulted with one another concerning the amount of homework assigned to make sure the students got their full three hours' worth. Nothing was left to chance. Every class had a "beadle," a student who was trusted to erase the blackboards, to manage the radiators, windows, and shades, and to run errands; everyone was expected to be in his assigned seat at all times. Absolutely nothing was permitted on the classroom floor; bookbags and clothing were to be placed on hooks on the back wall. Every class began with a short prayer, with all standing upright in a reverent posture. Slouchers were openly reprimanded. If pens were to be used for a certain exercise, then pencils were unacceptable, and vice versa. All students wore coats and ties, with the knot of the tie pulled tight, all the way up to the Adam's apple. All students stood to recite when called on;

others raised their hands to be recognized. Slovenly posture was immediately challenged. Except for the teacher's dialogue with an individual student and occasional group recitations, absolute silence was expected in the classroom. Jesuit teachers did meticulous class preparation and spent long hours correcting every item on student papers. In Greek class, points were taken off for incorrect accent marks or for missing iota subscripts. Memory was held to be a mental faculty on a par with intellect and will and was cultivated for its own sake. "Repetitio est mater studiorum," was the watchword. That repetition was indeed the mother of learning was not a concept to quarrel with, and students daily expected to be called on to repeat poems, lists, the steps in geometry theorems, and catechism answers from memory—verbatim.

If, when called on for recitation of a poem, you stumbled or were not prepared, the teacher, clearly annoyed, declared "quinquies" (Latin shorthand for "be prepared to recite the missed stanza *five times* the following day") and called on someone who was. Jesuits were not afraid to confront students who failed to uphold their responsibilities. They made it clear to you through the daily quizzes that, when they assigned something, they expected the task to be completed. When you did something right, you got immediate positive reinforcement. When drills took place, a dozen students would stand on one side of the room facing another dozen on the other side, competing over Latin phrases or vocabulary lists.

The Jesuit presence permeated everything, inside and outside of classrooms. Truly, Foucault's network of gazes permeated all the public space of a Jesuit prep school; as high school students we were not aware that the Jesuits were themselves subject to a network of gazes in their own formation.[6] We knew, or at least we imagined, that the Jesuits were peering down at us from the high vaulted porches of the neo-baroque church as we knelt, four to a pew, attending morning Mass. I can still feel their eyes on my back, making sure that I was paying attention to the service and not cramming for the upcoming Latin test. It was all the more vexing to have eyes that were normally friendly staring at you in reprimand.

If a Jesuit encountered a large group of students acting in a disruptive way, he had a simple way of quelling the disturbance. Without raising his voice above a soft whisper, he would single one student out from the crowd, stare intently at him, ignore all the others, and, with a deliberate motion of the finger, bring that student over to within a few inches of his face. (How my present graduate students would have enjoyed seeing me, clad in black soutane, perform this trick before 3000 screaming basketball fans in the crowded gym of a Jesuit university!) The usual effect on the rest of the crowd was immediate and electric. Everyone wondered what was transpiring (would the student be expelled?) as the Jesuit and the poor student walked off, talking quietly.

CONFRONTATIONAL CORRIDORS

All Jesuit scholastics were charged not just with keeping order in their classes but with the discipline of the whole school; each was deputized as an "assistant prefect of discipline" and made to feel responsible for all student behavior, not just that of his own classroom. Since teachers were considered schoolwide disciplinarians, there was not just one "prefect of discipline" patrolling the corridors, but dozens of them. A brand new teacher fresh from the Jesuit "scholasticate" (seminary) was expected to take on an upperclass bully or a senior athlete if he caught him in some corridor horseplay. All Jesuits had to be respected by all students, it was felt, or law and order would break down. What Jesuit teachers feared more than any arrogant student was a fellow teacher (Jesuit or lay) who did not know how to control a class; he represented a partial chink in the corporate armor that might affect the whole school. These techniques of control were incorporated quietly into each scholastic's personal style by learning gestures and attitudes as insignificant as a raised eyebrow or a slight variation in the tone of voice. Such school and classroom management tactics were not the exclusive province of the Jesuits; I only wish to emphasize that they actually did, for the most part, effect this discipline in a uniform way and that surveillance was not confined to "classroom management"—it permeated the corridors and the cafeteria, the auditorium and the playing fields, the whole school. Students of Jesuit prep schools were constantly reminded that their gentlemanly deportment should be such that they could immediately be singled out as coat-and-tie-clad "preppers" from amidst a large center-city crowd.

Jesuits believed firmly in the effects of original sin, and, if adolescents did not have an extra dose of it, they were at least never to be completely trusted until they reached the latter months of their school careers, at which point they were permitted to enter into a complete fellowship with their teachers. Fear was certainly not considered the best method for motivating students in these highly competitive schools, but neither was it disdained. "Jug," a two-hour after school detention period, was utilized whenever the occasion called for it, be it lateness for school or surly behavior. Excuses for tardiness were listened to, and then politely ignored, as the "jug slip" was written. The prefect of discipline relished his reputation as the most hated man on campus. Only the most boring exercises the prefect of discipline could dream up, such as copying declensions of Latin nouns over and over again, could be done during jug.[7] For serious breaches, expulsion was a distinct possibility, and everyone feared it, but in practice it was rarely used.

Exposure to Dialogue

I have already hinted at the existence of another side to life in Jesuit schools. In the corridors and the cafeteria, at school football games and class parties, there were often occasions for casual chats, relaxed talk, and "shooting the bull" with the "Jebbies." A sense of humor was somehow intrinsic to the Jesuit personality. In such dialogic settings, the personality of the student was subjected to challenge, to banter, to new insights, to friendly teasing and joking. Jesuit scholastics drove the team bus to out-of-town football games, accompanied students to Saturday night symphony concerts, and helped to organize class picnics and proms; as a group of celibates, they were not even permitted to spend much time with their own relatives and were on call for the students seven days a week. At the end of the school day, their interaction with the students was just beginning, whether through a pick-up basketball game or in a school newspaper office. Their self-imposed ideal was to combine a maximum exposure of their own personality to the students with the maintenance of a high energy level.[8] This out-of-classroom side of Jesuit education was the prime vehicle for constructing values, reflecting on moral rules, and pondering future careers (many a Jesuit began considering his own calling to the order in just this way). I cannot honestly say that "social justice" was primary among those values, although there were some outstanding Jesuits who began questioning the Catholic church's own racial and class practices as early as the 1930s.[9]

Was it the fact that Jesuits had first established such firm disciplinary control that permitted this other, more humane, side of schooling to unfold? Or should we, with Michel Foucault, read these informal, friendly contacts as a form of covert oppression? For him, the aim of all institutions (and, very specifically, the Jesuit schools of the seventeenth and eighteenth centuries) was and is to repress in the most totalizing way. No doubt Foucault would see such human contacts not as humane but as cooptation into a repressive regime. I addressed Foucault's disciplinary thesis more directly in chapter 3 in order to question whether his whole critique is valid when applied to urban education today, however applicable it might have been to the historical construction of bourgeois society. But it is important to note that even during the period when "monitored control" was at its height, there was always, paradoxically, another feature present, seemingly contradictory to the first: the relaxed bonhomie of a Jesuit school corridor.

But at the outset, one has to ask: are such remembered pasts just nostalgic illusions? Did such a controlled disciplinary regime ever really exist, or are these just tall tales told by enamored alumni? If it did exist, was it all that effective? It would certainly be an exaggeration to contend that Jesuits always conformed to their own ideology of firm but moderate discipline. I can still feel a vicarious tingle from the hard slap one of my overly loquacious friends received for continuing to chatter away when a young Jesuit demanded silence. As for adolescent sexual issues, it was felt that they needed no explanation—except from the vantage point of the pulpit or the confessional. I need not rehearse here all the failings of the Jesuit schools— especially in the area of sex education. Suffice it to say that these disciplinary practices, successful though they were in many respects, generated their own covert and overt resistances, both in the schools and even within the Jesuit order itself. And if strict rule enforcement did not always exist "on the ground," it was certainly an ever-present ideology. In the "schools" we have been discussing in this book, it is that disciplinary ideology that has gone.

"The Definition of a Gentleman"

Nor is my purpose to judge the merits of Jesuit education as such. I have, quite deliberately, excluded consideration of what would be considered the core intellectual substance of the old (i.e., pre–1950s) Jesuit education (intense concentration on the Greek and Latin classics in the original languages; mathematics, science, and literature of the Western humanist tradition;[10] a focus on clear thinking and persuasive oratory; and the imparting of a Christian philosophy and theology and the attendant values according to the norms of the Catholic church) in favor of a treatment of the disciplinary "externals." These two faces of Jesuit education, the Christian interior and the gentlemanly exterior, separable only in the abstract, were epitomized in Newman's famous 1853 essay on the definition of a gentleman, which was held up to us as the ultimate charter for proper behavior. We accepted this picture of the gentleman as the gracious host at face value; we were unmindful then of the elitist, patriarchal, British upper-class implications it conveys with its constant repetition of "he." In reading it, one must bear in mind that Newman himself was striving to present a kind of phenomenological description of the ideal of a "natural gentleman," one whose external behavior (manifested in gentleness, consideration for others, and good manners) might in all externals be indistinguishable from that of a "Christian gentleman" attentive to the promptings of supernatural grace and the principles of Christianity:

> Hence it is that it is almost a definition of a gentleman to say he is one who never inflicts pain. . . . The true gentleman . . . carefully avoids whatever may cause a jar or a jolt in the minds of those with whom he is cast—all clashing of opinion, or collision of feeling, all restraint, or suspicion, or gloom, or resentment; his great concern being to make every one at their ease and at home. He has his eyes on all his company; he is tender toward the bashful, gentle towards the distant, and merciful towards the absurd; he can recollect to whom he is speaking; he guards against unseasonable allusions, or topics which may irritate; he is seldom prominent in conversation, and never wearisome. He makes light of favors while he does them, and seems to be receiving when he is conferring. He never speaks of himself except when compelled, never defends himself by a mere retort, he has no ears for slander or gossip, is scrupulous in imputing motives to those who interfere with him, and interprets everything for the best. He is never mean or little in his disputes, never takes unfair advantage, never mistakes personalities or sharp sayings for arguments, or insinuates evil which he dare not say out. From a long-sighted prudence, he observes the maxim of the ancient sage that we should ever conduct ourselves towards our enemy as if he were one day to be our friend. He has too much good sense to be affronted at insults, he is too well employed to remember injuries, and too indolent to bear malice. He is patient, forbearing, and resigned, on philosophical principles; he submits to pain, because it is inevitable, to bereavement, because it is irreparable, and to death, because it is his destiny. If he engages in controversy of

any kind, his disciplined intellect preserves him from the blundering discourtesy of better, perhaps, but less educated minds; who, like blunt weapons, tear and hack instead of cutting clean, who mistake the point in argument, waste their strength on trifles, misconceive their adversary, and leave the question more involved than they find it. He may be right or wrong in his opinion, but he is too clear-headed to be unjust; he is as simple as he is forcible, as brief as he is decisive. Nowhere shall we find greater candor, consideration, indulgence; he throws himself into the minds of his opponents, he accounts for their mistakes. (Newman 1959, 217–19)

In Jesuit schools, Newman's essay was considered a kind of synopsized "manual of etiquette." This vision of good manners, it was felt, plus the example set by the lives of the Jesuits, would be the proper guide for conduct. These were the attitudes I carried with me and that ignited my imagination as I first began working within the New York City public school system in 1985.

Schools as Constructs

The more familiar I became with the public high school system, and the more teachers and principals I met, the more I became aware of the role of memory. These educators, like me, had their fantasies and memories of the way things were—memories of schools they had attended or previously worked in, memories not unlike my own, of strict disciplinarians and quieter corridors, of domineering principals and of kindly teachers, of the way a school "is supposed to be." More important, I began to understand that the school system, which at first sight appears so bureaucratically permanent as to be almost eternal, was itself nothing other than a historical-social construct and a compendium of the memories and imaginations of all those who had ever worked in or for the board of education or who had ever influenced it in any way—from principals and classroom teachers to architects, from legislators to superintendents, from custodians to security guards, from parents to the students themselves. The present occupants of the building were only the most recent users. Finally, I was able to appreciate that the students, too, have their memories of other school experiences—both here and in other countries—that have shaped their views of how a school should and should not be conducted and that these views are also constructive of the "sense of place" of the school itself.

I present this closing digression on Jesuit schools, then, as a more or less faithful representation of the mental and emotional baggage that I carried with me as I began my work in public high schools and that epitomizes that part of my identity that was to grapple with, be transformed by, and, in a very small way, transform everyday life in these same schools. I should quickly add that this does not represent my total identity: the Jesuit in me was becoming tempered (if that is the right word) in the 1970s and early 1980s by further training in anthropology and education.

Nevertheless, when it came to the simple question of running a tight ship (and ignoring momentarily the larger socioeconomic and political issues), Jesuit schools had, and perhaps still have, a well-deserved reputation for excellence. Many will shudder at such a distinction between politics and pragmatics, since it obscures the complete acceptance of the Western hegemonic and patriarchical tradition that such a system fostered. The whole idea of Jesuit education was not just to nurture the humanism of the Renaissance but to baptize it, to tie it back to its medieval and theological roots. All of that is beyond dispute; the single point I want to make about Jesuit education is that, from the point of view of the student, there was no doubt but that the Jesuits were in charge, not the students. However otherworldly Jesuit education was, it did not allow itself to lose touch with the contemporary youth culture nor to be intimidated by it. Youth culture, for the Jesuits, was just one more challenge to be faced squarely: you had to listen to it, charm it, confront it, even overwhelm it, and finally incorporate it. As children, we knew all this even before we ever set foot in a Jesuit school. While still in elementary school, most Catholic boys had gotten the word that these Jesuits knew what they were about when it came to education. As a result, parents and the Catholic community at large deferred to them as a matter of course. The Catholic grade school nuns, in particular, spoke of them with great reverence. Again, it is important to state that these recollections evoke experiences from four or five decades ago; I can make no comment about the state of Jesuit education today. If Scaglione (1986, 6) is right, the Jesuits of today may be as confused as everyone else seems to be about which directions education should take.

In Loco Parentis

My intention in concluding with this personal testimony on discipline in Jesuit schools has been to illustrate the way in which a "model" (albeit somewhat idealized) Jesuit teacher, be he scholastic or priest, combined (or at the very least was expected to combine) in his own persona four distinct roles: (1) teacher, focusing on cognition, scholarship, and instruction in classical learning or science; (2) disciplinarian, articulating and enforcing the behavioral standards and limits for an adolescent; (3) mentor, opening himself to engage in one-on-one dialogue or playful interactions with adolescents while still maintaining distance as an adult; and (4) spiritual guide, receptive to the most intimate manifestations of the student's spiritual life and willing to share his own deepest-held beliefs and values. At its very apex, Jesuit education was motivated by a desire to inspire the student to go out and accomplish great and even heroic deeds "with great courage and a magnanimous and liberal heart" after the example of Ignatius Loyola, who was in turn motivated by tales of medieval chivalry and of the lives of Catholic saints.

All of this, of course, was the stuff of an *in loco parentis* pedagogy, taken for granted as an organic part of Jesuit practice from the opening of their first college at Messina, Italy, in 1548. My graduate students today stare at me in disbelief when I relate to them how, as late as the 1960s, as a young priest-housemaster living in the student dormitory of a Jesuit university, I was doing midnight bedchecks, bailing students out of the local precinct when they got in trouble with the law, communicating with their parents, and checking to see if they were going to daily Mass, in addition to my regular teaching duties. Obviously, this all-embracing notion of the role of the teacher contrasts with the present notion—at the secondary and post-secondary levels—which has become so narrow as to encompass only the realm of the intellect.

The mere recollection of such memories, even when stated in such affectionate terms, should not be read as an endorsement of the get-tough approaches recommended by such conservatives as William Bennett (1992) and other reactionary commentators who like to speak of a "loss of nerve" on the part of school administrators (Bennett 1984, 19) or who reiterate the comparison studies between Catholic and public schools, which simply state in statistical form what everyone knows to be obviously true—namely, that in the Catholic schools, "disciplinary standards in every area measured are higher, and discipline problems, as measured by absenteeism, cutting classes, threats to teachers, and fights among students, all for students from comparable backgrounds, are lower than in public schools" (Coleman, Hoffer, & Kilgore 1982, 187).

On the contrary, my aim has been to interrogate the mentality underlying Bennett's ideology as well as the prevailing ethos in inner-city public schools. The question this ethnography attempts to pose is not whether earlier Jesuit educational practices, or even methods that were taken for granted in New York City public schools forty or fifty years ago, should be reimposed on today's urban educational scene. The issue of discipline has become far too complex for such simplistic solutions. This book argues that the current system, at least at the level of inner-city high schools, has, like the surrounding neighborhoods, become so ravaged by a culture of violence that it is now critically necessary to rethink all presuppositions before prescribing quick fixes for the violence. Traditional debates (e.g., McNeil 1988, 214) on these matters, which would seek to reduce student discipline problems to boredom over irrelevant course content (I do not deny that boring classes are a real problem!), further intellectualize the question and doggedly refuse to look at the teacher in terms of a relationship to the body.

Everyday life in inner-city schools, as we have seen, leave little space or time for the entire humanist enterprise with its disciplinary infrastructure. Inner-city school corridor life, with its squads of guards, high-tech equipment, and recurring incidents of violence, stands as a stumbling block to those who would restore any vestige of a demythologized humanist tradition. But these corridors are not just a contradiction to all that conservatives stand for; they represent a challenge to critical theory as well. Authors such as Spanos,[11] as we have seen, have set out to destroy humanism, seemingly unaware that in these "schools," at least, humanism and the disciplinary edifice that supports it are already in their death throes. Liberal and moderate discourse, too, have their own ways of hiding or avoiding sensitive questions regarding discipline and violence. My Jesuit school-public school fantasy, then, is about more than just a momentary, irritating incident, a case of middle-class mores clashing with the idiosyncrasies and alien etiquette of the cultural "Other." Although taken from what has come to be thought of as an elite private sector, it is a metaphor of the whole confrontation between the culture of violence and a public educational system that is struggling to imagine itself absent that culture of violence.

"Chaotic" or Complex?

This book has examined various discourses—at the level of everyday enactment in the school system as well as at the level of pedagogical the-

ory—that explicitly or implicitly profess to control or interpret school violence and are themselves constructive of student subjectivities and bodily
performances. Medical anthropological research has called into question
the givenness and "naturalness" of the physical body of Western medicine
and has established the body as a product of specific contexts rather than as
an ubiquitous cultural universal (Lock 1993, 134). The field of *educational*
anthropology, however, has not adequately theorized the body and has become fixated in decontextualized models that tend to stereotype and dichot-
omize high school students as either rebellious, resistant, feisty teenagers or
as compliant youth who are required to reject their ethnicity in order to
succeed in white society. These views are not incorrect. They are, however,
only partial. I differ from them in that I posit a culture of school violence
not only as a centralized dominant power that oppresses students from on
high but as an energy operating at the margins—in tight competition with
traditional schooling—for control over the construction of students' subjectivities and bodies as well as a force that has fragmented the school itself.
The culture of violence, rooted in the capitalist economic order, constructs
a violent student identity to do its dirty work of violence for it. The response
of the system to the real or imagined student violence is the techno-security
one, with conflict-resolution initiatives thrown in for public relations purposes.

My central thesis is that the culture of school violence destroys and re-
constructs the stable categories of social science: ethnicity, identity, subjectivity, institution, dominant culture, and counterculture. This approach is
analogous to Feldman's (1991) discussion of violence in Northern Ireland
society but adds a further dimension: a declaration that an ethnography on
the spatial margins of urban education (school corridors, stairwells, cafeterias, security guards' dressing rooms, custodians' boiler rooms, student
hangouts) as opposed to the traditional centers (classrooms, principals'
offices) presents a challenge to Michel Foucault's "surveillance" theory,
which was applicable to a modernity that no longer exists. Panopticism is
dead. In postmodern America, we are no longer gazing at our youth, even
with machines, in order to "discipline" them in a careful, minutely detailed,
forceful, and consistent fashion. We are all looking the other way.

The space of inner-city school corridors—the cutting edge of postmodern American culture—thus brings to our attention that that culture
is much more than merely depthless, fragmented, heterogeneous, indeter-

minate, diverse, eclectic, and playful. It is also, and perhaps primarily, violent.

The realities in inner-city schools are more complicated than the current discourses of the right or the left would have us believe, and this brings me back to the inconsequential doorway encounter at the neighborhood public high school, the source of my disjointed fantasy. As I tried to sketch out in the previous chapter, the task that lies ahead—for educational policymakers, for teacher educators, and for teachers—is not to revive humanism by returning to the panoptic past, nor to be satisfied with creating a few small exemplary schools as "replicable models," but to create a total public educational system of small, caring, manageable learning environments where teachers can once again play the complex mind-and-body roles that are needed and that youth expect of them, where they can actively take part in adolescent initiation rites, and where they can forge a unified code of conduct for a school communitas that will be respectful of today's heterogeneous urban society.

NOTES

INTRODUCTION

1. Here, as in much recent scholarship, discourse is conceptualized as constitutive not only of ideology but of the body itself. How the discourse of violence constructs an ideology peculiar to itself as well as a material counterpart manifested through the body and the bodily *habitus* (as conceptualized by Bourdieu 1977) will be elaborated in the following chapters. A simple illustration of how the code of violence becomes incorporated in the individual's cognitive mapping and also in the corporeal makeup is provided by the orientation process that new undergraduate students receive when they arrive at most urban universities today and are exposed to seminars on "street smarts"—formal lessons on ways to comport oneself on dangerous city streets to avoid being mugged. Presumably, the freshman's perception, imagination, and bodily demeanors are all affected, since warnings are given about the necessity to be alert at all times, to avoid daydreaming while walking on city streets, to walk erectly, briskly, and attentively, to appear to be in control, and the like.

2. The work of Drew Leder 1993 provides some interesting insights in how to penetrate this barrier between scholar and layperson. In his sessions inside a maximum-security penitentiary, he encouraged the inmates to read and interpret the writings of Michel Foucault, a task they accomplished most successfully.

3. A few of the interviews with students, faculty, or administrators were tape recorded when I felt that a particularly dense dialogue could best be captured that way. Ordinarily, however, references to school conversations are taken from my fieldnotes or from graduate student logs, which were written shortly after or, at times, during the event.

4. It is noteworthy that most recent commentators on Foucault—historians, sociologists, and cultural critics—accept Foucault's basic thesis that the "grid of discipline" is everywhere becoming more extensive in society. See de Certeau (1984, xiv). The now almost complete breakdown of any kind of careful rule enforcement in inner-city school life represents a direct challenge to this assumption.

5. The Arcades Project, or *Passagen-Werk,* was a book that was never completed, due to the untimely death of Benjamin as he fled the Gestapo at the beginning of World War II. It attempted to outline and interpret the origins of modernity (see Buck-Morss 1989).

6. I am indebted to my colleague Peter Lucas, who has recently completed a study of space, place, and time in an urban high school, for this information.

CHAPTER ONE

1. The first incident happened in one of the high schools that adjoins a high school (see the description of Alpha School in chapter 2) in which our program operates. The killings were admitted by a third student who was fifteen years old at the time. He said he had borrowed the pistol from a friend and claimed his life was in danger because one of the two students had shot at him in the street the previous day and had threatened to kill his mother. He was convicted of two counts of manslaughter and received a sentence of six and two-thirds to twenty years in prison. The mother of one of the slain boys was quoted as saying, "No parents can feel free and safe to send their kids to school anymore" (Fried 1993). This shooting occurred in the same school in which, five months earlier, another student was shot and killed and a teacher seriously wounded. Both incidents are described in detail in Donaldson 1993.

2. Literally, "a praiser of bygone times," *Ars Poetica,* l. 173.

3. In 1969, the New York State Legislature passed a decentralization law that "granted substantial operating powers to community boards over all education in their districts except high schools" (Ravitch 1988, 386–87). Control of all public high schools in New York City remains in the hands of the central board of education. All 126 regular high schools are managed through five superintendents' offices, one in each of the five boroughs; the five superintendents report directly to the central board. During the struggle over decentralization in the late 1960s, supervision of the high schools was never relinquished to the thirty-two school districts that were created throughout the city at that time. These districts, controlled by thirty-two different local boards, are empowered to manage only the elementary and junior high schools. In the current debates over school governance, all these arrangements are being called into question.

4. In recent years, the central board of education has permitted certain school districts to create some small high schools (e.g., 60–150 students), usually as outgrowths of local district-run middle and junior high schools. In addition, on March 18, 1993, then Chancellor Joseph Fernandez announced the opening of fifty small "Vision" schools to be collaboratively managed by the board of education, various school districts, and some community groups (see New York City Board of Education 1993). These new Vision schools fall under the jurisdiction of the Superintendent of Alternative Schools, which is a separate division of the board of education and has been responsible for the small alternative high schools, some having begun in the 1970s. The mission of this division is to serve those students who are not being served—or who cannot be served—by the High School Division, to which the 126 regular high schools report. Students in these alternative schools may have dropped out of one of the larger schools or have been suspended for various reasons. They may be returning from a stay in the criminal justice system or immigrating from overseas with little formal education. If all of these small new Vision and alternative schools are counted, there are currently about 197 high schools in the city. At the present time, a new wave of school creation, entitled Vision II, is underway.

5. The informal division described here is not to be confused with the board's

official classification of school types: (a) academic-comprehensive; (b) vocational-technical; (c) specialized high schools; and (d) alternative high schools (schools for those who have dropped out or have been "pushed out" of the other regular schools; see n. 4).

6. The previous year (1990–91), the number of incidents was forty-five; the year before that (1989–90), the figure was twenty. (Ed Muir, Vice President for Security, United Federation of Teachers, interviewed by author.)

7. A few of these schools, due primarily to politically powerful principals, have been able to keep the metal detectors out where the school leadership deems them counterproductive; how long they will be able to hold out, given the legal and insurance risks involved, is at present highly questionable. Given the possibility of a weapons incident and its dire consequences, the pressures on these principals from the central board and the union to accept this "security package" are enormous.

8. There is general agreement by all officials that the entire New York City system underreports violence (see Travis, Lynch, and Schall 1993; Dillon 1993a). The teachers union maintains its own independent crime-reporting system. It is also generally known that an individual principal can decide not to report a large number of incidents for fear of giving the school a bad name. When the list of schools having the largest numbers of serious incidents was recently published, people in the schools in which we work considered it laughable that some very large schools had not reported a single incident in an entire year. To correct abuses of this nature, the Chancellor's Advisory Panel on School Safety (Travis, Lynch, and Schall 1993) recommended that the reporting function be taken away from the principals and handed over to the school's chief security guard, who, in turn, does not report to the principal but to the central board. Principals tell me that most of the quantitative information (and not merely the violence data) reported to the central board is capable of manipulation and is, in fact, constantly manipulated by the principals. Yet these other reporting functions (attendance, dropout rates, etc.) would not be taken away, only the violence statistics. No one in the system seems willing to question the wisdom of this decision, which will strip the principals of the most basic item of trust—i.e., reporting to central headquarters the disciplinary situation in their individual schools. The political double-bind factor accompanying reporting operates throughout the system and is most noticeable at the top. The former chancellor (Cortines), convinced that serious crimes (assaults, robberies, rapes), though reported as rising for eight years in a row, were still being underreported, mandated a better information system (Dillon 1993a). When, the following year, reported incidents increased dramatically, he was excoriated by the mayor (Giuliani) for allowing this dramatic increase to happen!

9. Not all schools divert students to a side entrance. Some allow them to enter through the main lobby. Others use both the lobby and the auditorium for scanning. In all cases, it is a sizable production with a large cast of security guards and machines and with complicated logistics. Many schools have staggered schedules, which means that some students are scheduled to begin their day at the second period, some at the third period, and so forth. Students who arrive a bit early for

their first classes are kept waiting in a "holding area" (e.g., the auditorium) before being admitted to the corridors; in some schools, they wait on the front steps even in cold or rainy weather. The fear is that if large numbers of students are admitted early, they will roam the corridors, bang on doors, and disrupt classes that are already underway.

10. See Travis, Lynch, and Schall 1993.

11. She was permitted to switch schools late in her high school career because she was given a "safety transfer" to another school in the same borough. The school safety division of the board would no doubt interpret such incidents as exceptional; in recent years, however, more female security officers have been hired in order to interact with the girls.

12. Students, after entering the building (and after putting their cards in the computerized ID machines, which also record lateness, absences, infractions, etc.), are ushered through a maze of rope barriers into the auditorium, where they file down the left-hand aisle. Then they place their bags on the X-ray machine and step onto the stage, where, after they remove keys and loose change from their pockets, two or three guards scan them with handheld or upright metal detectors. Next, they proceed to their classes through a side door. Meanwhile, students who have been retained by the guards for any reason (they do not have their ID cards, their teachers have failed to show up for classes, or they are waiting for their first period to begin) sit in the audience and watch the whole spectacle. If an angry confrontation occurs between students and guards, the performative nature of the event is magnified. The whole process takes as little as five and as long as fifteen to twenty minutes, with as many as fifteen to twenty guards, deans, and paraprofessionals operating the machines.

13. In what many public school educators saw as a clear political move intended to placate a very vocal community organization, a former chancellor (Fernandez) permitted a group of church leaders to apply for public funds to create small Vision schools as annexes to the larger school, which the group was opposing. The church-state implications of this move have never surfaced for public discussion.

14. As part of the admissions procedure for high school, students are given the choice of (1) attending their local academic-comprehensive high school; (2) applying for one of the four specialized high schools; or (3) applying for a specialized program in up to eight of the ed op schools. For most of the students who are reading and writing at several grades below level, however, this choice is meaningless, since they will probably not be chosen by any of the schools to which they have applied and are thus forced to attend their local "zoned" (lower-tier) high school.

15. Lower-tier principals are masters at dealing with the complicated contradictions board policies can put them in. For example, a large lower-tier school may have 4000 students, 500 of whom may be long-term absentees (LTAs)—students whose names are on the school's rolls but who have never entered the building. The school thus has 3500 students in actuality but receives financial resources for 4000. If the school decides to reach out (through home visits by outreach workers) and bring the LTAs back, this hurts the school's attendance (because, once they have returned, these former LTAs—who were previously not counted as regular stu-

dents—are the students most prone to be truant or to cut classes) and hurts the school's discipline (because they are usually troublemakers). Therefore, the principal will have a better school—in the eyes of those examining the statistics—if no effort is made to recapture the LTAs, who thus remain at home or on the streets but not counted in the attendance figures. But here is where one top priority of the board (to get the LTAs off the street and into the school) conflicts with another priority (to improve attendance). Both priorities have their appropriate financial rewards and punishments. Smart principals know how to play this game and to make the correct decisions in order to look good on reports to the central board. They receive regular tax levy money (city funds) for the basic population and for good attendance. They get AIDP (Attendance Improvement/Dropout Prevention) money (state funds) to do outreach and to bring in the LTAs, thereby risking likely poor attendance in the future.

16. The board has, in fact, closed down three comprehensive high schools and attempted to convert each of them into three or four smaller schools. It is still unclear how different these restructuring efforts will be from the mid–1980s attempt to break the larger schools down into smaller houses (in which, in order to reduce anonymity, students were kept for several periods a day with a designated group of teachers and counselors)—an effort, to repeat, that did not appreciably affect student achievement or behavior. Almost all the lower-tier schools have been divided into houses for years now, but there is little evidence that these houses have reduced student alienation or violence. I will return to this topic in chapter 8.

17. Not only does the graduation rate of these lower-level schools suffer when a student transfers from lower tier to ed op, but, should the transferring student drop out of the ed op school, the lower-tier school, not the ed op one, gets charged with the dropout on the board's statistical profile, adding insult to injury. Thus, the graduation rate and the dropout rate of the lower-tier school are both negatively affected—as is the school's reputation in the community.

18. In an effort to prevent "skimming" or "creaming" (selecting only the best students), the central board has set down criteria for ed op schools and for the new smaller Vision schools. As part of the admissions procedures for these specialized schools, students are given a standardized reading test, the Degrees of Reading Power (DRP). These ed op or Vision schools are permitted to take only 16 percent of their students from the "above average" category. They must then take 68 percent "average" students and 16 percent "below average" students. Half the students are selected by the computer at random; half are selected by school officials. Lower-tier school principals have told me that they would welcome having these criteria applied to their schools. In other words, they would relish having 86 percent of their students reading at or above level on entry since in actuality they might have less than 20 percent reading "at grade level." In practice, these standards are so high that it is doubtful that even the ed op schools can attain these levels of literacy. (Students who score within the top 2 percent on the reading test are automatically accepted to the ed op program or school listed as their first choice on the application.)

19. This tendency to situate violence in past times matches a parallel discourse that attempts to locate violence in some other place. Journalists, intent on writing

success stories, often portray schools as currently having "no serious incidents" but as having been "lawless" just a few years previous. The remarkable change is usually ascribed to the leadership of a particular principal who has decided to get tough (Richardson 1993). Whether the violence is dispersed into a previous time or into a distant place, the result is the same: violence, in this genre, is viewed as not existing *here and now.*

20. A survey of 1400 students in fifteen New York City high schools (selected as a representative sample of the city's 290,000 high school students) conducted by the Federal Centers for Disease Control and Prevention reported that more than a third of New York City high school students say they are physically threatened during the school year, that nearly a fourth say they get into fights, and that one in five admit to carrying a weapon (McFadden 1993).

21. Throughout this study, all student names (sometimes expressed as initials only, sometimes as given names) are pseudonyms.

CHAPTER TWO

1. It is difficult to get detailed information on ethnicity or country of origin for the student populations in public schools. The school's official reports must adhere to the mandates of the Civil Rights Act of 1964 and so request data according to racial categories: African American, Asian, Hispanic, black, white, and Native American. In addition, the system requires schools to report on the country of origin for new admissions from overseas. A student's native language can usually be determined from the high school application form, although this process is far from being as straightforward as it might appear. New arrivals from rural Jamaica, for example, fluent in Jamaican Creole but with little exposure to any form of standard English, will often, when responding to questions about native language, indicate English as their home language when they have problems communicating with their teachers. For an excellent analysis of the relationship of Creoles and "standard" languages, see Carrington 1988. By putting together several different sources at one school in our program (Beta School), I was able to compile the following approximate profile: the term *Hispanic* covered students from Panama, Honduras, Nicaragua, El Salvador, Guatemala, Colombia, Venezuela, Costa Rica, Puerto Rico, and the Dominican Republic; the term *black* covered students from Liberia; Angola; Nigeria; Antigua; Jamaica; Barbados; Trinidad; Grenada; Surinam; Guyana; Nevis; British Virgin Islands; U.S. Virgin Islands; St. George; St. Kitts; St. Lucia; St. Vincent; Haiti; St. Lucia; Canada; Britain; Germany; and the United States (i.e., native-born African Americans). In addition, there were students from Cambodia and from Yemen. Immigrant students may, of course, also enter the United States after having moved for a few years to a third country, e.g., Canada, England, France.

2. Graduate students, rather than undergraduates, were recruited for both programmatic as well as pragmatic reasons. Initially, it was felt that the presumed greater maturity of the graduate students would be a definite plus. It was far more practical to schedule graduate students into the schools, since the university's courses for graduate students were mainly in the evening, whereas the undergradu-

ate courses were held during the day, at the same time that we were expected to be in the schools.

3. During the summer of 1986, the university and the state collaborated in developing legislation for a school-college partnership program (Stay in School Partnership Program or SSPP) that would assist potential high school dropouts. In its first year, the legislation provided $1.5 million for ten colleges and universities throughout the state to ally themselves with high schools in the dropout-prevention effort. Our small pilot program, begun during the prior spring term, served as the prime model in the design of this new state law. SSPP was phased out in 1989–90 and the Liberty Partnership Program (LPP) took its place; again, state legislators looked to our program as a model in drafting the LPP legislation. Currently (1995), our funding comes from LPP at the state level, from the School, College, and University Partnership Program at the federal level, and from Project Achieve at the New York City Board of Education level (funded through the United Way of New York City), as well as from several private foundations (CBS, Harry Frank Guggenheim, Morgan Stanley, and Penates). Each graduate student receives eighteen credits of tuition remission each year plus a $7,000 stipend in exchange for twenty hours of work in the program each week. The program receives about $950,000 each year in external funding and serves about 950–1000 students.

4. The New York City Board of Education's criteria for admission to its Project Achieve program, which brings local community-based organizations into the schools to work with at-risk students for "attendance improvement/dropout prevention" purposes, are as follows: poor academic performance; poor attendance; behavior/discipline problems; family or peers have history of dropping out of school; negative change in family circumstances; history of child abuse or neglect; homeless/residence in a shelter; substance abuse; limited English proficiency; teenage pregnancy and/or parenting; referral by the teacher for other reasons. Under these criteria, it is easy to justify placing almost any child in the program. The analogy with special education is pertinent: just as the 1970s produced a whole new profession (special education) with its own degrees, courses, specialists, and student population, the 1980s witnessed the creation of a subdiscipline with its own experts (dropout-prevention coordinators and specialists who work with at-risk children), literature, curricula, techniques, and national conferences. Roughly speaking, the at-risk population falls somewhere between the special-education students and the general school population. Ineligible for the sometimes stringent legal criteria for disability, the at-risk students nevertheless were seen as alienated from the general population and therefore as needing extra help. In practice, the lines were often blurred, and we ended up seeing many students who were in the special-education program solely because they were deemed to be discipline problems for the regular school. These heavily funded local special-education programs in the schools began to see us as a valuable resource to which they could refer students, but neither they nor their evaluators or special-education professionals at the university level officially acknowledged this dependency.

5. Both in New York City and elsewhere around the country, school districts are

planning to start small schools under an ideology that espouses all African American schools for young black males; the same ideology is also at work in the promotion of some all-Hispanic schools. Because this ideology is in direct conflict with Supreme Court decisions on desegregation, these schools are being publicly announced simply as "multicultural" sites. See, e.g., New York City Board of Education 1993.

6. It has been over forty years since *Brown v. Board of Education* became the law of the land, yet one of the common denominators of the lower-tier schools throughout the city of New York is that many do not have any white students. However one explains this phenomenon (e.g., housing patterns, "white flight") and whatever judgments one places on it, the fact remains that these inner-city students have some white teachers but no white peers.

7. As Rabinow (1986, 244) has pointed out, the scientific authority of the anthropologist has traditionally rested on the experiential "I was there" element and its suppression in the text, giving the ethnography a characteristic ring of absolute certainty. In the shift I am attempting to make, it would appear that an even deeper danger must be avoided: by highlighting the more or less permanent presence of the service provider over the more or less temporary presence of the researcher, it would be easy to slip into an "I was *really* there" interpretation. Such an outlook would presuppose a renewed faith in the viability of an accurate representation of the other—the equivalent of checking with the local missionary to find out what the "natives" are *really* like after the anthropologist has gone back to the university!

8. See N. L. Gage 1991.

9. At times, the principals come to participate in the seminars, as do local heads of community-based organizations who work in the schools.

10. See Gottlieb 1986.

11. An article in the *New York Times* (Gottlieb 1993) describes the changes that have taken place in this neighborhood since the early 1980s, most especially the realization of a large urban reclamation project. The article is as optimistic as Gottlieb's 1986 article is depressing. A walk through the neighborhood, in fact, reveals that all of these perceptions can be verified at the same time—the tenuous coexistence of tidy houses on one block with crack houses on the next.

CHAPTER THREE

1. It is becoming increasingly clear that such a response to violence is not limited to large cities but has become the standard solution. The *New York Times* (see Steinberg 1994) reported on the death of a student, a star athlete, who was killed with a knife in the crowded corridor of a suburban school. The school superintendent was quoted as saying: "I can't say that violence is the order of the day in our schools. But I'm sure that under the circumstances we are going to look again at the issue of metal detectors."

2. See Travis, Lynch, and Schall 1993. In addition to the nearly 3000 uniformed officers, the Division of School Safety employs 123 civilians and has an annual budget of nearly $73 million and a fleet of ninety vehicles. In 1968, this division did not even exist. The first 200 employees, seasonal guards who were hired in the fall and

fired at the end of the spring semester, were appointed in 1969, during the wide-spread disturbances that occurred at the time of the decentralization disputes and teacher strikes.

3. The alternative schools, which have small student populations of 250 to 350 students, have only one guard at the front door to keep out intruders and to staff the sign-in desk. The alternative schools will be discussed more fully in chapter 8.

4. School safety officers make between $18,000 and $24,000 per year.

5. Scarry (1985, 33–34) demonstrates how, in serious pain, "the claims of the body utterly nullify the claims of the world" and of the self and how "physical pain . . . obliterates all psychological content, painful, pleasurable, and neutral." Although school-corridor encounters between guards and students certainly cannot be equated with the torturer-prisoner situations Scarry is referring to, both single out the body and bodily functions and separate them from the remainder of the self and its relationship to the world. In the schools, the management of the student's "self and world" are, in theory (and, to a large extent, in practice), consigned to the school's professional personnel (guidance counselors and teachers), while the body is handed over to the guards, and, in many situations, to the police.

6. The door systems, isolated stairwell landings, metal gates, and large, empty, unused spaces in the older school buildings form extremely complex architectural mazes and provide a wide variety of areas for mischief for unsupervised adolescents. Some of the very large, troubled high schools have as many as eighty exterior doors (Dillon 1993b).

7. The guards, as "peace officers," have the right to make arrests but not to carry weapons. The police officers who are also present *do* carry weapons in the schools.

8. In a two-year period in one of our schools, two arsons gutted entire class-rooms.

9. One of the major developing problems for lower-tier schools is the presence of older students (e.g., seventeen- to nineteen-year-olds) who are still in the ninth or tenth grade, are often absent, and have accumulated few credits. Previously, when counselors or administrators saw that a seventeen-year-old ninth grader (known as a group among counselors as "bad LTAs") was going nowhere, they could counsel the student to go to another school—for example, to an alternative high school, where in a more sheltered environment the student might stand a chance of finishing high school or at least getting a high school equivalency degree. In this way, the lower-tier schools were thus able to get rid of some students who were really making no progress in their schools. This is now no longer possible, since the board has recently shifted its policy. It is now no longer permitted to "counsel out" a student until the end of the semester following the student's eighteenth birthday. School officials tell me that the change in policy was due to the fact that there were "too many kids on the street with nothing to do." The lower-tier schools are now forced to retain these students, the "hallwalkers," in school. The result is that the lower-tier schools have been forced to create another specialized program (in addition to evening schools, Saturday schools, "houses," and a host of other programs) especially adapted to this population. This usually takes the form of a high school equivalency program (GED) specifically designed for these students. The struggle behind

this move is part of the systemic tension that exists between the lower-tier schools and the system of alternative schools. The alternative schools are run by a separate superintendency. Lower-tier schools complain that almost all the alternate programs are closed by October of any given year. "Our kids are bad for their stats," one assistant principal for guidance told me. Faced with handling 3300 students annually, he referred disparagingly to alternative and Vision programs as "their little sinecures." It is his job to get students into these alternative programs, but he found in his day-to-day work that the resources were just not there. He told me of his frustration in spending weeks trying to motivate a student to apply for an alternative program only to find that when the student finally got there she or he was turned away. "They arrive on a Tuesday and are told that the school only does admissions on a Monday." Thus, both the student and the counselor become discouraged in seeking for alternatives within the system.

10. Under the union contract, principals are permitted to give only 35 percent of homeroom teachers a building assignment for one period per day. These building assignments, due to union pressures, have for the past decade tended to be to extra-classroom duties other than hall and cafeteria patrols. Examples include performing tasks in the guidance office or the health clinic or working at curriculum construction. At the present time, some principals are trying once again to extend these duties of teachers into the area of discipline and security.

11. In the fall 1995 debate raging in New York City about the ways to prevent school violence, none of the participants (the mayor, the chancellor, the board of education, the United Federation of Teachers) questions the basic premise that the core of the problem consists in a need to strengthen the security guard system. The highly contested proposal of allowing the Police Department to manage the school safety division merely takes this proposition to its logical conclusion. Six major reports in the past twenty-five years have all been variations on this basic theme (Toy 1995). In all of these efforts to "rethink" school safety, none of the panels has been willing to rethink its own basic suppositions.

12. The point being made here, it should be noted, has nothing in common with the now fashionable and counterintuitive argument that, if we really investigated, we would find that the students "in the good old days" were doing much more than just throwing spitballs (O'Neill 1994), another line of reasoning some conservative academicians have mobilized as an excuse for doing nothing to respond to the current crisis of violence. "The dropout rate was big then, it's big now. It was violent then, it's violent now—what's the big deal?" they seem to be implying.

13. Again, the reference here to "undisciplined bodies" should not be read as denoting urban schools to the exclusion of suburban and rural ones. Many educators throughout America would probably concur in the legitimacy of this question. The present ethnography, however, did not encompass such a broad spectrum of schools.

CHAPTER FOUR

1. Bourgois makes the connection between the micro- and the macro-levels by demonstrating the analogies between the localized violence of the "street" fre-

quented by drug dealers and their customers, on the one hand, and the world of the legitimate businessman on the other. This analogy may be extended to yet another level by interpreting all of modern culture (Benjamin 1968) and postmodern culture as inherently and irrevocably violent (Girard 1977; McKenna 1992).

2. The educational issues raised by adolescents transferring from Caribbean educational systems to those of the United States and other more highly industrialized countries (e.g., Canada), of course, involve more than the differential disciplinary practices referred to here. For a partial review of some of the underlying linguistic assumptions, see Carrington 1988, in which the author contrasts some of the traditional attitudes toward Creole languages with newer, more open, and less colonial attitudes.

The process of constructing transitional educational settings for students transferring from the Caribbean to New York schools is controversial, because it can also be interpreted as an attempt to lump all Caribbean students into one group without adequate diagnosis of their previous educational status. Many Caribbean students migrate to New York and finish high school as class valedictorians and go on to prestigious American colleges.

Many of the students referred to our program—which has itself become an important resource for entering migrants—have been incorrectly assessed and placed in inappropriate math or language classes. Even after being "correctly" placed, students discover teachers who are often insensitive to educational, cultural, and linguistic differences.

A complete educational system in the receiving country would demonstrate an awareness of the different needs of entering students and would provide for specialized teacher training sensitive to such issues as the structural differences in Caribbean educational systems; the history and evolution of Creole languages; the traditional and evolving attitudes about Creole languages; the lack of formal educational systems in some countries due to political circumstances; issues peculiar to teaching English to Creole-speaking students; an introduction to the various Creole grammars, dictionaries, and bibliographies for Jamaica, Trinidad, Barbados, etc.; a review of the literature and poetry of particular Creole languages; and some familiarity with the Caribbean newspapers and magazines available in the United States. Carrington's work presents an excellent summary of the educational issues involved in establishing programs for students making transitions from the Caribbean.

3. References to "the Caribbean" in this loose way can be misleading, since they do not take into account the differences between social classes or the variations among different countries' educational systems. Especially in the Caribbean, those in rural areas may experience schooling quite different from those in urban areas. Due to extreme political conditions (in Haiti, for example), some students may have no opportunity to attend school for years on end. In other places (e.g., Guyana), children may not attend school for long periods, because their family's economic circumstances require them to work. All public educational systems in the Caribbean have suffered in the 1980s and 1990s due to local budget deficits, the American recession, and reduced foreign capital. Nevertheless, *expectations* about schools and schooling can exist independent of actual school experiences, and it is this contrast

between Caribbean—or other international—students' expectations of American schools and their experiences in U.S. schools that we are dealing with here.

4. The schools we are in actually never have "all school" assemblies partly because the auditorium would not hold the entire student population but primarily because administrators fear they are not able to control the entire group. Smaller groups of students (the bilingual "house" or the graduating seniors) are usually gathered together in the auditorium for a specific purpose.

5. See, for example, deJonge (1993, 30–38), in which National Basketball League "trash talking," defined as "the various gratuitous ways by which players distract, intimidate and infuriate their opponents," is uncritically accepted by the author. Apparently without any awareness on the part of the author as to the racist implications, he characterizes this as "an overwhelmingly black phenomenon," referring to the way some white basketball stars (e.g., Larry Bird of the Boston Celtics) become even more accomplished in this art than their black fellow players. DeJonge blithely likens trash talking to other inner-city speech styles, thereby confusing acceptable and unacceptable behaviors within the inner-city community itself and obscuring the ways in which the dominant sports culture and the major media glamorize, co-opt, and normalize the practices of inner-city violence.

6. But Buck-Morss (1984, 312; 1989, 117) also points out that the sandwichman himself, as an extension of Benjamin's thought, can be seen as undergoing a further metamorphosis. To these images of the flaneur and the sandwichman she juxtaposes a photograph of a Jewish man being paraded by the Nazis, barefooted and without trousers, and carrying a sign, "I am a Jew but I have no complaints about the Nazis." The connections between these disparate images are not all that far-fetched: the sandwichman (who was usually a Parisian *clochard* [tramp]) is advertising the very capitalistic system that is destroying him; the hallwalker (a marginalized inner-city youth) likewise wears and publicizes the latest fashions of a consumer economy that is indifferent to the urban blight surrounding him. Furthermore, as stated in the text, the adolescent's agency, no longer part of a network of communal relations, is now confined to her or his own "body space" struggling to defend itself, unaided by the pseudo-protection of the policing arm of the state (whether guards or police).

7. Union officials and former teachers interviewed also complained that the "special-ed lobby"—those advocating most strongly for the rights of special-education students—have made it almost impossible to apply disciplinary standards to these students. The result is that special-ed students, in a distinctive way, are deprived of the benefits of confrontation and discipline. The "professionalization" of special-education staff in the schools has become a serious problem for many schools. Principals who approach special-ed psychologists for help in ascertaining whether a particular student may or may not be psychotic, for example, are told that these "professionals" accept referrals only if the student in question is "potentially eligible for special education." Generally speaking, our tutors have found that the special-ed rooms in the high schools (only five students to a room) are passive enclaves where students can be seen with their heads on the desk most of the day. The heavily funded "resource" staff (psychologists, social workers) never appear to have a very heavy caseload and never appear to have very much work to do. Often,

industrious special-ed teachers and assistant principals refer the special-ed students to our program, where individual interaction with the tutors is simultaneously more relaxed and more intensive.

8. Although there is no question but that the teacher "burnout rate" is enormous in inner-city schools, the hidden ideology in individual teacher biographies such as Samuel Freeman's *Small Victories* (1990), which portrays the seemingly heroic endeavors of an idealistic teacher in an inner-city school before she finally quits, is supportive of an essentially conservative theme that stresses the importance an individual contribution can make in the face of the bureaucratic lethargy of others. In glamorizing an individual teacher, such works fail to focus on the even more impressive performances of those other individuals who stay to teach and run the school, year in and year out. One is also left wondering if the "superstar" teachers portrayed in such accounts would not have burned out in any school environment due to the idiosyncrasies of their own personalities. Such accounts are counterproductive in that they draw attention away from the complex underlying infrastructural and systemic processes at work in schools and produce Hollywood-like caricatures of schools whose staff members consist of "good guys" and "bad guys." Even serious studies of school reform seem to be satisfied with these low (because purely individualistic) levels of explanation: e.g., Patricia Alberg Graham's *Sustain Our Schools* (1992, 9): "Teachers who bring about improvements frequently find themselves exhausted by the effort, unappreciated and unsupported by the school system. Therefore they have to leave the schools."

9. See Sizer 1984.

10. See Brown 1981.

11. To cite one small example, here is the advertisement for *Street Fighter II,* one of the most popular video games of the 1990s: "Get Ready to Rumble! From across the globe come eight of the wildest fighters the world has ever known. Choose your champion, gather your courage and prepare to battle opponents in a bare knuckle brawl. Face Ken and his devastating 'Dragon Punch'! Watch the temperature rise as Dhalsim incinerates you with his mystical Yoga Flame! Hear your spine crack as Zangrief smashes you to the pavement with his spinning pile driver! Cover your ears as Guile breaks the sound barrier with the awesome power of the Sonic Boom! Annihilate your competition and claim the right to test your skills against the bone-crushing power of the Grand Masters! Can you survive? Can anyone?" (CAPCOM USA Inc., Santa Clara, Calif., 95054).

CHAPTER FIVE

1. New York City Board of Education reactions are typical of school administrators' discourse nationwide in that they tend to minimize serious crime and violence inside the school buildings. See, for example, the remarks made by Jack Isch, administrative assistant to the superintendent, Oklahoma City Public Schools, in a statement made before the House Subcommittee on Elementary, Secondary, and Vocational Education in Colhoun, ed., 1984: "Getting to and from school is the real problem for many students. . . . Schools are in fact much less a place of crime and violence for young people than the streets. As stated earlier, I believe "disorder" in

schools is decreasing. Recently, I was in attendance with a group of administrators from the eastern half of the nation. Overwhelmingly, they believe disorder is decreasing in their schools."

Later, in the same set of remarks, he cites positivistic research data to convince the committee that most school crimes against school personnel are committed by intruders, not by students, and that a logical protection against this outside adversary is more security guards: "Oversight by this committee would certainly find that many school districts are doing what we are doing in Oklahoma City, placing security officers in school buildings to keep intruders out." The underlying assumptions here are (1) that the ultimate causes of disorder are external to the school; (2) that they can be excluded by means of the guards; (3) that the main function of the guards is to deal with the problem of intruders rather than with student discipline; (4) that the school is essentially a harmonious community united against a common enemy on the outside: "Students, teachers, and administrators obviously still have some encounters involving violence, theft, vandalism and arson—but not nearly as much with each other as with outsiders."

2. See Honderich, ed., 1995, 855.

3. For a useful summary of critical pedagogy ("critical ethnography," "radical pedagogy,") see Anderson 1989 and Ellsworth 1989.

4. Mandated disciplinary hearings, one phase in the student's appeals process, take up hours of a principal's time each day.

5. In dialogical anthropology the "subject" is considered an entity that turns to the Other; the subject of dialogue is not conceptualized as the autonomous rational and linguistic individual (Maranhao 1990; Buber 1970; Gadamer 1975; Bakhtin 1981; Levinas 1969; 1987). "In the act of turning to the Other the subject gains identity, that is, meaning. . . . Bakhtin's dialogical principle unfolds from the notions of Self and Other as mutually constituting" (Maranhão 1990, 4).

CHAPTER SIX

1. Fine implies (1991, 87) that "activist faculty" and "paraprofessionals" who live in the community ("in central Harlem"), presumably of the same race, gender, class, and ethnicity as the students, are more understanding, more respectful, and more open to students' disclosures than others. Our tutors find that the exact opposite may also be true: teachers and paras from marginalized groups may be either extremely empathetic or the last persons in whom students wish to confide. Contrary to the conventional wisdom, black teenagers may often relate extremely well to white tutors from the "majority culture." The same may be said for Hispanic students.

CHAPTER SEVEN

1. In passing, I note that social reproduction and resistance theorists are made uncomfortable by mentions of abuse and neglect, perhaps because even the mere allusion to it seems to smack of cultural deficit theory. One searches in vain for a reference to abuse or violence in the indexes of these works (Apple 1982; Aronowitz and Giroux 1985; Giroux 1988).

2. Freire 1971, cited in Spanos (1993, 199).

3. "Banking education" is Paulo Freire's way of characterizing a traditional educational style in which the student's head is envisaged as a kind of empty bank. The teacher, presumably rich in knowledge of anything from chemistry to literature, deposits information into the student's head (cited in Spanos 1993, 203).

4. Having the temerity to criticize rap, of course, does not imply that the tutors and I totally reject this musical and artistic form. On the contrary, some of our program's work with inner-city youth has consisted precisely in helping them produce performances featuring rap music and dance. Some art and music critics are reluctant to assert any kind of disapproval of rap, even when acknowledging that violence is seriously intended. Shusterman (1992, 226–27) seems inclined to accept and defend rap's and hip-hop's explicit threats of violence because of their unquestionable popularity. Any critique of the violence is interpreted as censorship, and rap's popularity is apparently seen by him as reason enough to justify it.

5. Noticeably absent from Spanos's list of repressive practices laid at the feet of traditional liberal education (prejudice against gays, women, blacks, etc.) is prejudice against the elderly. Following Nietzsche, the only age group endowed with "force" for him seems to be youth (1993, 204). "Ageism" and elder abuse are missing from all of his several catalogs of oppressions.

6. Deconstructing logocentrism, for Derrida, does not involve a denial of self-presence, just a displacement and deferral of it.

7. Many of these authors (e.g., Spanos, 1993, 213; Giroux 1988, 189) imagine that they themselves have gone beyond the cognitive and dealt with the body because of their focus on an "emancipatory practice" that would translate into more democracy in school and thereafter. They interpret all school disciplinary problems as traceable to the failure of teachers and administrators to reform the curriculum adequately (Giroux 1988, 127) and to destroy Western humanism.

8. Needless to say, this is not to imply that, on an individual level, *post factum,* teenage pregnancy and childbirth should be interpreted in a negative light for the individual concerned. It is possible to withhold judgment and disapproval on an individual basis, and even to celebrate, with the mother, the joys of parenthood, while still condemning the phenomenon as a social pathology.

CHAPTER EIGHT

1. See McKenna (1992) for a more profound understanding of how the process of scapegoating serves to prolong violence and how the interpretation of this phenomenon in the works of René Girard and Jacques Derrida may serve as a theoretical foundation for eliminating it.

2. "Borough Academies," the euphemistic name for these schools for the most violent and troublesome students, have already been started in two boroughs (Manhattan and Brooklyn). They present several legal and regulatory concerns for the New York City Board of Education right now, not the least of which is the thorny set of standards and laws that protect the "special education" population. These borough academies are considered to be a "general education" program for violent students and have not yet been equipped to provide services for "violent" special

education students. As a result, there is no place to send aggressive, "acting out" special education students—even though, de facto, many students currently enrolled in the borough academies would probably qualify as "special education." Under the new federal law, special education students who carry guns will be treated in the same way as other students unless their weapon-carrying behavior can be shown to be related to the "handicapping condition" that originally identified them as eligible for special education. One can imagine the panoply of legal challenges that will ensue.

3. There is one dubiously hopeful exception to this statement. The board is attempting to shut down two or three of the larger "lower-tier" schools and then reopen them as several smaller schools. Although at first blush this development sounds most hopeful, I cannot be very optimistic about it, given the preliminary reports that even this restructuring is being done in such a way as to download the most troublesome or least promising students to the surrounding lower-tier megaschools.

4. This document, the "Travis, Lynch, Schall Report," referred to earlier, was commissioned by a former chancellor who appointed an Advisory Panel on School Safety, which he charged with the job of reviewing school safety policies and approaches.

5. In essence, the panel is recommending to the Division of School Safety a "problem-solving policing" approach that involves (1) an analysis of "criminogenic locations" (the spots, presumably, where students raise the most hell) to be combined with sophisticated monitoring technology and electronic detection systems; (2) strategic patrols (based on a history of crime trends in and around the school) instead of random patrols; (3) intergroup mediation instead of so many arrests; (4) involvement of community groups and the use of various resources inside and outside the school in defining the safety problems and in designing strategies to address those problems; (5) reliance on a broad-based team-building approach that includes, among other ideas, a greater sensitivity to the local police, who complain that they try to respond to incidents and sometimes get no cooperation from schools. Note the concern for involvement of community groups and local police, the passing reference to mediation, but the total absence of any reference to teachers.

6. See, for example, an article in the *New York Times* (Barbanel 1993) that proclaimed that "educators see school-based management as one of the main tools to reinvigorate faltering public schools over the next decade." A former chancellor permitted high schools the option of joining or not joining the School Based Management/Shared Decision Making (SBM/SDM) initiative. Contrary to the *Times'* glowing appraisal, however, the scuttlebutt among principals was that those principals who opted into the program regretted it because the ensuing meetings (which were overtly designed to give teachers and guidance counselors more of a say in school administration) resulted in endless bickering, the holding up of appointments, and an increase in union grievances.

7. The principal is suspect because the board has reason to believe that serious incidents are underreported. As the Travis panel states, "in some cases principals apparently determined that an incident should not be reported at all because it gives

the school a bad name" (13). The underlying assumption here is that the board does not know, absent this reporting system, which schools are the most violent. This allows the system to keep up the pretense that, if only the central board knew about such incidents, it could offer some help to prevent them. Both assumptions are highly questionable. Nevertheless, the crucial task of deciding which incidents are "serious" and which are not, it appears, will be taken out of the hands of principals and placed under the authority of head guards, who do not report to the principal but to the central Division of School Safety. The principal's authority is thus further undermined. Board policy is consistently going in the direction of strengthening the supervisory chain from the guards to the head guard to central Division of School Safety; the principal is kept out of this line of command except for cosmetic and deferential references.

8. In a recent court case, for example, two fourth-grade boys, special education students classified as emotionally disturbed, recently accused the principal of a New York City elementary school, a man who held this post for fifteen years, of hitting them with a metal object. In New York State Supreme Court the principal denied the boys' testimony and claimed that he had simply broken up a violent fight between the two youngsters, aged nine and ten. The jury chose to believe the boys with the result that the principal—who is now appealing the case—finds himself facing a sentence of up to a year in jail and $2000 in fines on two counts of child endangerment. The principal's lawyer, who described his client as extremely distraught and overwhelmed, was quoted as saying that the jury's verdict "sends a message that no teacher in the city school system should break up a fight, maintain control, or otherwise assert themselves." The Schools Chancellor said that he would seek the principal's dismissal from the school system (Fried 1994).

9. In recent years, articles encouraging interdisciplinary and "humanistic" approaches to teaching mathematics and writing have appeared in a number of journals such as *College Mathematics Journal, Mathematics Teacher, The Physics Teacher, College English,* and *Journal of Curriculum Studies,* among others. This movement, which has much in common with the "writing across the curriculum" approach, is closely related to what has come to be called humanistic mathematics, family math, or ethnomathematics.

10. See, for example, Powell and Frankenstein 1989.

Epilogue

1. James Q. Wilson (1993, 249) has aptly pointed out, as noted in the introduction, that schools are inevitably involved in the process of teaching morality whether they are consciously doing so or not.

2. See Scaglione (1986, 164–85): The "rules and established customs" of the Royal College of Savoy in Torino, which the Jesuits conducted exclusively for the sons of the nobility, for example, set down a detailed list of regulations governing every minute of the day, from wake-up time and morning Mass to nightly prayers and retirement to bed. These prescriptions and the penalties for infractions are minutely detailed and cover every aspect of student life. Some sample excerpts: "The valets must awaken the students. . . . The signal for prayers is given half an hour

after wake-up call. . . . Whoever is late at prayers, and more so if he misses them altogether, shall dine without dessert, and if such failures are frequent, the Superior shall be notified. . . . After prayers each shall retire to his room in silence. . . . Those who are bound to recite their homework must do so at this time. . . . The teacher must not assign additional homework too lightly, but if he deems it necessary to do so he must demand that it be executed on schedule, and the negligence of the students must not be overlooked." A daily schedule for a typical school day during the winter term was as follows:

> 6:30—Wake-up time; 7:00—Prayers, combing of hair, study, recitation of homework with the Prefect; 8:00—Mass and Breakfast; 9:00—School; . . . 11:30—End of school, going to the refectory; 11:45—Lunch, then Dance and Fencing lessons; 2:00—School; 4:30—End of school, Snack; 5:15—Study; 7:45—Rosary, Dinner, Recreation; 9:15—Prayers, then all retire to bed.

3. Scaglione, (1986, 179): "The principal goal for being in College is to acquire piety, to study, and to learn good manners. The Prefect is charged with this goal, which he must strive to achieve with his counsel, his example, and those methods that he will find here recorded and that the Superiors will suggest to him. In the exercise of his task he will always join good and attractive manners to firmness and resolution, since with the former alone he will obtain little, and with the latter alone he will antagonize everyone, but with these qualities together he will be more obeyed, respected and loved."

4. Lacouture (1991, 241) cites, among many others, a certain Languet, a Calvinist of the late sixteenth century, who wrote: "Les Jésuites font tomber peu à peu les Sorbonistes dans le mépris. Le collège de Clermont est le plus florissant de la ville. Ses professeurs surpassent tous les autres en réputation."

5. Historians have often reflected on the reasons for the success of the early Jesuit schools of the sixteenth and seventeenth centuries: "The secret of [the Jesuits'] success is partly to be found in the fine enthusiasm and devotion with which they combined learning and piety in the performance of their duties." Boyd and King (1975, 207). Scaglione (1986, 51) calls the Jesuit pedagogical system "undoubtedly the most successful and influential to come out of the Renaissance" due to its adaptation of humanistic postulates to the new needs of the times. Lord Bacon, commenting on the accomplishments of the Jesuits of his day, said (addressing them directly): "You are so good, I wish you were ours [i.e., on the Protestants' side]" ("Talis quum sis, utinam noster esses"). Cited in Boyd and King (1975, 207).

6. The Jesuits' own discipline stressed the internalization of the gaze rather than any external oversight by the gaze of superiors. Control of the eyes was strongly emphasized in the Jesuit course of training. In the constitution of their order, the Jesuits were exhorted by their founder, Ignatius Loyola, to guard "most diligently" the "gates of their senses," especially the eyes, in order to "preserve themselves in peace and true internal humility." They were told that "for the most part they should keep the eyes lowered, neither inordinately raising them nor gazing about here and there" (Oculos demissos ut plurimum teneant; nec immoderate eos elevando, nec in hanc aut illam partem circumflectendo) (Thesaurus Spiritualis Societatis Jesu 1948,

433). Jesuit novices were instructed to remain close to the walls as they walked down the corridors of the novitiate with their eyes cast down and fixed slightly ahead. These and other "rules of modesty" were not considered mere external prescriptions; rather they were part of a spirituality that stressed honoring and reverencing others, striving to see God's image in them, yielding preference to them, and mutually growing in devotion to one another and to God. In supervising schoolboys, this gaze switched from *ad intra* to *ad extra,* from being intrasubjective to being intersubjective; but the goals were identical.

7. There was a certain congruence between modern Jesuit schools and Jesuit education in the sixteenth and seventeenth centuries in the practice of a moderate discipline. None of the historical evidence supports the stereotypical image of the Jesuits as a kind of ecclesiastical paramilitary force. Cf. Boyd and King (1975, 207), commenting on Jesuit discipline: "Yet, though repression of the natural impulse was an essential part of the system, the discipline of the schools was never harsh. Hours of study were kept few . . . [There was] the use of emulation and rewards.".

8. I do not mean to imply that there was a standard "Jesuit personality." Jesuit scholastics and priests, like teachers everywhere, varied a great deal in their approaches to students. Some were very sensitive to becoming too friendly with the students and restricted their interactions to more formal and scholarly contacts. Students, perceiving these disparities, might inquire of other, more approachable Jesuits why a certain priest or scholastic chose to remain so distant. Such rapport was an expectation and, when absent, was noticed and mentioned. (I am not concerned here with historical perceptions of the Jesuits, a topic closely related to their important role in the Counter-Reformation, their suppression in the eighteenth century, and their complex role in modern European history.)

9. See McDonough 1992.

10. The education of a Jesuit in modern times (until the 1970s) usually involved fifteen years of training after high school and was arranged by stages in various "houses of formation" beginning with the novitiate (two years) and followed by the juniorate (two years), the philosophate (three years), "regency" (the three-year period in which the Jesuit scholastic taught at a Jesuit high school or college), the theologate (four years, with ordination to the priesthood after the third year), and tertianship (a final year of spiritual training). It was only at the conclusion of this long period that the fully formed Jesuit was deemed ready to meet the challenges of the ministry in university or parish work. Many Jesuits, in addition, later pursued advanced degrees in various fields at secular universities. The humanistic studies, beginning with the Latin and Greek classics in the juniorate, explored a sizable portion of what would now be called the canon of Western literature (with the exception of works that were on the Vatican's "Index of Forbidden Books," whose reading required special permission). Although the philosophical and theological training centered on the schoolmen of the Middle Ages, especially St. Thomas Aquinas, many Jesuit houses of study, especially the European ones after World War II, began showing an openness to historical criticism in biblical studies and to Christian existentialism. The beginnings of "liberation theology" date from that same post-World War II historical context in Western Europe. Many Latin American Jesuit seminari-

ans received their theological training in the ferment of postwar Europe before returning to their homelands. A few Jesuits (usually those who were destined to teach philosophy at Jesuit universities) studied Marx or Heidegger; others became geologists, nuclear scientists, astronomers, or chemists. The social sciences were, by and large, regarded with suspicion until the 1960s. See McDonough 1992.

11. William Spanos envisages a "destructive pedagogy" that entails a complete rejection of Western humanism, given its hegemonic history; his lack of an ethnographic base, especially one rooted in urban secondary education, leads him to neglect the deleterious effects the culture of violence has already wreaked on the educational institutions shaped by the humanist enterprise. See Spanos (1993, xxii).

Acland, Charles R.
1995   *Youth, Murder, Spectacle: The Cultural Politics of "Youth in Crisis."*
       Boulder: Westview Press.

Althusser, Louis
1971   *Lenin and Philosophy, and Other Essays.* Bristol, England: Western
       Printing Services.

Alves, Julio
1993   Transgressions and Transformations: Initiation Rites among Urban
       Portuguese Boys. *American Anthropologist* 95(4): 894–928.

American Psychological Association
1993   *Violence and Youth: Psychology's Response.* Washington, D.C.: Public
       Interest Directorate.

Anderson, Gary L.
1989   Critical Ethnography in Education: Origins, Current Status, and New
       Directions. *Review of Educational Research* 59(3):249–70.

Anyon, Jean
1979   Ideology and United States History Textbooks. *Harvard Educational
       Review* 49(3):361–86.

Apple, Michael W.
1982   *Education and Power.* Boston: Routledge and Kegan Paul.

Aronowitz, Stanley, and Henry Giroux
1985   *Education under Siege: The Conservative, Liberal, and Radical Debate
       over Schooling.* New York: Bergin and Garvey.

Bakhtin, Mikhail
1981   *The Dialogic Imagination.* Austin: University of Texas Press.

Ball, Stephen J.
1990   Introducing Monsieur Foucault. In Stephen J. Ball, ed., *Foucault and
       Education: Disciplines and Knowledge.* London: Routledge.

Barbanel, Josh
1993   School Financing Not Less for Poor, Study Says. *New York Times,*
       October 5:B3.

Benjamin, Walter
1968   Theses on the Philosophy of History. In *Illuminations,* ed. Hannah
        Arendt. New York: Schocken Books.

Bennett, William J.
1984   To Reclaim a Legacy: Report on Humanities in Education. *Chronicle
        of Higher Education.* November 28.
1992   *The De-Valuing of America: The Fight for Our Culture and Our Chil-
        dren.* New York: Summit Books.

Bourdieu, Pierre
1977   *Outline of a Theory of Practice.* Cambridge: Cambridge University
        Press.

Bourdieu, Pierre, and Jean-Claude Passeron
1977   *Reproduction in Education, Society, and Culture.* London: Sage Publica-
        tions.

Bourgois, Philippe
1989   Crack in Spanish Harlem: Culture and Economy in the Inner City.
        Anthropology Today 5(4): 6–11.

Bowles, Samuel, and Herbert Gintis
1976   *Schooling in Capitalist America.* New York: Basic Books.

Boyd, William, and Edmund J. King
1975   *The History of Western Education.* London: Adam and Charles Black.

Brantlinger, Patrick
1983   *Bread and Circuses: Theories of Mass Culture as Social Decay.* Ithaca:
        Cornell University Press.

Briggs, Charles
1986   *Learning How to Ask: A Sociolinguistic Appraisal of the Role of the In-
        terview in Social Science Research.* Cambridge: Cambridge University
        Press.

Brown, Daniel E.
1981   General Stress in Anthropological Fieldwork. *American Anthropologist*
        83:74–92.

Buber, Martin
1970   *I and Thou.* Translated by Walter Kaufmann. New York: Scribner's.

Buck-Morss, Susan
1984   The Flâneur, the Sandwichman, and the Whore: The Politics of Loiter-
        ing. *New German Critique* 99–153.
1989   *The Dialectics of Seeing: Walter Benjamin and the Arcades Project.* Cam-
        bridge: MIT Press.
1995   The City as Dreamworld and Catastrophe. *October* 73:3–26.

Caputo, John D.
1993   *Demythologizing Heidegger.* Bloomington: Indiana University Press.

Carnegie Corporation of New York
1994   Saving Youth from Violence. *Carnegie Quarterly* 39(1):1–15.

Carrington, Lawrence D.
1988   *Creole Discourse and Social Development.* Ottawa: International Development Research Center.

Clark, Joe (with Joe Picard)
1989   *Laying Down the Law: Joe Clark's Strategy for Saving Our Schools.* Washington, D.C.: Regnery Gateway.

Coleman, James S., Thomas Hoffer, and Sally Kilgore
1982   *High School Achievement: Public, Catholic, and Private Schools Compared.* New York: Basic Books.

Colhoun, Frederick S., ed
1984   Educational Research Service. *School Research Forum,* nos. 46–47.

Coon, Carleton
1971   *The Hunting Peoples.* Boston: Atlantic-Little Brown.

Damon, William
1995   *Greater Expectations: Overcoming the Culture of Indulgence in America's Homes and Schools.* New York: Free Press.

Davis, Susan G.
1986   *Parades and Power: Street Theatre in Nineteenth-Century Philadelphia.* Philadelphia: Temple University Press.

de Certeau, Michel
1984   *The Practice of Everyday Life.* Berkeley: University of California Press.

deJonge, Peter
1993   Talking Trash. *New York Times Magazine* June 6:30–38.

DeWitt, Karen
1993   Teachers Ask for Help with School Violence. *New York Times* January 15:A14.

Diggins, John Patrick
1994   *The Promise of Pragmatism: Modernism and the Crisis of Knowledge and Authority.* Chicago: University of Chicago Press.

Dillon, Sam
1993a Board Report Played Down Crime, Cortines Says. *New York Times* November 24:B1.
1993b On the Barricades against Violence in the Schools. *New York Times* December 24:B1.
1994   Cortines Proposes New System to Educate Violent Students. *New York Times* October 1:25.

Donaldson, Greg
1993   *The Ville: Cops and Kids in Urban America.* New York: Doubleday.

Drabelle, Dennis
1993   The Jesuits Made Me Do It. *Washington Post Education Review* April
       4:27.

Ellsworth, Elizabeth
1989   Why Doesn't This Feel Empowering? Working through the Repressive
       Myths of Critical Pedagogy. *Harvard Educational Review*
       59(3):297–323.

Erickson, Frederick
1984   What Makes School Ethnography "Ethnographic"? *Anthropology and
       Education Quarterly* 15(1):51–66.
1987   Conceptions of School Culture: An Overview. *Educational Administra-
       tion Quarterly* 23(4):11–24.

Feldman, Allen
1991   *Formations of Violence: The Narrative of the Body and Political Terror
       in Northern Ireland.* Chicago: University of Chicago Press.
1994   On Cultural Anesthesia: From Desert Storm to Rodney King. *Ameri-
       can Ethnologist* 21(2):404–18.

Fine, Michelle
1991   *Framing Dropouts: Notes on the Politics of an Urban Public High
       School.* Albany: State University of New York Press.
1992   *Disruptive Voices: The Possibilities of Feminist Research.* Ann Arbor:
       University of Michigan Press.

Foucault, Michel
1973   *The Order of Things.* New York: Vintage Press.
1974   *The Archaeology of Knowledge.* London: Tavistock.
1977   *Discipline and Punish: The Birth of the Prison.* Translated by Alan Sheri-
       dan. New York: Vintage Books.
1980   *Power/Knowledge: Selected Interviews and Other Writings, 1972–1977.*
       Edited by Colin Gordon. New York: Pantheon Books.

Freadman, Richard, and Seumas Miller
1992   *Rethinking Theory: A Critique of Contemporary Literary Theory and an
       Alternative Account.* Cambridge: Cambridge University Press.

Freedman, Samuel G.
1990   *Small Victories: The Real World of a Teacher, Her Students, and Their
       High School.* New York: Harper and Row.

Freire, Paulo
1971   *Pedagogy of the Oppressed.* New York: Herder and Herder.

Fried, Joseph P.
1993   Youth Receives Maximum Prison Term in Two Students' Killings. *New York Times* September 8:B3.
1994   Jurors Find Principal Hit Two Students. *New York Times* December 13 B:3.

Friedlander, Bernard
1992   Violence and the Schools: A Crisis of the Nineties. *Journal of the Connecticut Association of Boards of Education.* January:1–22.

Gadamer, Hans-Georg
1975   *Truth and Method.* New York: Continuum.

Gage, N. L.
1991   The Obviousness of Social and Educational Research Results. *Educational Researcher* 20(1):10–16.

Geertz, Clifford
1973   *The Interpretation of Cultures.* New York: Basic Books.

Gilligan, Carol
1982   *In a Different Voice: Psychological Theory and Women's Development.* Cambridge: Harvard University Press.

Gilligan, Carol, Janie Victoria Ward, and Jill McLean Taylor
1988   *Mapping the Moral Domain: A Contribution of Women's Thinking to Psychological Theory and Education.* Cambridge: Harvard University Press.

Gilmore, Perry
1985   Silence and Sulking: Emotional Displays in the Classroom. In Deborah Tannen and Muriel Saville-Troike, eds., *Perspectives on Silence.* Norwood, N. J.: Ablex.

Girard, René
1977   *Violence and the Sacred.* Baltimore: Johns Hopkins University Press.

Giroux, Henry A.
1983   *Theory and Resistance in Education.* South Hadley, Mass.: Bergin and Garvey.
1988   *Schooling and the Struggle for Public Life: Critical Pedagogy in the Modern Age.* Minneapolis: University of Minnesota Press.
1996   *Fugitive Cultures: Race, Violence, and Youth.* New York: Routledge.

Goffman, Erving
1963   *Behavior in Public Places: Notes on the Social Organization of Gatherings.* New York: Free Press.

Gottlieb, Martin
1986   F.H.A. Case Recalls Bushwick in the 1970s. *New York Times* February 2:35.
1993   Bushwick Hope Is a Public Project. *New York Times* August 15:38.

Bibliography

Graham, Patricia Alberg
1992 *SOS: Sustain Our Schools.* New York: Hill and Wang.

Guthrie, Grace Pung
1985 *A School Divided: An Ethnography of Bilingual Education in a Chinese Community.* Hillsdale, N. J.: Lawrence Erlbaum.

Heath, Shirley Brice
1989 *Ways with Words: Language, Life, and Work in Communities and Classrooms.* Cambridge: Cambridge University Press.

Henry, Jules
1963 *Culture against Man.* New York: Random House.

Honderich, Ted, ed.
1995 *The Oxford Companion to Philosophy.* Oxford: Oxford University Press.

Jones, Fredric H.
1987 *Positive Classroom Discipline.* New York: McGraw-Hill Book Company.

Kenway, Jane
1990 Education and the Right's Discursive Politics: Private versus State Schooling. In Stephen J. Ball, ed., *Foucault and Education: Disciplines and Knowledge.* London: Routledge.

Labaree, David F.
1988 *The Making of an American High School: The Credentials Marker and the Central High School of Philadelphia, 1838–1939.* New Haven: Yale University Press.

Lacouture, Jean
1991 *Jésuites: Une Multibiographie.* Paris: Éditions du Seuil.

Leder, Drew
1993 Live from the Panopticon: Architecture and Power Revisited. *Lingua Franca.* July/August:30–35.

Leitman, R., and K. Binns
1993 *The Metropolitan Life Survey of the American Teacher: Violence in America's Public Schools.* New York: Lewis Harris and Associates.

Levinas, Emmanuel
1969 *Totality and Infinity.* Pittsburgh: Duquesne University Press.
1987 *Hors sujet.* Paris: Fata Morgana.

Lock, Margaret
1993 Cultivating the Body: Anthropology and Epistemologies of Bodily Practice and Knowledge. *Annual Review of Anthropology* 22:133–55.

Lockwood, A. T.
1988   High School Choice and Students at Risk. *Newsletter of the National Center on Effective Secondary Schools* 3(2).

Maranhão, Tullio
1990   Introduction. In Tullio Maranhão, ed., *The Interpretation of Dialogue.* Chicago: University of Chicago Press.

Marcus, George E.
1986   Contemporary Problems of Ethnography in the Modern World System. In James Clifford and George E. Marcus, eds., *Writing Culture: The Poetics and Politics of Ethnography.* Berkeley: University of California Press.

McDonough, Peter
1992   *Men Astutely Trained: A History of the Jesuits in the American Century.* New York: Free Press.

McFadden, Robert D.
1993   Report Finds 20 Percent of Students in New York City Carry Arms. *New York Times* September 16:B3.

McKenna, Andrew J.
1992   *Violence and Difference: Girard, Derrida, and Deconstruction.* Urbana: University of Illinois Press.

McLaren, Peter
1986   *Schooling as a Ritual Performance: Towards a Political Economy of Educational Symbols and Gestures.* London: Routledge and Kegan Paul.

McNeil, Linda M.
1988   *Contradictions of Control: School Structure and School Knowledge.* New York: Routledge.

Mendler, Allen M.
1992   *What Do I Do When?: How to Achieve Discipline with Dignity in the Classroom.* Bloomington, Indiana: National Educational Service.

Mukerji, Chandra, and Michael Schudson
1986   Popular Culture. *Annual Review of Sociology* 12:47–66.

Narayan, Kirin
1993   How Native Is a "Native" Anthropologist? *American Anthropologist* 95:671–86.

Newman, John Henry Cardinal
1959   *The Idea of a University.* New York: Image Books.

Newman, Maria
1995a Disciplinary Schools Planned for Students Carrying Weapons. *New York Times* March 8: A1.

265

1995b Giuliani Chides Cortines for Resisting Use of Police. *New York Times* June 1:B3.

1995c School Safety Chief Resigns, Urging Job Be Done by Police. *New York Times* May 31:A1.

Newmann, Fred M.
1981 Reducing Student Alienation in High Schools: Implications of Theory. *Harvard Educational Review* 51(4):546–64.

New York City Board of Education
1989 *Don't Risk Your Education: No Guns in School.* New York: Author.
1993 *Addendum to the High School Directory: The New High Schools, 1992–93.* New York: Author.

New York State Department of Education
1994 *Violence in the Schools: A National, State, and Local Crisis.* Albany: Author.

Norris, Christopher
1987 *Derrida.* Cambridge: Harvard University Press.

Ogbu, John
1978 *Minority Education and Caste: The American System in Cross-Cultural Perspective.* New York: Academic Press.

O'Neill Barry
1994 The History of a Hoax. *New York Times Magazine* March 6:46–50.

Ong, Walter J.
1990 *Orality and Literacy: The Technologizing of the Word.* London: Routledge.

Powell, Arthur B., and Marilyn Frankenstein
1989 Empowering Non-Traditional College Students: On Social Ideology and Mathematics Education. *Science and Nature* 9/10:100–112.

Prothrow-Stith, Deborah, with Michaele Weissman
1991 *Deadly Consequences.* New York: HarperCollins Publishers.

Rabinow, Paul
1986 Representations Are Social Facts: Modernity and Post-Modernity in Anthropology. In James Clifford and George E. Marcus, eds., *Writing Culture: The Poetics and Politics of Ethnography.* Berkeley: University of California Press.

Rappaport, Roy A.
1993 Distinguished Lecture in Anthropology: The Anthropology of Trouble. *American Anthropologist* 95:295–303.

Ravitch, Diane
1988 *The Great School Wars: A History of the New York City Public Schools.* New York: Basic Books.

Richardson, Lynda
1993   Where Law and Order Is the School Rule. *New York Times* December
       9:B1.

Rofel, Lisa
1992   Rethinking Modernity: Space and Factory Discipline in China. *Cultural Anthropology* 7(1):93–114.

Rosenau, Pauline Marie
1992   *Post-Modernism and the Social Sciences: Insights, Inroads, and Intrusions.* Princeton: Princeton University Press.

Rumberger, Russell W.
1987   High School Dropouts: A Review of Issues and Evidence. *Review of Educational Research* 57(2):101–21.

Ryan, Alan
1993   Reasons of the Heart. *New York Review of Books* 40(15):52.

Sante, Luc
1991   *Low Life: Lures and Snares of Old New York.* New York: Farrar, Straus, Giroux.

Santner, Eric L.
1986   *Friedrich Holderlin: Narrative Vigilance and the Poetic Imagination.* New Brunswick, N.J.: Rutgers University Press.

Scaglione, Aldo
1986   *The Liberal Arts and the Jesuit College System.* Amsterdam: John Benjamins Publishing Company.

Scarry, Elaine
1985   *The Body in Pain: The Making and Unmaking of the World.* Oxford: Oxford University Press.

Scheper-Hughes, Nancy
1992   *Death without Weeping: The Violence of Everyday Life in Brazil.* Berkeley: University of California Press.

Shusterman, Richard
1992   *Pragmatist Aesthetics.* Oxford: Blackwell.

Sizer, Theodore
1984   *Horace's Compromise: The Dilemma of the American High School.* Boston: Houghton Mifflin.

Spanos, William V.
1993   *The End of Education: Toward Posthumanism.* Minneapolis: University of Minnesota Press.

Steinberg, Jacques
1994   Student Slain at School in Mt. Vernon. *New York Times* October
       25:B1.

Taussig, Michael
1992   *The Nervous System.* New York: Routledge.

Thesaurus Spiritualis Societatis Jesu
1948   *Regulae Modestiae.* Vatican City: Typis Polyglottis Vaticanis.

Toy, Vivian S.
1995   On School Security, Perennial Problems, Familiar Advice. *New York Times* August 15:B2.

Travis, Jeremy, Gerald W. Lynch, and Ellen Schall
1993   *Rethinking School Safety: The Report of the Chancellor's Advisory Panel on School Safety.* New York City Board of Education (unpublished manuscript).

Turner, Victor
1969   *The Ritual Process: Structure and Anti-Structure.* Ithaca: Cornell University Press.

Tyler, Stephen A.
1986   Post-Modern Ethnography: From Document of the Occult to Occult Document. In James Clifford and George E. Marcus, eds., *Writing Culture: The Poetics and Politics of Ethnography.* Berkeley: University of California Press.

U.S. Department of Education
1991   *America 2000: An Education Strategy: Sourcebook.* Washington, D.C. U.S. Government Printing Office.

U. S. Department of Health and Human Services
1993   *The Prevention of Youth Violence: A Framework for Community Action.* Atlanta: Centers for Disease Control and Prevention.

Wexler, Philip
1990   *Social Analysis of Education: After the New Sociology.* New York: Routledge.

Wigley, Mark
1992   *Heidegger's House: The Violence of the Domestic.* Columbia Documents of Architecture and Theory (D)1:91–122. New York: CBA Rizzoli.

Willis, Paul
1977   *Learning to Labor: How Working Class Kids Get Working Class Jobs.* New York: Columbia University Press.

Wills, Gary
1995   To Keep and Bear Arms. *New York Review of Books* 42(18):62–72.

Wilson, James Q.
1993   *The Moral Sense.* New York: Free Press.

Wilson, William Julius
1987   *The Truly Disadvantaged: The Inner City, the Underclass, and Public Policy.* Chicago: University of Chicago Press.

Wolcott, Harry F.
1973   *The Man in the Principal's Office: An Ethnography.* New York: Holt, Rinehart, and Winston.

INDEX

Acland, Charles, 6
Advisory Panel on School Safety, 254n. 4
African American students: as conditioned
   to expect little from schools, 107–8; immigrant students compared with, 34, 107,
   111; relating to white tutors, 252n. 1; segregated schools for young black males,
   246n. 5
all-school assemblies, 109, 250n. 4
Alpha School, 69; ethnicity of principal,
   69; ethnicity of student body, 48, 54; ethnicity of tutors, 54; origins of, 69; standardized test ranking, 48; teachers on the
   students' cafeteria, 99; weapons scanning
   as routine at, 77
alternative high schools, 240n. 4; "family"
   groups in, 212; individuality in, 211–12;
   older students counseled out to, 247n. 9;
   security staff of, 247n. 3
Alves, Julio, 27
Americanization of immigrant students,
   110–14
Anderson, Gary L., 136
anthropology: applied, 61; dialogical, 252n.
   5; educational, 237; medical, 237. *See
   also* ethnography
antihumanism, 190–93
antiviolence programs. *See* violence-
   prevention programs
applied anthropology, 61
Arcades Project (Benjamin), 15–17, 239n. 5
Aronowitz, Stanley, 135, 141, 195
Asian students: Bengali students, 107, 110;
   scope of term, 70
at-risk students, 16, 49, 50, 245n. 4

Bakhtin, Mikhail, 252n. 5
banking education, 192, 253n. 3
Bengali students, 107, 110

Benjamin, Walter, 15–17, 26, 103, 115–16,
   193, 239n. 5, 250n. 6
Bennett, William, 11, 20, 134, 235–36
Beta School, 69–70; ethnicity of principal,
   69; ethnicity of students and tutors at,
   54; Jamaican students' image in, 114;
   origins of, 69; as too quiet in 1950s, 117;
   total security force at, 78
black students: the dozens among, 153–54;
   relating to white tutors, 252n. 1; scope of
   term, 70, 244n. 1; stylized sulking among
   male, 154. *See also* African American
   students; Caribbean students
Borough Academies, 201, 253n. 2
Bourdieu, Pierre, 12–13
Bourgois, Philippe, 12, 88, 103–5, 248n. 1
boxcutters, 203
Boyd, William, 256n. 5
Briggs, Charles, 65
Buck-Morss, Susan, 115–16, 250n. 6
building assignments, 91, 248n. 10

cafeterias: doors bolted to prevent students
   from leaving, 85; security guards controlling access to, 82; teachers avoiding,
   98–99
Caribbean students: Americanization of,
   111–14; Creole languages among, 244n.
   1, 249n. 2; as critical of lack of discipline
   in schools, 107–10; social differences
   among, 249n. 3; transitional educational
   settings for, 249n. 2
Carrington, Lawrence D., 249n. 2
Central High School (Philadelphia), 147–48
Chancellor's Advisory Panel on School
   Safety, 241n. 8
character training, 134, 224
choice, 20, 29
Clark, Joe, 134

271

Index

inner-city high schools (*cont.*)
overcrowding in, 30; as part of larger society, 199; peer group now controlling, 109; perception of progress in, 35; as places to avoid, 28–31; porosity of boundary between street and, 71; poverty of surrounding neighborhoods, 68; as in presocietal state, 108; Regents' diplomas obtained in, 32; as remnants of modernity, 116; small schools skimming students from, 32, 34, 210, 211, 242n. 13; stairways, 82, 92, 99; street culture introduced into, 12, 27, 82, 86–87, 89, 95; toilets, 99; transforming into ed op schools, 31–32; violence as normalized in, 1; as war zones, 37–44, 244n. 20; what students encounter in, 26–28, 241n. 9, 242n. 12; white students as rare in, 55, 246n. 6. *See also* cafeterias; classroom, the; corridors; principals; school discipline; school violence; security forces; security technology; students; teachers
interviews, 65–66
intruders, 85–86, 123, 251n. 1
Isch, Jack, 251n. 1

Jamaican Creole, 244n. 1
Jesuit education, 224–36; attention to detail in, 226–29; dialogue in, 230–31; disciplinary techniques, 229–30, 257n. 7; dress code, 227; education of a Jesuit, 257n. 10; Foucault on, 226–27, 230–31; Jesuit scholastics, 225–26, 229, 230; the Jesuits not the students as in charge, 234; jug, 230; the model Jesuit teacher, 235; network of gazes in, 228, 256n. 6; Newman's gentleman as model for, 231–33; reasons for success of, 256n. 5; Royal College of Savoy, 255n. 2; sex education, 231
joning, 153–54
jug, 230
junior high schools, 33

King, Edmund J., 256n. 5
Kohlberg, Lawrence, 162, 168

Labaree, David, 147
Lacouture, Jean, 256n. 4
Landry, Tom, 8
Leder, Drew, 239n. 2
left-wing theorists. *See* radical theorists
liberal theorists (mainstream theorists): on

inner-city schools, 5; muting of discourse of violence by, 157; responses to violence of, 13, 19, 20–21
Liberty Partnership Program (LPP), 244n. 1
list-notice students, 28, 33
long-term absentees (LTAs), 242n. 15
lower-tier high schools. *See* inner-city high schools

magnetic lock systems, 26, 86, 247n. 6
magnet schools. *See* educational option schools
mainstream theorists. *See* liberal theorists
manners, 223, 224, 226
Maranhão, Tullio, 252n. 5
Marshmallow Effect, 108–9
mathematics, 33, 215, 255n. 9
maturity-immaturity dichotomy, 14, 190–92
McKenna, Andrew J., 253n. 1
medical anthropology, 237
mentoring, 56–58, 220, 235
metal detector systems: archway detectors purchased, 80, 201; as criterion of lower-tier school, 23, 25; hand-held scanners, 27; as image of the response to violence, 132; principals opposing, 241n. 7; as standard response to school violence, 246n. 1; as unsuited for minute surveillance, 220
Metropolitan Center for Urban Education, 4
morality. *See* values
multicultural sites, 246n. 5

Narayan, Kirin, 59
National Rifle Association (NRA), 203
neo-Marxism, 137, 147
network of gazes, 12, 97–98, 144–45, 228, 256n. 6
New Haven Plan, 20
Newman, John Henry, 232–33
New York City high schools: admissions procedure, 242n. 14; Advisory Panel on School Safety, 254n. 4; Borough Academies, 201, 253n. 2; central administration of, 240n. 3; Chancellor's Advisory Panel on School Safety, 241n. 8; Marshmallow Effect in, 108–9; official classification of, 240n. 5; Project Achieve, 245n. 4; Regents' diploma, 22, 32, 70; school-based management, 205, 254n. 6; "600

274

Index

students (*cont.*)
  dents; dropouts; Hispanic students; immigrant students
stylized sulking, 154
subaltern cultures, 148, 177
Superintendent of Alternative Schools, 240n. 4
symbolic violence, 134, 157

Taussig, Michael, 26
teachers: academic skills focused on by, 10, 131; as armed, 126; behavioral standards not enforced on, 144; broad spectrum of behaviors in, 171; building assignments for, 91, 248n. 10; burnout among, 119, 251n. 8; cafeteria avoided by, 98–99; as caring persons, 135; class preparations, 121; complaints about security guards, 89; on conflict resolution as curricular specialty, 163; as critics of dominant and subaltern cultures, 177; Dewey on, 148–49; dialogic relationship with students, 191; directed to not intervene in violence, 11, 83, 209; gaze averted from trouble, 126, 131; as going through the motions, 216; immigrant students' criticisms of, 108; as informed of security equipment only after its appearance, 78; *in loco parentis* role, 128, 131, 164, 208; as isolated in their classrooms, 118; the Jesuit teacher, 235; memories of other school experiences, 233; mentally relocating the violence, 43–44; older teachers comparing past and present, 116–18; reconceptualizing teaching as vocation not profession, 215–19; school discipline transferred to security forces from, 2, 27, 82–83, 91–94, 115, 204; security force numbers compared to, 78; street culture imported into school by, 126; street vernacular used by, 27; students blamed for the violence by, 35; teacher-principal relationship as having fallen apart, 207; teaching load, 121; tough street style adopted by, 128; traditional role fragmented, 10, 116; as transformative intellectuals, 133, 134; Travis report ignoring role of, 207–8; values in teacher-student dialogue, 149–55; withdrawing into passivity, 127, 172, 194. *See also* teachers' unions
teachers' unions: building assignments re-

stricted by, 91, 248n. 10; as complicit in culture of violence, 128–29; crime reporting system, 241n. 8; guard apparatus as creature of, 82; policy on school violence, 11, 83, 209; security package supported by, 241n. 7; strengthening guard apparatus supported by, 75, 132; United Federation of Teachers, 82
technology, security. *See* security technology
teen pregnancy, 194–95, 212, 253n. 8
toilets, 99
traditional values, 149
trash talking, 250n. 5
Travis, Lynch, Schall Report, 202, 204–8, 254nn. 4, 5, 7
Turner, Victor, 55, 141
tutors, 50–51; Americanization of immigrants countered by, 111; cavalier treatment of, 66–67; coherent plan required by, 153; eating with the students, 50–51; as ethnographers, 58–62; forging a role for, 52–54; going the extra mile for the student, 179–88, 189–90, 192; heterogeneity of teams of, 54–56, 67; making themselves available and vulnerable, 213–14; as mentors, 56–58; minority students relating to white, 252n. 1; as often the only ones who listen to students, 172; seeking students out, 213; seminar for, 52; students asking personal questions of, 175; students code-switching to emulate, 195; switching students from one tutor to another, 51; tutoring room as relaxed and secure space, 58, 60; tutoring seen as sign of disrespect, 51
Tyler, Stephen, 8, 62

unions. *See* teachers' unions
United Federation of Teachers, 82

values: character training, 134, 224; code of conduct, 164, 213; courtesy, 208, 226; gentlemanly, 231–33; manners, 223, 224, 226; permissiveness, 219; in teacher-student dialogue, 149–55; teaching moral values, 175–77, 224, 255n. 1; traditional, 149
video games, 251n. 11
violence: in rap music, 141; in street culture, 104–5, 176; structural violence, 134; symbolic violence, 134, 157; in video